Life Is an Opportunity To Joyfully Celebrate!

Becky Mulkern, ND

BALBOA.
PRESS
A DIVISION OF HAY HOUSE

COVER ART: 'SAILING HOME' original painting by Huntington Barclay, sold to St.Pauls School Science Center, Concord, NH. Archival quality prints are available from the artist in several sizes, framed and unframed. Contact Mr. Barclay at hunt@roadrunner.com or call direct (603) 986-0900

Balboa Press books may be ordered through booksellers or by contacting:

Balboa Press
A Division of Hay House
1663 Liberty Drive
Bloomington, IN 47403
www.balboapress.com
1 (877) 407-4847

Because of the dynamic nature of the Internet, any web addresses or links contained in this book may have changed since publication and may no longer be valid. The views expressed in this work are solely those of the author and do not necessarily reflect the views of the publisher, and the publisher hereby disclaims any responsibility for them.

The author of this book does not dispense medical advice or prescribe the use of any technique as a form of treatment for physical, emotional, or medical problems without the advice of a physician, either directly or indirectly. The intent of the author is only to offer information of a general nature to help you in your quest for emotional and spiritual well-being. In the event you use any of the information in this book for yourself, which is your constitutional right, the author and the publisher assume no responsibility for your actions.

Printed in the United States of America.

ISBN: 978-1-4525-9608-2 (sc)
ISBN: 978-1-4525-9610-5 (hc)
ISBN: 978-1-4525-9609-9 (e)

Library of Congress Control Number: 2014907221

Balboa Press rev. date: 4/21/2014

Dedication

I am honored to dedicate this book to my amazing mother. If not for her unconditional love and acceptance, I may not have written this book. Without judgments or expectations, she allowed me the freedom to be myself and freely explore the world. I was blessed to have such an awesome mother.

I also dedicated this book with gratitude, appreciation, and love to those individuals and lightworkers who have been committed to creating a joyful, unconditionally loving, environmentally sustainable, and socially just world. I heartedly salute your efforts.

I offer this book with heart felt love to all who choose to evolve and grow even in the face of overwhelming challenges. As greater numbers of us believe, trust and commit to creating a world that values acceptance, unity and peace, we gather strength and in turn create a world that radiates light and is based in the heart and unconditional love.

This book is especially dedicated to Pachamama, which is the earth, the sky, the universe, and all time. I love you very deeply. I have such gratitude for your endless and bountiful gifts. May we all remember to give thanks and pray every day for her! (She really needs it!)

Acknowledgments

I hold such deep gratitude for everyone's support!

Many, many thanks are felt for all my "Indiegogo" Supporters, friends and family who helped to make this book a reality. Your emotional and financial support, provided the resources and time for the writing, publishing, editing, and marketing of my book. I felt so blessed and appreciative of the many individuals from around the world who showed up for me. I am still so overwhelmed by the response and support. Thank-you all so much! Heart-felt thanks, is offered to all my contributors. I am so grateful for you. Thank-you! Thank-you! Thank-you! I could not have done it without everyone's support.

A very heart-felt thank-you goes to the following contributors: Bruce and Muf, Marc, Casey, Corny, Michael, Kat, Sebastian, Karen, Jesse, Jessica, Ric, Gabe, Jim, David, Jane, Dick, Janet, Michael, Laurel, Jelena, Heather, Mary Lou, Sarah, Olivia, Ray, Kylie, Mary, Tim, Deb, Peg, Kristy, Martina, Hal, Chris and Elaine, Joana, Cyndi, Mary Anne, Kristin, Anna, Beth, Kathy, Deb, Tom, Michael, Jackie, Ozzie, and Kevin.

I am grateful for my very dear friend Laurel. She is such a beautifully loving and brightly shining light in my world. Thanks so much for starting the Indiegogo book launch. You were my first contributor! That was so heart-warming and exciting.

There are so many individuals who were part of this process of bringing this book to you. I am thankful for all their support and the many blessings that I have received in this process.

My mother was very inspirational to me. Her example taught me to very naturally and unconditionally love and accept those around me. It wasn't a conscious choice, but a way of being that I learned from her. I am so thankful that she was always there just loving and accepting me as I was.

Thanks to the Great Spirit/Infinite Intelligence/Source for supporting and guiding me through all my challenges, even when I lost faith and trust. Archangel Azriel, thank-you for assisting me in releasing old ways of being and limiting beliefs, while moving through transformations on the path to finding my Authentic Self. I know he was laughing with me at times when I was slow to change but he was always deeply loving and supporting me in my process. Thanks to all my guides and angels for being my connection to unseen worlds.

I am so deeply grateful for the bounty of Mother Earth. She nourishes and reenergizes me every day. The peace and serenity that I feel in the natural world sustains me at very deep and healing levels. For that I am very grateful. I enjoy the *Oneness* and the freedom and connection that I feel when I am in her presence. She has given me/us so much. I pray daily for her sustainability, vibrancy, and health.

I hold such deep gratitude for my artist friend Hunt Barclay who graciously allowed me to use his painting for the cover of my book. I loved his artistry the moment I saw it. He must have designed it for us. It is an extraordinary work of art.

My couch surfing friend Dominic Casserley gifted his photographic artistry to me. Thank-you so much! Dominique donated a wonderful video for my Indiegogo launch site. I appreciate his time and talent and his creation of a professional video for the site.

My dear friend Jane Biggio has been so extremely supportive and loving. As my personal editor she taught me how to go a step above in my own editing. Wow, I really learned a lot from her about fine tuning my writing. I am so grateful and appreciative of her enthusiasm and dedication to me and my book. She really spurred me on at times when I needed it without even knowing what she was doing. I celebrate and thank-you Jane, from the bottom of my heart. I pray that you are blessed with many new opportunities in your life.

I deeply thank Jesse (& Jessica) my loving son and support system. From giving me breakfast in bed when he was in grade school to bringing flowers, great food, and love to my book launch party. He has always been there for me when I needed emotional, financial and loving support.

Casey my first born son, I am so grateful for your help with computer and art work. You are always there with enthusiastic support and celebration of me. I love it. Thanks so much for your generous and loving way of being.

My youngest son, Gabriel thanks for your artwork, Facebook advertising and marketing help. Thanks so much for your eager and loving support on the book launch! I love your genuine and present nature. Thanks for your loving support.

I am so grateful to my friend Karen Payne for her continued support throughout this process. Thanks for organizing my first presentation as an author. Wow, that was very exciting! I hold such gratitude for the photo that you took for the cover of the book. I love you Karen.

Thanks to dear Raymond for being one of my best and caring supporters. You have helped me to grow and evolve into a loving partner. I have learned to always return to love. Unconditional love and acceptance has always been the best answer to all my questions.

Grateful thanks to Tiana Robinson who helped with marketing and computer work. I appreciated your efforts.

Thanks so much to Bart at the Conway Daily Sun for helping me with press release information and design work.

Thank-you to all the local people who acknowledged my new book and wished me well.

I feel so blessed.

Becky Mulkern ND

Contents

Foreword

I attended Becky's *Life is an Opportunity* course when I was in my early thirties, was married, and had one child. Motherhood was exceptionally challenging for me. The emotional challenges that surfaced after the birth of my first child were associated with my own childhood. I went to therapy and realized I had a lot of old "stuff" from my past that I needed to address. I tried many avenues of help, but it was the *Life is an Opportunity* class that was the most helpful. This class provided me with a "tool box" of life skills that I have carried with me ever since. The cool thing about tools is that with practice you learn how to use them. In practicing them often, they become an extension of your own self. In time you become a master craftsman. The tools even seem to develop and take on a life of their own. While taking the concepts I learned from Becky and applying them in my daily life, I began to create my own personal life skills tool belt.

The most powerful and beneficial result was found in my unconditionally loving relationship with my children. I was able to provide a beautiful, stable and powerful foundation for my relationship with them. We can be honest with one another, share delicate feelings, and have enough faith in our relationship to share exceptionally difficult feelings like anger and disappointment. Through a relationship based on unconditional love and trust, an emotional strength develops that provides us the courage to deal with things when we open to our feelings of vulnerability and fear.

The greatest impact of the *Life is an Opportunity* approach resulted when I learned to let go of the polarities of good/bad and right/wrong. My entire childhood was steeped in these words. I always felt like I wasn't good enough or smart enough. I felt defeated before I ever started anything. If something I did or said wasn't right then it had to be wrong. If my behavior wasn't good then it had to be bad. Looking back now I can see how exceptionally limiting that kind of thinking is. There is nowhere to go from there, you are always stuck.

By learning to simply live in unconditional acceptance and noticing "what is" without deciding to judge anything, I opened up an entire world of possibilities. I could be anything! If you don't label with good/bad or right/wrong, what is left? Everything is available then! I could be "in process," "working towards," waiting for the right timing, listening for clues from the universe, or simply being and accepting what is happening. It felt so much better than judging that I must be wrong or bad since I couldn't see myself as right or good.

I practiced using my new tools and ways of being with my children. I learned how to let them just be without making them good/bad or right/wrong. I practiced letting go of judgment and I let them experiment with their own decision making and thought processes. It became enjoyable to watch their thoughts progress and to notice how much they could learn and figure out on their own, with me being a listener instead of a dictator. I loved to encourage them by asking questions and wondering about their ideas. This was a refreshing change from my own childhood in which I was told I couldn't have an opinion. While growing up, I was also told what I could or couldn't feel. Raising my children differently and unconditionally became a healing and growth process that changed my perception of myself and the world.

One exercise we did at home between classes was to look in the mirror, and say "I love me. I'm fine the way I am." At first, it felt wrong and very strange to do. It was hard for me to say it to myself and believe it. I had to practice for a long time before it felt true, and not a lie.

Learning these new skills gave me the courage to notice and acknowledge when I had hurt my children's feelings and to have the strength to apologize. This simple but powerful act is one of the greatest aspects of my relationship with my children. It means a lot to a child when an adult apologizes in a real and meaningful way. You can see it in their eyes. I am glad I learned how to let go of judging myself and allow just myself to be me. One of my favorite sayings that I learned in this class is: "when we know better, we do better" or "we are always doing our best." It became something like a life saver that kept me from "drowning" in self judgment and instead swimming in self-love.

This course has given me the wisdom to encourage my children to accept themselves and to believe they are lovable, amazing, and fine just the way they are. I am exceptionally grateful to have developed this perspective and insight. Being able to hold a space of non-judgment with them is the greatest accomplishment in my life.

These are a few of my favorite tools that I rely on regularly. They have taken on a unique personal meaning since I have been working with them for many years now. Everyone may interpret them differently, but I know what they mean to me and how helpful they have been.

Seek joy.
Laugh often.
Trust myself.
It's okay to feel anger and pain, just notice it fully then let it go.
Repeat if necessary.
Judging is limiting, discrimination is important.
Listen to my body.
Listen to the universe.
Be present.
Exist.
Allow.
Accept.

I am confident that you will thoroughly enjoy this amazing book that Becky has written for you!!! Reading *Life is an Opportunity* and practicing what you learn will guide you to feel light in your body, relaxed with yourself and able to look in the mirror and say "I love me. I'm fine just the way I am."

Have fun with it, and enjoy yourself!
Jane Biggio

Preface

~ఌౖఁ • ౖఌ~

NAMASTE: I honor the place in you in
which the entire universe dwells.
I honor the place in you which is of love, of light,
of truth and of peace.
When you are in that place in you,
and I am in that place in me.
We are ONE.

We are not here to focus on "what's wrong with you." That is an outdated way of the past. The present evolutionary time is about supporting ourselves and recognizing the magnificence of who we truly are. Many individuals have learned to think and believe that they aren't OK the way they are. At this time of the end of an old evolutionary cycle and the beginning of a new era, we are waking up to realizing our connection to each other, our spiritual heritage, and Source. We are certainly truly blessed to be leaving the Age of Darkness and to be heading toward the Age of Light.

It is time to think differently and create our lives differently. Now is the time to go beyond thinking "outside the box" and to envision a world without boxes. Can we all change that radically? I believe that we can and that we are…… Begin to look around you….

On the cover of this book is a painting by a dear friend of mine, Hunt Barclay. It is an unusual cover. I adored his painting the first time I saw it. I knew that I wanted his extraordinary work of art on the cover of my first book. The colors are heavenly and the art work feels Divine. It immediately held great significance for me. It represented how we can choose to move through life with faith, unconditional acceptance and certainty. Though there may be storms, turbulence or challenges surrounding us, we can remain conscious, present and centered. We can choose to be guided and supported by the Universe, while focusing on our strengths, our blessings, and our destination, while sailing safely home to the Light. The name of Hunt Barclay's painting is "Sailing Home."

I chose the name "Life is an Opportunity" for my course and book over 25 years ago. It evolved from a workshop that I was teaching and what I believed in my heart to be true. The title was perfect. The course originally evolved from a volunteer training program, which was based in unconditional acceptance. I offered the program during my social work degree internship. Individuals volunteered to participate in a 6 month non-traditional therapy program for a 26 year old autistic male client. Their free training was offered at a local agency for developmental disabilities. The program was modeled after a home based child centered program that Barry Neil and Suzie Kaufman had implemented with their son Raun who had been severely autistic. Within 3—4 years of participation in their program, by the age of 6, Raun was healed… cured, his autism was gone and he was living as a normal little boy (actually above normal, he was called the class genius). This type of healing through unconditional acceptance is totally authentic and was unheard of at the time that it happened. It really led me to contemplate what real healing means and what contributes to it …on every level.

The Kaufman's' focus on unconditional acceptance seemed key not only to health, but to a healthy body, mind, and spirit. My program evolved from this original inspiration. What was interesting was that the key emotion that I observed in my autistic client was fear. It appeared that fear caused him to contract and severely withdraw from life. I observed various changes in him when he was exposed to individuals around him sharing unconditional acceptance and love. He came out of the shell that held him in. He became more interactive, animated, cried and actually told his mother that he loved her. (If you want to read more about this process, read the book "Son-Rise" or watch the Kaufman's video.)

After the six month program ended, I was inspired to try a similar approach with challenged individuals who were interested in changing and creating their lives anew.

While I was teaching the *Life is an Opportunity* classes for over 25 years, I saw amazing changes occur in individuals' lives when they became unconditionally accepting and loving. They were floored. I was too! In situations where they didn't know what to do, they just stopped and became unconditional and watched everything around them change. Wow! It was pretty simple and miraculous.

Five years ago I was very surprised to find a greeting card with the following poem on it:

<blockquote>
Life is an opportunity, benefit from it.
Life is beauty, admire it.
Life is bliss, taste it.
Life is a song, sing it.
~Mother Teresa
(*The original poem is longer.*)
</blockquote>

Author's Note

For many years, I observed individuals who attended counseling and psychotherapy sessions, who often reported, feeling worse instead of better. It seemed that as they delved into the past, going over and over it in their mind, they often came out feeling depressed, unhappy, and were unsure as to what to do with their feelings and their future. I questioned how helpful it was for them just to talk about their past. I felt that it was possibly beneficial but somehow incomplete. I am also often surprised how long clients will participate in a therapy program that is providing them with no positive results.

When I attended the University of New Hampshire in the early 90's, I acquired a degree in Social Work. Previously, I believed that Social Work and counseling didn't work very well for many individuals. I had observed individuals who went through counseling, who didn't feel that it helped them or that it significantly changed their lives. While at UNH my feelings were supported in an unexpected way. One of my required courses related research studies concerning the effectiveness of professional casework services (social work). Joel Fischer wrote a research paper labeled "Is Casework Effective?" The following is revealed in his paper:..... in about fifty percent of the studies reviewed, clients receiving casework services "tended to deteriorate,"....a lack of effectiveness in helping clients seems to be true, ...in intensive service programs the differences "were negligible,"........"there was no difference between experimental and control groups on all major methods of evaluation though the workers felt that they had substantially helped their clients," ....again and again, there was no significant change reported and some groups actually got "worse," and "lack of effectiveness seems to be the rule rather than the exception." What they found was that 1/3 seemed worse, 1/3 seemed better and 1/3 remained the same.

Though most of the studies were taken from the 50's and 60's, it does get one to thinking. How effective are the approaches that are being used today in professional counseling services? Could non-traditional psychotherapy yield far greater results for clients in a less time? (Actually a psychotherapy training called *Guided Self-Healing* that I was involved with in the past seemed to demonstrate that it was possible.) Certainly *Emotional Freedom Technique* has presently shown extreme effectiveness in shorter lengths of time.

I have an *ONDAMED Pulsed Biofeedback* system which I have used with clients for many years. I have seen not only significant healing changes in clients' ability to deal with stress, PTSD and anxiety, but their overall level of stress and anxiety was significantly reduced as well.

Many times there are cultural belief systems in place that do not work, but are accepted because they are the *norm* and everyone has learned to live with them. They are what is available. Whether it is different types of psychotherapy, cancer or medical treatment, different types of diets or flu shots, many people may accept these as the *norm and appropriate* without any questioning.

In my eight week, *Life is an Opportunity* classes, individuals experienced tremendous healing shifts and dramatic changes in their lives. Many participants returned to class with miraculous stories. My course was focused on living with unconditional acceptance and love. Participants learned to let go old beliefs, limitations and judgments and instead choose to be empowered through joy, love, meditation, celebration and unconditional acceptance. These were people from all walks of life...lawyers, psychologists, mothers and fathers as well as depressed, burnt-out, anxious and deeply stressed individuals. ***Participants benefited because they were given simple and easy to use tools that deeply impacted their lives.*** I offered them many possibilities that provided opportunities to create their life as they chose. They no longer had to be a victim or continually feel powerless in their lives. Their lives changed radically because they were deeply in touch with their personal power to choose and their authentic loving self. Their choices became effortlessly empowered and the results were miraculous.

Through my own personal growth and life experience, I have come to realize that there is a great deal that I *know*. For many years, I underestimated, didn't value, or accept the wealth of my own knowledge, my wisdom, experience, or intuition. As I have grown wiser and become more appreciative of myself, I really support, acknowledge and trust the *sense of knowing* that I and we all inherently have. I base much of my healing work with clients in helping them to see and recognize how much they truly know. Most individuals completely underestimate themselves.

Mark Twain addressed well our (inherent) capabilities:

> Inherently, each one of us has the substance within
> to achieve whatever our goals and dreams define.
> What is missing from each of us
> is the training, education, knowledge and insight
> to utilize what we already have.

It is not how much we don't know that is of importance, (although recognizing this fact can bring great humility), but really it is the process of discovering how much we really do know that is truly enlightening!

Introduction

An experience of eternal being seeps through the
seams of late twentieth century human contentions,
seeping beneath the stage props and undermining the
assumptions that have fostered these past millennia of
history. This experience of being is slowly uplifting
the hearts of millions, not yet breaking lavalike—as it
soon will—through the crust of illusion into general
human acknowledgment, but bubbling beneath
the surface of human lives, altering subconscious
predispositions, shifting the deeper things.
~Ken Carey, *Starseed - Living in a
Posthistoric World (1991)*

Now is a time of profound opportunity. Now is the time of
evolutionary shift and change. The present time brings with it
creative and exciting possibilities for moving beyond our past
and present paradigm, but with it there is an obligation for us to
consciously create a new and glorious future, filled with hope,
truth, justice, and sustainability for all. We may feel unsure as to
what this new future may look like, but have faith that if we can
hold in our hearts the key values that we want to see in our new
future... in our new paradigm, we will bring these values with us
and to all life. We can do that together. We can be our authentic
selves, connect to one another, and our divine inheritance.

Many of the individuals who read this book may already be
on the path of enlightenment and spiritual growth. Hopefully this
will give all of you additional support, guidance, and clarity to

do more of what you already know. This book may bring greater purpose to your journey, lessen your daily stress and bring ease to an overly busy life. In applying many of these easy concepts that I am presenting, you will understand better every day that you can truly grow, evolve, and live without pain. We don't always need pain to grow.... as in the *no pain, no gain* theory. If you choose to be awake and present each moment, you may make choices that allow you to learn without pain, discomfort and tribulation. It is possible to experience life without choosing to look at it or experience it in a negative way.....as hard, failed, wrong, or a struggle. Emotional learning and spiritual evolution can come with ease, passion and joy if you believe it is possible and design it that way, but you have to let go of the struggle and let divine order unfold. Our essence is love, our truth is Oneness and we are all here to serve and bring value to the whole. We can eliminate focus on what makes us different but on what make us whole and connects us. Let us bring love, hope and trust to the new consciousness that is unfolding.

What we need to do most is unconditionally love and accept ourselves...starting this very moment. The core of life is unconditional love. There is nothing more important than this.....

How can we connect with our loving spiritual self?

By manifesting love and compassion.
Why? Because love and compassion are far more
than the abstractions many of us believe them to be.
They are real. They are concrete. And they make up
the very fabric of the spiritual realm.
~Eben Alexander, M.D., *Proof of Heaven*

This book is about waking from deep sleep and fundamental unconsciousness. We now have an opportunity to consciously choose to awaken and to recognize our purpose in this present evolutionary process. It is about letting go of distraction, fears, conditioning, limitations, trauma, numbness, unexamined negative beliefs, and redesigning our lives so that we are in charge of ourselves. We can choose to be profoundly dedicated to continually making choices that lovingly support and empower us (and in turn everyone) at all times.

Over time you will more easily learn to recognize the many faces of fear and illusion, and you will let them go as you see that everything is really not just OK, but even truly amazing. You will see that your life processes are a stepping stone and an opportunity that plays a purpose in your life, growth, awakening, and authenticity. (Look back at some of your challenges and see how those challenges brought you here and how your life may be better because of them.) There are no accidents, failures or mistakes. Everything occurs in our best interests, whether we recognize it or not. All *seeming* obstacles redirect us, help us to let go of limitation, self-sabotage, and impossibility, and at the same time, gently nudge us forward (or sometimes not so gently, if we don't listen to the first few nudges) toward our infinite and unlimited potential. Every challenge brings with it an opportunity that brings us beyond the limiting stories in our mind and toward our destiny. There is always a gift embedded in every challenge. How wonderful!

What I am offering in this book can support you to creatively make choices that you didn't think were possible. It may help you to change in unexpected ways. You will see that you can transcend the ordinary and begin to see each moment as extraordinary. You will begin to see everything that you have created. You will realize that you can choose to take charge of your life and begin to create it exactly as you want. ***Understand that you can choose how to think and feel at all times.*** Wow, that is powerful!

The past has been about learning to live with the ego and logical mind, and all that it brings with it…. fear, doubt, restriction and limiting beliefs. We are presently moving toward living from the heart and making choices based in unconditional love. We are no longer thinking in polarities but deeply feeling our connection to our hearts, each other, and the Universe. We are leaving polarities behind and moving toward living with heartfelt being.

We have lost touch with the deep mystery at the
center of our existence—our consciousness.
~Eben Alexander, M.D., ~*Proof of Heaven*

Each moment, each experience holds the opportunity to spiral upward or spiral downward, to move toward the light, or away from it. Each moment contains seeds of fear, negativity, powerlessness, frustration, and limitation OR peace, ease, joy, love, and unlimited possibilities. (Both contain opportunities for learning and evolution.) The choice is always yours!

As you become aware of the inner dialogue of fear, pain, judgments, and negativity that you have held, you will learn that you can look at these feelings, accept them without judging them, experience and feel the pain, and then let them all go. This will free you to be more and more your authentic self. Feeling our feelings allows us to heal, release them and let them go.

You will feel continually freer and lighter as you release and transmute negative, fearful and unloving emotions. These feelings have been part of you. They aren't bad. They may just be your aspects of your struggle to do your best in every experience, though you may be feeling *inadequate, not enough, or wrong.*

While reading this book, enjoy the opportunity to recognize the ways in which you can choose to create more of the following in your life: consciousness, honest communication, healthy choices, personal integrity, creativity, empowerment, passion, fulfillment, the ability to let go of control (while truly recognizing how much control you really have), gratitude, reverence, serenity, and unconditional love.

See the *Life is an Opportunity* way of life as an ongoing workshop and/or experience that can dramatically change your life, health, and future. Read the material, follow the recommendations that work for you, and practice and apply the ideals daily in your life. You may wish to read one chapter at a time and apply it in your daily life for one or two weeks, before reading further.

This is a time in history when more than ever before new doors are opening, and many, many new amazing possibilities are available to everyone. It is a time of tremendous change and opportunity. All you have to do is recognize and let go of old fears, limits, beliefs, and impossibilities and *focus with your heart on what you want to create.*

First and most important, this book is not about fixing what is wrong with you... there is nothing wrong with you. This book is about guiding you to access that magnificent Child of God and the Universe that you are.

We are moving from focus on the outer world to focus on the inner world and our connection to ourselves through Oneness, God, Source, Infinite or Universal Intelligence or the Great Spirit. (Choose the name that works for you.)

I want to know God's thoughts; the rest are details.
~Albert Einstein

The ideas and information that I am presenting are merely tools offered to you to use in ways that will benefit your evolution. There is no right or wrong way for you to enlighten or lighten yourself. There is only *your* way. Use what you feel will work for you, adapt and change what you feel you need to, and place on hold those ideas that seem not to apply at this time. During this process have an open mind, integrate and apply these ideas in your life, and always take care of yourself. Always love yourself unconditionally. Most of all enjoy and embrace this journey....it's yours. *Our greatest growth can come when we walk into unknown territories with an open heart and mind. We will find ourselves when we love, have gratitude, and hold reverence for all that we are and all that is.*

I say to mankind, be not curious about God. For I,
who am curious about each, am not curious about
God—I hear and behold God in every object...
~Walt Whitman

This book wasn't intended to include my process, but as I was finishing it, I realized that I had to add in personal stories about my struggles and challenges and how I rose above them through learning to see *Life as an Opportunity*. My stories include some miraculous turnarounds, rewards for my patience, and enlightening discoveries. Many experiences occurred that surprised me and taught me about the larger universe beyond the limitations that I had previously believed in. I began to see a world that connected me to unseen phenomenon and supported my faith in the Divine. I was rewarded for my perseverance, faith and belief that I was truly taken care of and watched over by a truly Divine Universe.

There are many quotes in this book from others who have been on this path…. scientists, philosophers, authors, shaman and visionaries. They understood what I have written about …they were living it. Many of them knew/know of this evolutionary time. Their quotes are here to cheer you on and let you know that you are not alone at this evolutionary time but are supported by many beings of light from the past and present. We all want you to reclaim your joy, authentic self and your understanding of how important you are in this Universe. You are totally loved and cherished by the Creator and all life.

I hope that this book will serve as a beacon of hope as you awaken to the present evolutionary shift and change and this life-enhancing transitional period.

Before you go any further

Please write out answers to the following: (either here or on a separate sheet of paper)

Beliefs that I hold about myself and my life that I would like to *let go of or change*: (Here are some possible categories)

Work related
Relationships

Personal
Stress
Love, Happiness, etc
Financial
Life
Time
Aging
Fears
Future

An example for the first category of "work" is: "The harder I work the less I receive" or "I am never appreciated for the work I do," or "The work I do never pays off." Remember, these are <u>beliefs that you want to let go of</u>....

More examples:
Work is hard. Life is hard.
I never make enough money.
I am never happy with my partner.
I am always late for everything.
I am afraid to speak up.
I am unlovable.
I don't deserve to be happy.

These are some possible examples, please create your own. Remember, these are beliefs that you want <u>to release</u>! Set the list aside and look at it again once you have finished this book. (Place it at the end of the book.)

At the end of each of the upcoming chapters, I am including information from some of the handouts in my "Life is and Opportunity" program. The information provides additional support and reading for the program, and is written in many different formats. The participants in my workshops have found them very helpful. I hope that you do as well.

1

Just Being

You are a human being. What does this mean? Mastery
of life is not a question of control, but of finding a
balance between human and Being. Mother, father,
husband, wife, young, old, the roles you play, the
functions you fulfill, whatever you do—all that belongs
to the human dimension. It has its place and needs to
be honored, but in itself it is not enough for a fulfilled,
truly meaningful relationship or life. Human alone
is never enough, no matter how hard you try or what
you achieve. Then there is Being. It is found in the still,
alert presence of Consciousness itself, the consciousness
that you are. Human is form. Being is formless.
Human and Being are not separate, but interwoven.
~Eckhart Tolle, *A New Earth*

Read this quotation two or three times if you need to, really take it
in, really grasp its meaning in your life. We are not human *doings*,
but human *beings*. That is the key. We need to keep a balance of
the physical, mental, emotional, and spiritual if we are going to
manifest a life of health, wellness, passion, and truth. There is no
other way.

Today, life is changing and evolving at a phenomenal pace. We
have arrived at a juncture in our path of evolution, and we now face
a shift in planetary life that requires everyone to consciously choose
a healthier and more sustainable future, if we are going to make it
to the next level. I am hopeful. I believe that we hold this vision
in our hearts and souls. More than 2,000,000 organizations are

spiritually activated and presently working toward environmentally sustainable, socially just, and thriving world. This is the largest social movement of all time and so few know that it is happening. Shift and change are happening in all fields and everywhere around us. You will be amazed if you look deeper.

The arc of the moral universe - bends toward justice.
~Dr. Martin Luther King Jr.

Certainly we can see an uprising of change in the *Arab Spring*, the spread of local food and farms, the *Occupy Movement*, sustainability, and wind and solar projects. There is a wider acceptance of gay rights and gay marriage. Women are speaking up against the broad prejudices and abuses aimed at them.

As we move into a feminine-based world, we are seeing more women as heads of state and in positions of power. A male-dominated competitive and warring world is being transformed into a female, energetic model that will be a more peaceful, loving, and conscious world. We are balancing masculine and feminine energies as we move toward a co-creative, cooperative venture that embraces both our female as well as our masculine aspects. Men's hearts are awakening and they are more vocal in embracing their own divine life. Men are finally ready to open themselves to their gentler, heart-centered, and more feminine characteristics. What a sigh of relief I am hearing.....

People everywhere are speaking up and demanding change. We are now standing for what we want, and we are no longer resisting what we oppose. This shift involves a global uprising and a worldwide spiritual awakening. Mankind and womankind together are recognizing their power as a conscious force. The impulse of evolution, based on non-traditional and evolutionary paradigms, is bringing in new values, new ways of being, and fresh solutions to our challenges. This growing movement toward a unified, global community of oneness is a tremendous change in the very foundation of human consciousness. Those involved in this movement understand that we must focus on achieving sustainability and on loving, respecting, and revering both Mother Earth and ourselves. ***We must live as nature does, in not taking more from nature than we truly need.*** We must live a heart-centered life and serve the whole and not just ourselves. There is no other way that we can truly be.

Humanity is going to require
a substantially new way of thinking
if it is to survive.
~Albert Einstein

Many spiritual philosophers say that nothing like this movement has ever happened in the history of our world. Many of us have been waiting and praying a long time for this. This is very exciting!

When we can just Be, connect with our heart, inner wisdom, and spiritual intelligence (whatever that may mean to you—God-Force, Spirit, Christ, I AM, Higher Self, Buddha, etc.) we will find that we are *moving mountains*. ***We have to connect with that part of ourselves that is timeless, powerful, compassionate, and fulfilled in a state of just being.*** That is our fate.

Rudolf Steiner, the brilliant mystic and author, talked in depth about unseen worlds in many of his books. He felt that during his generation, people had lost touch with a deeply spiritual connection to God. He shares his feelings in his book *Staying Connected*:

Dying is part of living. Yet, during the last few centuries, we have preferred to deny death by making it an end so final that it is unthinkable—a void, absolute negation. We thought we did so because we loved life. In fact we did so because in our obsession with material things occupying space, we lost the ability to understand that life extends far beyond the limits of our five senses. We lost the sense that the visible world is merely the tip of an unquantifiable, qualitative, invisible reality. That is to say we "lost" the spiritual world and, having lost it, can no longer imagine that life can take forms other than the purely physical form we have made supreme: the only reality.

Andrew Cohen, author of *Evolutionary Enlightenment* speaks of God in the following way: "God represents the creative principle, the First Cause, or Eros, the elemental driving force behind the evolving universe. God is what I call the 'evolutionary impulse' that overwhelming urge to Become that emerges from the deepest dimension of Being itself, which of course, is not separate from your very own consciousness."

When we continually live in the space of form and the physical, we disconnect with formlessness. We actually operate in a different way than if we incorporate both. When we choose to incorporate both we go beyond the physical. Then we live with spirituality in all that we do and all that we are. We find our way Home.

A human being is part of the whole, called by us
"Universe," limited in time and space. He experiences
himself, his thoughts and feelings as something
separated from the rest—a kind of optical delusion
of his consciousness. The striving to free oneself
from this delusion is the one issue of true religion.
~Albert Einstein

Einstein felt that the key to true peace of mind was through overcoming the delusion of separation and feeling our connection to the whole and to the Universe.

Our home resides in heart-based consciousness and peace-filled being. This is where our present and future rests. We are moving from operating out of the power-craving ego and logical mind to being present in our heart and to feeling Oneness with all life. This is where a dynamic gift is waiting. We are releasing and letting go of the ego identity, blessing it for all it has taught us, and regaining the energy of the newborn child, that of innocence, love, unity, and connection to the infinite universe.

The God who existed before any religion
counts on you to make the oneness of the
human family known and celebrated.
~Desmond Tutu

2

Breaking Free from Old Patterns and Limitations

*There is no greater gift to yourself and to
those around you than your deciding to dump struggle,
for struggle is an unholy battle
that you fight with yourself.*
~Stuart Wilde, ~Life was never meant to be a Struggle

Ninety-five percent of individuals repeat the same patterns and the same choices day after day, year after year, throughout their entire lives! Are you one of these individuals? Based upon everything that they have learned growing up, and believing that they have only certain choices and possibilities, these ninety-five percent operate within believed "limits" and parameters. By operating "inside the box," they unconsciously accept the limits they believe to be real. These acknowledged limits then determine their choices and, in turn, every moment of their lives. As they repeat the same patterns and choices with which they feel secure with, they continue to produce the same results indefinitely into the future. They embody the saying: *"If we keep doing what we've always done, we'll keep getting what we've always got."*

By leaving behind and freeing ourselves of our past history, we can create life anew. We can even begin to break up some of these old patterns by doing things as simple as parking in a different place, going to a new group meeting, doing something unexpected or different on your day off. Just for fun, start with little things and see what happens. It can feel really refreshing when you do this.

5

Some of our greatest growth can come when we break free from the old, repetitive patterns and unfounded fears and push into unknown territories. We have arrived when we leap "empty handed into the void" (as is said in the *Runes*), silencing the mind, recognizing our true nature and who we *truly* are. When we can believe boldly in ourselves with absolutely no doubt in our minds and hearts, we can truly create all manner of things in our lives. This is not a question of discipline. It is a passionate and committed choice we make for ourselves and the whole world, dedicating us to conscious evolution.

One of my favorite quotes that I strive to live by is the following one that was thought to be authored by Johann Wolfgang von Goethe, but was originally written by William Hutchinson Murray (1913—1996) and found in his *The Scottish Himalaya Expedition, 1951*:

> Until one is committed, there is always hesitancy, the chance to draw back, always ineffectiveness. Concerning all acts of initiative (and creation), there is one elementary truth the ignorance of which kills countless ideas and splendid plans: that the *moment* one definitely commits oneself, the providence moves too. All sorts of things occur to help one that would never have otherwise occurred. A whole stream of events issues from the decision, raising in one's favor all manner of unforeseen incidents and material assistance, which no man could have dreamt would have come his way. I learned a deep respect for one of Goethe's couplets: Whatever you can do or dream you can do, begin it. Boldness has genius, power, and magic in it.

Years ago, I had an experience that demonstrated how Providence works in my favor. I understood deeply that I am always being taken care for by unseen powers.

I realized that it was time to buy a new, used car. I observed the many miles on the old one and the rust and new sounds, noises, klunks and sputters that seemed to appear more often. I had planned to look for another car on a Friday, but due to lack financial resources, decided to put it off again.

On early Saturday morning I was headed out at 6:45 AM to a workshop which was over a mountain pass, one hour from home. When I had driven about 15 minutes the car started sputtering and shaking. I kept driving hoping that it would go away, but it didn't, so I turned around. Thinking that there may have been water in the gas, I filled the tank. It seemed to run better, so I headed north again. Soon it started to sputter a little, but not really as much as previously. My intuition guided me to turn around. I listened. It seemed to drive fine on the whole trip home. I decided that since I had the time I would go to a dealer and look for another used car that morning, so I cleaned out the car when I got home.

I called and made an appointment with the sales manager. I was unable to see my regular salesman because he had been out of work for a month after being in an auto accident. My salesman called however while I was there and came right down with his crutches and all. He showed me a car that was truly perfect, for both me and my budget and it had arrived just the day before. He gave me what seemed to be a great deal, even with a warranty. Since the new car hadn't been cleaned yet, I had to wait till Monday to pick it up.

I drove my car home, but it wasn't sounding too good. It was still sputtering. I decided not to drive it over the weekend, but I would stay home and work on my book.

I was concerned about needing money for insurance and future car payments and I had no vehicle to get my son to work for a few days. I put all concerns aside and just decided to move ahead. Once I made the decision to buy the car, everything fell into place. My associate was working that day and she let me borrow her car to drive my son to work and do some errands. I called a friend who lived nearby. She said that I could use her husband's truck since he was away for a few days. My associate's last client lived in Jackson and she gave me a ride to my friend's house to pick up the truck. I called another friend and she offered to wire the insurance company the money needed to cover the insurance. It all easily fell into place with a little organizing. I even had calls from new clients who scheduled for the following week. When I decide to move toward what I wanted without any thoughts of doubt in my mind many things happened which I would not have expected. I was extremely grateful. We are so graciously supported by the Universe!

Committing ourselves to live with faith and moving in the direction of our hopes and dreams is an important priority in this evolutionary process. ***The Universe always says "Yes" to whatever we affirm.*** So, affirm the best for yourself. Affirm what you truly want. Avoid saying and thinking what you do not want to happen, because the universe affirms our every thought, so keep saying "Yes" to life. The more we have faith, focus on our passion, and begin creating our goals, the more support we shall have from the Universe.

Commitment is what transforms a promise into reality. It is the words that speak boldly of your intentions. And the actions that speak louder than words. It is making the time when there is none and coming through time after time, year after year. Commitment is the stuff character is made of, the power to change the face of things. It is the daily triumph of <u>integrity</u> over skepticism.

~Schoerson Lohman

More than 35 years ago I was feeling depressed, unfulfilled and uncertain as to what to do with my life. I wasn't inspired, content or feeling spiritually "alive." I prayed and asked for guidance and soon found myself directed to read *Autobiography of a Yogi*. One of the themes in this book that Yogananda wrote was to "serve or suffer." That was where he had found his peace and his calling. It struck a truth in me and from that point forward I have dedicated my life to "serving." My dedication is focused on inspiring individuals to find their way and passion. I feel blessed to have been a support system and provide guidance for so many individuals. Teachers can certainly be inspirational in our process of finding our way to peace, love and fulfillment.

3

Understanding Fear

The brave man is not he who does not feel afraid,
but he who conquers that fear.
~Nelson Mandela, *Long Walk to Freedom*

From the time we are conceived, we are bombarded with imprints and patterns of both positive and negative electromagnetic frequencies. We are too young to understand the difference between them and we have no filter system to discriminate and/or repel the harmful energies. Frequency imprints and feelings from others may impact us so deeply that before the age of 7 many of the patterns for our life are fully imprinted and already determining our life experiences. Certainly we have free will, but we don't always see through the illusion and conditioning that we perpetuate from the patterns and beliefs that our parents, family and culture held. Many become stuck in these patterns. When our parents said to us, "be a good girl/boy," they meant well, but they contributed to our holding guilt as we tried to conform to their/societies desires. In a sense, we may have felt that if we didn't do what they wanted, we were "bad." We may have carried that guilt forward, feeling it again, every time a similar experience arose. The negative, destructive, and depressed frequencies that we adopt can continually affect our ability to draw to us what we most want in our life.

David R. Hawkins, MD, PhD author of *Power vs. Force, The Hidden Determinants of Human Behavior,* shares research in his book, on how different emotions including shame, fear, courage, love, peace and enlightenment relate to individual existence, survival, and egocentric focus. They extend up a scale to broad interest in the well-being of others and a dedication to living for the salvation of humanity. Shame is rated at a low of twenty, fear at 100, anger at 150 and courage at 200. Upper levels incorporated acceptance at 350, love and reverence at 500 and peace and bliss at 600. Enlightenment spreads a range from 700 to 1,000. Most individuals were in the range of 200. Levels below 200 were weakening and levels of 200 and above were strengthening. Two hundred is the mid-point between attracting negative experiences or attracting well-being and having interest in the well-being of others. I know for myself when I was in my twenties and thirties, I could see that some people I knew had a great interest in the welfare of others, but at that time, I couldn't live beyond being a single parent and taking care of myself and my three boys. It wasn't until I was older, more evolved, emotionally stable and open hearted that I began to have a deeper interest in the welfare of others around me. I was glad to reach that level. It felt expansive and transcendent.

> What is not love is always fear and nothing else.
> *Course in Miracles*

Fear and aspects of fear (everything that is not love is fear) resonate at such low levels that they become not only destructive, but they magnetize and attract more of the same experiences. We are all connected by what some people call morphic fields or morphogenetic fields and the collective consciousness. Rupert Sheldrake in his book, *A New Science of Life* speaks of morphic fields as invisible as the effects of gravity, magnetic fields and cell phone electromagnetic fields. Even the fields of our minds extend far beyond our brains. Author Sheldrake states: "Through morphic resonance, the patterns of activity in self-organizing systems are influenced by similar patterns in the past, giving each species and each kind of self-organizing system a collective memory." Though we can't see them, they are present, are affecting and will continue to affect our lives. Deepak Chopra often talks about the "collective unconsciousness" in his lectures. Depending on our focus and identification with certain beliefs, we could actually be held back or helped to move forward. Seems important then to really be aware of what we thinking and are focusing on.

Collective unconsciousness or morphic fields are like the "hundredth monkey effect" that Ken Keyes Jr. talked about in his book *Hundredth Monkey*. This effect may provide a momentary transference of knowledge throughout a species when a certain number of them have learned a new idea or action. This new knowledge then bypasses the traditional physical barriers and limits and becomes a mind to mind jump… a leap in consciousness. The concept came from Dr. Watson who wrote about studies of Japanese monkeys in his book, *Lifetide* (1979). He related that some Japanese scientists observed monkeys over a span of thirty years and saw that one monkey called Imo solved a problem of dirty raw potatoes by washing them in a nearby stream. Soon his mother, playmates and then other mothers began exhibiting the same behavior until monkeys in all of the community were washing potatoes. At that point monkeys on other islands began exhibiting the same behavior. They called this the "hundredth monkey affect."

What is important about this concept is that once enough of us do something to change our future, more and more people may automatically start doing it without knowing why. But there is a point at which if only one more person tunes-in to a new awareness, a field is strengthened so that this awareness is picked up by almost everyone! Pretty amazing!

> The first peace, which is the most important,
> is that which comes within the souls of people
> when they realize their relationship, their oneness
> with the universe and all its powers,
> and when they realize that at the center of the universe
> dwells the Great Spirit, and that this center
> is really everywhere, it is within each of us.
> ~Black Elk

There may be a tipping point that is reached when enough individuals become aware of choosing a behavior or way of being.

As more and more people shift creatively and tap into the collective unconsciousness, we may all choose new behaviors or ways of being that truly benefit everyone. Peter Diamandis (on *Ted Talks*, his book *Abundance* 2013) believes that if enough people begin to shift into the new paradigm, the new reality, and new ways of being, we can leave behind the old fear-based paradigms and move ahead exponentially. He believes that we can exponentially create and manifest from our thoughts and will power any number of amazing things.

Morphic fields may provide avenues of connection between animals (and people) through communication, though they are many miles from one another, This provides an explanation for telepathy, which appears to be normal for many animals. Telepathy may be more "normal than paranormal, natural than supernatural, and is also common between people who know each other well." (Rupert Sheldrake)

Recently I read in *Serpent of Light* by Drunvalo Melchizedek, that native shaman around the world communicated psychically, from one community to another, for thousands of years. I believe that the worldwide computer connection that we experience today is just a metaphor for the worldwide psychic connection that we could have with each other at any time. We are all connected whether we feel it or not. Maybe that is part of our future reality?

It is powerful to think that our attitudes, feelings and energy can affect so many more people than we ever imagined. Our impetus to change negative and fearful attitudes could be inspired by an altruistic feeling of wanting to spread joy and love instead of negativity and fear. Certainly the last thing you or someone else wants to feel or share is fear, but we aren't always aware of what we are feeling or sharing. Sometimes we are asleep....

First of all, let me assert my firm belief
that the only thing we have to fear is fear itself.
~Franklin D. Roosevelt, *1932 presidential election campaign*

Even though most people don't realize it, fear is an ever present aspect of many individual's lives. Through the media we are fed a non-stop dialogue and pictures of everything that we should and could fear. How often do you hear inspiring, uplifting or cheerful news? Not often. We are constantly barraged by many forms of negativity and fear-intended information, though we don't always recognize the impact of most of this information.

Many of the decisions that people make and actions that they initiate are based on fearful beliefs that the world outside of them is "threatening and unsafe". They believe that what they fear is outside of them. But fear is always in our mind and not outside of it. Fear is something that we hold within ourselves and project outwards, making all of our decisions based upon it. Fear is something that we may unconsciously live with and choose, possibly due to an onslaught of stressful, as well as traumatic experiences in our past. Egocentric living stems from fear and looking outside of ourselves to get value from other sources. Feeling whole doesn't come from others or somewhere outside us, it comes from within ourselves and our connection to the Divine.

What if we are already complete? When we value ourselves and release the need to be valued by others we may find the wholeness that already exists within us.

Here is a great tool….When you are feeling "scared" transpose the letters in that word and instead choose to feel "sacred." You are a divine child of God.

Though some people think that we live in one of the most abundant times ever, many individuals are continually focused on scarcity and lack. With the media focusing on "what's wrong," we are unable to see "what is amazing, changing quickly and beneficially working" for the greater good. There are more technological systems available to more people than ever before. By 2013, 70% of the world enjoyed cell phones! The cost of solar power dropped 50% just last year! The US presently supplies 60% of its own fuel for powering cars and heat, etc. from wind, solar, natural gas and oil. There is a technological revolution going on. Volkswagen car manufacturers just came out with a car that gets over 200 miles per gallon of gas. Hopefully we shall see more of these advances that contribute to a more sustainable and healthier future.

When you start turning off the negative media and plugging into the positive and creative endeavors that are happening in the world, you can feel a sense of joy about our collective future. Investigate… don't take my word for it. Try turning off your TV and watch hopeful news on your computer for a week. Think about how you can be part of the solution to today's challenges. There are so many possibilities including: buying local, recycling, consuming less that can't be recycled, supporting local businesses, meditating, growing a garden (you can always start small), and enjoying nature more. We all need to be active participants in our collective future.

The effects of traumatic injuries and abusive experiences can accumulate over time and later become anxiety, poor physical and emotional health, and Post Traumatic Stress Disorder (PTSD). Individuals experiencing trauma, usually internalize the experience, and in time become more fearful and anxious as other similar experiences occur. These patterns of internally held trauma may be carried forward for years in their lives or for lifetimes. I believe that a high percentage of people today hold severe stress, trauma and PTSD in their body and mind without even knowing it. As we become aware of our emotional reactivity and fear, we can begin to feel it first and then to slowly let it go as we change our behavior and ultimately choose to respond in other ways. We <u>can</u> learn to healthily and creatively respond instead.

I experienced PTSD after being in an unexpected car accident. There were 3 impacts in a matter of seconds…another car hit the back left of my car, the right side of my car hit a tree, and my head hit the interior of the car door. After that experience, I realized that I wanted a seat belt in my kayak, on my bike and anywhere possible to assure my safety. That was my fearful reaction after being hit unexpectedly from behind. The suddenness, injury and trauma were deeply internalized into my being. I didn't realize how traumatic it had been for a number of years. I did however, slowly work it through, by riding on a motorcycle of all things….It took some courage, through practice, to let go, relinquish control, and just enjoy the ride. I can celebrate that I had courage to do that! I even got to the point where I felt like I was flying through the mountain valleys instead of riding a motorcycle. It became exhilarating!

The first step in healing and change is recognizing fear and how many different fears we hold. ***Once we identify the fact that we are constantly choosing both consciously and unconsciously to live in fear, we have accomplished a major step in self-awareness.*** Fear provides us a wonderful opportunity to evolve and grow. If we can just witness and simply watch what happens when we experience fear, it is a second major step. Don't try to make anything go away… just be with your feelings. You don't have to do anything more. Witness your anxieties, and unconditionally accept them instead of reacting to them, and everything will change….

Living in fear may first be experienced in utero. It can be passed directly from mother to child. It is often learned from a very early age. Ken Carey shares the following in *Notes to my Children*:

> We have begun to see that as children grow older, they usually lock the child spirit up. Do you know why? It starts because they believe a lie <u>that they have to worry.</u> This is the first lie. When a little child first begins to believe that he or she has to worry, that's when the child spirit starts getting locked up in prison. That is how the bars of the prison are built. The bars that lock the child inside are built out of fear. Fear enters in and mixes up all their thoughts so that they can't think clearly anymore. They get more and more mixed up. They feel like they don't know what to do so they start copying. But it is all because they believe that people have to worry.

Children are born with a wonderful ability to live in the present moment and to be present where they are and with what they are doing. They don't sit around thinking about the past and future the way many adults do. They are totally present and involved in enjoying each moment as it presents itself....they laugh, play and investigate. Everything is new and exciting to them. They are curious about life.

Adults who live with regret about the past and fears about the future, have unconsciously learned and somehow believe that they have to live a life filled with fear and worry. Their mind is filled with a non-stop inner dialogue that supports their acquired need to worry, be anxious and fearful.

Silencing the mind is definitely "easier said than done," for the mind itself often seems to have "a mind of its own." *Most individuals are totally unaware of their mind and its constant dialogue that often rambles on incessantly, fearfully and seemingly beyond their control.* Most people, who are anxious, fearful and uncomfortable in life, don't even know it.

When individuals take my workshops and counseling programs, it is often a "wake up call" for them. They awaken sometimes dramatically, when they first begin to realize that they hold fear and constantly live in fear. They begin to see the degree to which they hold fear and the degree to which fear governs their life, including every choice, decision, reaction and response. Until taking the workshop, many participants had no idea that most of their thoughts were based in fear.

Look at the following statements and see and understand how they all have underlying issues with fear:

"I better hurry or I will be late...."

"I hope I'm dressed appropriately..."

"I didn't do that right...."

"What if....

"I'm afraid to speak up...."

"What if I share my feelings…"

"What if they don't like me…"

"If I get too close, I might get hurt…"

"I can't…."

"What if I'm wrong…"

List of Fears

Trauma from our past can dictate the quality of our life and future. It may show up as fear. Fear arrives in many shapes and forms, mostly in reaction to what we imagine and perceive to be true. The following is a list of possible fears that individuals live with:

Fear of loss (material, financial, emotional, etc.)
Fear of gain (do I really deserve? how would my life change?)
Fear of physical and emotional pain
Fear of being wrong, rejected, abandoned
Fear of responsibilities or freedom
Fear of death (but also fear of life)
Fear of success and/or failure
Fear of intimacy
Fear of being alone or separated
Fear of fear itself
Fear of acting inappropriately, not doing it "right"
Fear of love and loss of love
Fear of not being enough or too much
Fear of being powerful or not powerful
Fear of being unworthy or worthy
And especially: Fear of letting go! What would happen if I let go?!

We may constantly try to protect ourselves from and avoid what we fear. If we don't face our fears directly, we end up living in fear and running from it much of the time. What is most curious though is that few individuals realize how much of their life is consumed by fear, worry and anxiety. I had a counselor in one of my classes that appeared fearful to me right away. He didn't see it, most people don't. People often understand fear better once it is labeled and described. The light goes on and then they see the amount of fear that they hold. It took about 4 classes before the light went "on" for this man. His life changed dramatically when he got it. It was a life-changing difference. (When I say that the "light goes on," try thinking of it as living with hope, faith and joy instead of the dark quality of fear, anguish and anxiety.)

Fear is an accepted "norm" in our society. *Worry seems to be a way to use up present moments and be consumed fearfully in those moments. To the degree that we hold doubt, fear and worry we are less effective in all that we do.* Suffering in fear is created from wrong thinking and perception and believing somehow that we are imperfect.

> Nothing that is Real can ever harm you,
> And nothing other than that which is Real
> Can ever bring you the Peace that you seek.
> ~*Course in Miracles*

When we experience anxiety, tension, doubt and fear, others will feel our fears and feelings as well. They may not actually recognize that it is our feelings that they are sensing. They may actually misinterpret it for being their own fear. They might even think that you are fearful of them.

> Doubt is created in the mind and brought to life there.
> It is first a whisper.... Then a denial ....
> It becomes infectious in nature, and a place
> where light cannot penetrate.
> It is a major foe of our time.
> ~*New Teachings for an Awakening Humanity*~

In reading about Native American ritual, I realized that our energy field may extend out from our physical body up to 100 feet or more. If that is true, then everything we feel radiates out from our being for quite a distance. What we feel will be felt by others as well. They may experience our nervousness, frustration and anxiety without knowing that it belongs to someone other than themselves. This can be a wonderful exchange if others are in an uplifting and loving space, but if they are not, then it may not be quite so wonderful.

A personal experience of mine will illustrate more clearly how we affect others with our fear, feelings and judgments.

When my one of my sons was learning to drive, I let him practice driving while I was in the car. Sitting in the passenger seat while someone is learning to drive has not been my favorite pastime. I understand that it is due to the helplessness and lack of control that I felt at those times. I am definitely more relaxed about it than I used to be, but I still can learn to relax better in these circumstances, let go and accept what is going on.

The first time that I experienced these fearful feelings with his driving, he was in stop and go traffic in one of our local towns. I was nervous and was being challenged to relax. I wasn't doing very well, though he was driving very well. In no time at all, he said, "I'm feeling tense and I don't know why." I didn't say anything, but was sure he was feeling my tension and not his own. He is generally very adept at everything that he does, whether his studies, a sport, meeting new people or his job, so I felt it was unusual that he feel any tension with his driving. He had actually been driving off and on for over a year and was a very good driver.

Another day he was practicing driving again on the way to the post office. With all the traffic that was present, I was again feeling somewhat tense. Within a short period of time, my son said, "I don't know why I'm feeling tense." I didn't say anything, but after we got the mail, I focused on looking at the mail, relaxing and just letting go and letting him drive. Within no time at all, he said, "I'm not feeling tense anymore, I feel comfortable driving now. I don't know why I was feeling tense before."

How amazing to experience this. Our thoughts and feelings not only affect us but can have a powerful effect on others as well! What an important lesson for me to learn and continue learning.

If we look at all the negative feelings, anger and fear that so many people are feeling, is it any wonder that so many individuals feel little peace, relaxation or joy. We could all be feeling each other's unrest.

If you are feeling out of sorts and anxious and you are wondering why, you may be absorbing energy from others who are nearby or from the greater world. You might try the following exercise: Sit quietly and breathe and just relax. As it feels right, ask yourself, "Is this energy mine?" Allow an answer to come and don't hurry it. You may or may not receive an answer, but the intensity of the negativity will diminish if the energy and origin is not you/yours. The more we can experience our personal autonomy, integrity and spiritual connection the less we will be affected by those outside our energy field. Try to do daily practices that contribute to your personal integrity. It could be meditation, a walk in nature or quiet time or anything that brings you a sense of peace and spiritual connection.

Individuals often experience a very profound realization of their anxious and chaotic mind when they try to meditate. Often they find that they cannot silence their mind of the endless dialogue that just "doesn't quit." *Meditation though can be learned by anyone.* There is no such thing as not being able to do it. Anyone can learn. It is like learning to walk, you take one step after another until you simply do it. You have to be motivated to do it. You have to choose and intend to do it. You can't "try" to do it. You can't discipline yourself to do it. You "do" it and enjoy it by learning at whatever pace is best for you. Do it your way.

Many individuals have taught themselves some form of meditation without going to a class or workshop. I don't believe that it takes a lot of knowledge to do it, just desire and awareness .....

awareness of the breath, quieting the mind, upright and open posture and learning just "to be." (You can get CD's and do on line courses as well. Deepak Chopra has wonderful courses and meditations that you can down load.)

In order for some individuals to slow down to meditate or do yoga, they may need to do some form of activity first. A friend of mine told me that she needs to exercise first. When I taught a children's yoga class, I would have them run around the gym 4 times before we started the after school program. That worked really well...they were very ready to relax and focus on the class after expending their pent up school energy...

Most people don't pay much attention to their breathing because it is a semi-automatic function which seems to regulate itself. Once our breathing unconsciously regulates itself to a stress filled and traumatic life, it changes dramatically from what is considered to be healthy, normal and relaxed. When we endure stress, whether it be real or imagined, our breathing changes and usually becomes rapid and shallow. These short, quick breaths are part of the body's "Fight or Flight Response," which allows us to fight or run in reply to the stress that we are experiencing (even if that stress is only imagined!).

FEAR...False Evidence Appearing Real
~unknown

Because stress and trauma often resides in the body even after an original stressful experience has ended, rapid and shallow breathing can become an ongoing, habitual process in the physiological system. If an individual is always reacting to life in a tense and fearful way, the fight or flight response continues to operate and may in time wear out the hormonal systems as the body stays in a 'hyper alert' and 'ready to react' state. The internal systems stay in constant readiness to fight or run. The circulation changes, a depressed immune system results, the adrenals become "burnt out" and rapid shallow breathing continues indefinitely, even though we may have been reacting to an imagined stress. In time the hormonal system moves from hyperactive to hypoactive, and can no longer respond in appropriate ways. The system is "burnt out."

There was a time when I experienced an immobilizing fear that I could not ignore. I was terribly afraid of losing my boys during my divorce from the boys' father. This intense fear originated around the fear of losing custody of my children. I just couldn't bear the thought of it happening. I was so afraid that I remember sitting in my office, trembling and paralyzed with fear. I couldn't do more than just sit! I was so immobilized with fear. I finally asked myself what was the worst thing that could happen? I sat down at my desk, because I couldn't do anything else. I imagined what I would do if it happened. I realized in that moment that I wouldn't die of fright or become immobilized indefinitely, I could bear the change if it happened and I could go on living…..I could go on living. I went over all the possible outcome scenarios and the fear was gone and I realized not only would I survive, I could thrive. I wouldn't really be losing the boys totally, I just wouldn't see them as much. I could do it! In that moment my mind shifted 180 degrees and I felt totally different. To my great and amazing surprise, the fear was gone and I was no longer immobilized. In seeing that my fear was fear of fear itself, it all changed. In being in the moment with the fear, it evaporated. I myself, had made it bigger than it was, and allowed myself to become an immobilized victim of the circumstances. Sometimes when we face the fearful illusions that we are afraid of, they disappear in that moment and we are free to move on. We see that we are not a victim or bound by our fears. Once I looked at it realistically everything changed and I felt powerful. I was as amazed as I could be at the result.

> Let us search then for his strength—for his largeness of spirit somewhere inside ourselves. And when the night grows dark, when injustice weighs heavy on our hearts, or our best laid plans seem beyond our reach—think of Madiba (Nelson Mandela), and the

words that brought him comfort within the four
walls of a cell: "It matters not how strait the gate,
how charged with punishments the scroll, I am the
master of my fate: I am the captain of my soul.
~President Barak Obama
~*Mandela's Funeral Service, December 2013*

Every crisis and trauma has a built in opportunity. There is actually *one* Chinese symbol that represents both of these, which very interesting. We need to remember that within each challenge there is an amazing opportunity for us as well!

The divorce actually inspired my oldest son to create greater peace in the world. He is an entrepreneur and has created a number of innovative and successful businesses. One of the businesses that he created is called *Couchsurfing*. It is a website that socially connects people through giving them a free place to stay with another person or family on the website. One may have to be (a non-fearful), open, community minded and welcoming person to be happy to have a total stranger from somewhere around the world staying in their home. The web site has safety guards in effect and users relate wonderful heartfelt sharing. I have had hundreds of guests stay with me, which means I have places around the world where I can visit and be hosted. I usually welcome all with a big hug!

Interestingly enough, I have had many clients that breathe shallowly long after their traumas and stressors appear to be gone. (I sometimes see them lying on my massage table with clenched fists before I begin a massage.) Breathing shallowly, muscle tension and cold hands and feet are a sign that the fight or flight or stress response is still plugged in and trying its best to protect you. Sometimes the body doesn't quickly deprogram and reprogram the breathing and circulation patterns to do anything differently after the stress has occurred. The breathing may be a certain way for so long that individuals don't even realize that it is abnormal or unhealthy.

> Awareness means Presence, and only Presence can dissolve
> the unconscious past in you.
> ~Eckhart Tolle, ~*A New Earth*

We may actually have two different selves that we identify with.... the ego or lower self who identifies with FEAR and separation, and the integrated, higher, and authentic self who identifies with love, oneness and connection. The ego when unhealthy is focused on itself and its safety, always afraid of "what might happen." The integrated-self lives in love, with faith in the future, and is based in the present moment. The integrated-self lives connected to the Divine, Spirit, God (whatever your belief system wants to call it) and a Spiritual Belief in Oneness and connection with all life.

> Only if you have ego is there conflict between the dark
> and the light. If there is no ego, there is no fight.
> There is only Divine vulnerability,
> which is your very best shield and defense.
> ~Lynn Andrews, ~*Shakkai*

In my "Life is an Opportunity" class I offered an exercise where the participants shared what they identified with the ego/separate self and the spiritually connected/ Integrated Self. The following is a partial list. You can really feel the difference between the two. Which one do you want to spend most/all of your time identified with?

The ego self (duality) and the Divine Self (Oneness)

Separate Self/Ego/ Personality (FEAR)	Integrated Self/Spiritual/ Divine (LOVE)
Empty	Full
Separation	Connected/Oneness
Divided	One
Fragmented	Whole

Incomplete	Complete
Defective	Integrity
Insufficient	Absolute
Lack/scarcity	Abundant
Partial	Unity
Fearful	Loving
Powerless	Powerful
Doubtful	Certain
Destructive	Creative
Unconscious	Conscious/awake
Rejecting	Accepting
Imperfect	Perfect
Unlovable	Lovable
Conditional	Unconditional
Victim, irresponsible	Responsible
Imprisoned	Free
Isolated	Connected
Illusion	Real/truth
Impure	Pure
Guilty, blaming	Innocent, autonomous
Reacts	Responds
Selfish	Selfless, self-reflective
Loser	Holding/embodying
Discipline	Choose
Impatient	Patient
Starving	Nourishing
Burnt out	Energized
Self-righteous	Respectful

I once heard a spiritual teacher say that *we are the most invincible when we are the most vulnerable.* If you think about it, what could be more powerful than that? It immediately made sense. I heard this over 20 years ago and I never forgot it, because it was very true.... being vulnerable is a stance of humility and power.

Fear may be useful if there is a tiger chasing you but the kind of fear that most people live with on an ongoing basis is destructive, depleting and a waste of energy. Fear is definitely not a beneficial motivator nor does it serve any purpose other than running from that tiger to save your life. It was an evolutionary mechanism that was useful when tigers, etc. were plentiful. Now is the time to move out of the fear and separation paradigm and into the light of love and spirituality. Fears have held us back in the old outdated paradigm for long enough. It is time to let them go. Now is the time to choose the new paradigm of love, Divine harmony and Infinite possibilities.

> All healing is essentially the release from fear.
> ~*The Course in Miracles*

Stuart Wilde is another favorite author and speaker. He wrote the following inspirational quote that I used in my course:

> What is important to remember is that through introspection you create the inner particle state—the Inner You. It gains strength as you focus upon it. By quieting the ego, the celestial light of the spirit shines through, giving your inner self life. The spirit is immensely powerful, but it has little influence in your life until it is freed from the debilitating racket made by the intellect. Then it can pervade your inner self, which in turn, pervades your outer conscious self. It's the spirit that gives the outer you energy and provides vision to your inner and outer self through a heightened sense of feelings. Spirit grants you feelings because everything is energy, so everything radiates a message. The Spirit is connected to everything via the God Force. The Spirit can connect your inner Self or your conscious outer self to the energy signals emitted by every aspect of life.
> ~Stuart Wilde, ~*Whispering Winds of Change*

Our challenge at this time is to unite the healthy ego and the Divine so that they are never separate again. As the authority of the ego matures and unites with the masculine and feminine Higher Selves, we will finally feel complete as a whole. There will no longer be these separate aspects of ourselves living in isolation, opposition and duality. We shall finally live from the heart and have complete access to all aspects of our being.

Going Deeper ~ (take time to write answers in your journal, if you like)

~Are you aware of how many fearful thoughts you have?

~What have you learned to fear? Who taught you? What are your biggest fears?

~Can you quiet your fears? Be aware of your fears, without judging them, observe them and then let them go.

~Are there fears that you live with daily?

~Do you notice that when others feel anxious, fearful and "out of sorts." Can you feel their disharmonious energy whether they tell you about it or not?

~What percentage of the time do you feel peaceful and calm?

4

Meditation – a Vital Tool for Growth and Evolution

The first Peace, which is the most important, is that which
comes within the souls of the people when they realize
their relationship, their Oneness, with the universe and
all its powers, and when they realize that at the center
of the universe dwells the Great spirit, and that this
center is really everywhere, it is within each of us.
~Black Elk

Over the past 50 years, hundreds of research studies on different
kinds of meditation have been performed in hundreds of independent
universities and research institutions in 33 countries. They have
found that meditation can:

~ Reduce stress, irritability, blood pressure, tendency to
   dominate, inhibition, and addiction

~ Increase creativity and intelligence (I actually had
   a student in one of my classes say that she felt more
   intelligent once she started meditating)

~ Improve memory and learning ability

~ Increase inner calm, energy, self-reliance, and
   psychological health

~ Reduce anxiety, depression, nervousness, aggression, and insomnia

~ Improve relationships (I have seen many relationships improve)

~ Increase happiness, self-confidence, sociability, and self-esteem

~ Promote a younger biological age

~ Reduce medical care including less hospitalization for cancer and heart disease

Meditation, relaxation and quiet time are beneficial in promoting healthy living. They provide the opportunity to connect with our mind and body, our "authentic" Self, and true spiritual nature. Through meditation we walk an inner path to self-realization and open the doorway to peace of mind. ***Through our willingness to be conscious and let go of constant thoughts and mental dialogue, we can slow and empty our minds, and become masters of our thoughts, our health and our lives.*** We are less bothered by petty things in life and in turn become more creative, focused and relaxed. In turn, we hold a greater sense of well-being.

By letting go of mindless chatter, our minds are free to live in the present moment. We find new freedom, receptivity and tranquility. Through valuing a quiet mind, mental stillness and inner peace, we are no longer a "victim" of our worries or unwanted thoughts and fears. In time, *we learn that we can choose our thoughts, alter our thinking and create the world we wish.* In turn and in time, we become free. The idea is not that you necessarily have to meditate, especially if that doesn't work for you. What is important is finding a way of "chilling" and connecting to a place within yourself, where you experience centeredness, balance, "aliveness" and a conscious connection to your inner self. Within ourselves is a place of passion, faith in the unknown and readiness to embrace new opportunities. You may feel that quiet time, music, dance, singing, painting or yoga are the best avenues for you to experience this. See what works best for you and do it.

> I love feeling thrilled by the small things in life—a
> new pair of sunglasses, a perfect cup of coffee or
> tea, a rainbow, a sunset, or a brightly colored bird.
> Admittedly, I notice them more when I remain faithful
> to my meditation and work with my connection to the
> light. The light makes everything more beautiful.
> ~Julia Griffin ~*One True Self Newsletter*, January 15, 2014

When we truly live in the moment, we are present for ourselves and others. We are clearly conscious and "here," not constantly somewhere else, or lost in our thoughts while living with regrets of the past and anticipation and fears of our future. Incessant streams of thoughts about our past and future occur, when our thinking is unattended and when we have little or no conscious connection with our mind. The average mind is constantly enduring unconscious states of thinking which impulsively carry it places it never really intended to go.

I added meditation to my therapies as a Naturopathic Doctor and to my "Life is an Opportunity" course when I realized how important it was for challenges like depression. I myself have been challenged with depression at times. One time when I was depressed, I questioned what I could do for myself and what might also help my clients. Meditation came to mind. Over the years, I had done some meditation but not always on a regular basis. I decided that it was time to start. It really helped because it released me from the past/future continuum and held me in the present moment where I felt safe and peaceful.

The Course in Miracles relates that depression comes from a belief in "lack." If we are somehow (consciously or unconsciously) feeling that one or more things are missing in our life, do we feel it enough so we end up feeling depressed? We certainly don't consciously choose it, but we do feel the "lack" or that something is missing. I believe that what we are feeling is really a product of the time that we live in and the disconnection to each other, our spiritual life and something deeply meaningful. Certainly we can't live in a superficial and meaningless way and feel very peaceful or fulfilled. We would probably be in a deep state of "numbness."

When I taught individuals in my *Life is an Opportunity* class to meditate, I recommended that they meditate daily. When they came back to class, some had practiced it and some had not. So I decided that I had to make it easier for them. I made an audio version for them to take home and listen to. That was interesting! Some individuals still had their excuses. In one class of 15, at the beginning of the second class, I asked participants about their meditation practice for the previous week. Interesting results, again, ... some had done it, some had done it some of the time, but the last person to speak was a mother of 5 who was meditating twice a day! After that, I realized, "no excuses" and that I needed to suggest that individuals make more of a commitment to themselves.

In doing a practice such as meditation, it has to be done as a choice and not a discipline, if we are to succeed in making it an important part and committed part of our life. A choice is something that we want to do and a discipline is something we feel that we "should" do. Making something a "choice" really creates a difference for many individuals, and empowers our process.

We can choose to make time for anything that we value. There are truly no excuses that are good enough for something that is beneficial for our mental health and wellness. If it is a process that enriches our lives and promotes our health, it is advantageous to let go of other things that are not beneficial for us. Through meditation we actually gain time. A relaxed state actually produces more energy, clarity and efficiency.

If we are free to make choices that are best for us, we can decide to choose whether we want to live in a state of sleepy unconsciousness—dull and disconnected to life, or in a vibrant state of consciousness, where we consciously direct our mind, while being totally connected with who we are. This becomes a shift that occurs over time. ***First, we have to realize that sometimes we are unconscious and sleeping through life.*** Awakening a little at a time, we begin to recognize that in an awaken state we really have more choices and options available to us than when we continue living in the "collective unconsciousness." We begin to see many choices that were not visible from our state of sleep. Unconsciousness is like a drug that keeps us from participating in life. If we honestly want to participate then we need to slow the mind and become more awake in each moment. Really open your eyes and see what is going on. Meditation can be a key that opens this door for you.

As we become more aware of our choices, we can free ourselves from the world of negative thoughts, judgments, and always "doing." We can slow down the mindless chatter and at the same time we can be more present to each new moment. We can choose and allow ourselves just "to be" and to meet each moment fully. Shallow, anxious breathing drains our energy, whereas slow, deep breathing helps us to feel the potential in each moment and touch the power of "NOW" with our whole being...body, mind, emotions and spirit. Conscious, deep breathing reduces stress. It is the key that unlocks the realm of quieting the mind, self-mastery, letting go of limitation and impossibility and achieving mindful living.

Try an exercise for yourself to increase your oxygen intake and healthily change the way you breathe. Oxygen carries 19 times more energy than food. It can help to release toxins and wastes from the body. Dynamic breathing affects the life force in ways that create and maintain health. You will notice the difference when you change the way you breathe. Try this exercise:

Inhale slowly as long as you can until you hear a voice that says, "That's it, that's as far as you can go." Then exhale in the same way, very slowly as long as you can until you hear that voice that says, "That's it, that's as far as you can go." Continue breathing this way for a while then begin to count to yourself as you do this.... 1...2...3...4, etc. up to 10. See how high you count for each inhale and exhale. Most people may start out at 3 or 4. With practice you should be able to reach 7—10 or more. Notice how it feels as you inhale and exhale longer and deeper. Expand your belly as you inhale...draw the air deep into your diaphragm and allow your shoulders to rise as you finish the inhale. Then reverse this pattern and continue to slow the breathing down as much as possible.

Meditation is a relaxed and peacefully conscious state that is very different from a "normal" daily state. During meditation, one is choosing mindfulness, and to be a silent witness to an awakened state. You are not active, passive or doing. You may recognize the constant chatter of the mind. Each time you do, understand that "it is only a thought." Through meditation an individual reaches a heightened state of awareness which plugs into the deep recesses of the mind and different dimensions of reality. It takes great inner strength, patience, commitment, intention and conscious choosing to just sit and peacefully watch your mind...... It takes letting go of everything....everything.

It is more precise to say that mysticism and science
are converging and that both point to a universe
whose nature transcends them both.
~David Spangler, ~*Emergence-The Rebirth of the Sacred*

When we choose meditation and mindful living, we become accepting, tranquil and unconditional. We begin to choose wisely and consciously each moment. As we let go and surrender to each moment, fear and resistance to change dissolves. We let go of struggle and relax into the "the flow" of life, choosing to be *really* alive instead of being half-asleep or just existing.

We can use our meditation time as a time of prayer, connection to the Divine, receiving inner guidance, communion with self, just being still or focusing on one feeling, thought (such as peace or love) or mantra. The most important aspect of this time is clearing the mind of all thoughts and attachments, while sitting in a state of stillness, awareness and just being.

When Shakespeare said, "To be or not to be," maybe he was talking about this state of mind—this state of just being. ***Can you just be?*** That is the question.

As we meditate, we learn what a rich experience deep breathing can be. We find our awareness, receptivity and creativity increases while fear, anxiety and depression diminish. In learning to still the mind and let go of thoughts, we find peace instead of conflict and unconditional acceptance instead of judgments. In the "gap," or the space between thoughts, is a place where in the stillness, you can connect with your Higher Self and the field of pure potentiality. In this place you can plant seeds for your intentions and create a flourishing future. It is here that you will feel your connection to God, the infinite universe and all life. In the stillness, stress and worries melt away and you become free. As you taste the rich experience of breathing, you will begin to taste the rich experience of life and all that it can bring you.

I love the following quote which differentiates between a "busy" mind and an "active" mind:

> A tranquil mind is never busy, but is more active
> than the busy mind. It does things better than
> the busy mind. It is free from the confusion of
> the busy mind and it does things in an easier and
> other than mechanical way of doing things.
> ~*Yoga & Spiritual Healing Magazine*

An active mind can be more efficient, relaxed and healthier than a busy mind. An active mind contributes to optimal health whereas a busy mind would have a destructive effect on health.

I recently had a guest who stayed with me, who spoke incessantly. She filled every space, every second with her words. It was very tiring and overwhelming to have her speak non-stop without any need for interaction or to leave opportunities for others to talk. On and on she went, as if it was a race, to see how many words she could fit in a minute. I don't think she had any idea what she was doing. My mind would shut off and I would finally have to interrupt her so I could then ask her husband a question or two about their homeland and his interests.

If we truly want to connect with others, we need to leave space for interaction, communion and connecting at a level that feeds us both.

If we really care about other people and what they have to say and we truly want to listen, then we have to slow down...s..l..o..w... ..d..o..w..n. Everyone is moving so fast and is so busy. People are overworking and on a perpetual treadmill. There is too much homework for the kids and no time for anyone to even be creative, dream, relax or just be. Some people appear to be unconscious robots trying to keep up with life on a treadmill, in which the speed is picking up and going faster and faster. Others are obsessed with accomplishment and consuming....the "how much can we accomplish and consume in how little time" mode.

Lack of presence in each moment diminishes the quality of life. Many individuals are noticing this. That is why the "Slow Food" Movement has begun. They are trying to say to everyone, slow down and be a healthy contributor to life....eat slowly at a local slow food restaurant and buy locally produced food. The movement started in Italy and has evolved to other Slow Movements in Italy including "Slow Cities" and "Slow Sex." Sounds healthier already.....

Many institutions are noticing that though people work longer, they are less productive. There is no time to nurture the creative process. Harvard University has actually sent out a letter to new freshmen...and it is called the "Slow Down" letter. It actually advises freshmen students to slow their life down so that they will become better students, learners, business professionals and scientists.

Well-intentioned parents are often over-homeworking their children so that they can "achieve" more. But some schools are actually initiating homework bans for certain ages (to the dismay of parents), according to Carl Honore who wrote, *In Praise of*

Slowness. Carl noticed the ill effects in his life when he wanted to do "fast track" bedtime stories with his son. He suddenly realized that he was out of control and missing quality time with his son. As he began making changes, he enjoyed more moments of his day, story time with his son and even believes that he has found his "inner tortoise." You can find him on *TED Talks.*

When I was attaining my social work degree at University of New Hampshire, I found group work extremely interesting. We would each work with a group of 12 of our fellow students and take turns leading the group. It was one of the most interesting and useful aspects of my degree work. One day in a group session, only 3 individuals spoke and they monopolized most of the time. Very little was said by anyone else, because they couldn't get a word in without cutting off or interrupting the speakers. At the next session a week later everyone was encouraged to take part and speak in turns. It was fascinating to see the difference from the previous session. It felt completely and wonderfully different. The individuals who hadn't been able to speak in the previous session, spoke briefly, but had more profound thoughts to share than those who spoke incessantly. That was eye opening. Please ask quiet individuals what they think sometimes.....

When I have worked with groups in my office over the years, I have made sure that everyone has an opportunity to talk and I have encouraged the quieter participants, because I found as in years earlier that they had a great deal to share that was of interest to everyone.

One time in a juice fasting class I encouraged an older woman to speak about why she had chosen to attend the class. She shared that she thought maybe juice fasting would help her nightly leg cramps. She said that, although she had no support from her husband or friends for attending the class, she had decided to come anyway.

After a couple of weeks I asked her how she was doing and she shared with everyone that her nightly cramps had gone away. If I hadn't encouraged her to speak, we would all have missed her story. Moral—please allow everyone time to talk. Don't take up every moment with your words. Encourage others and gladly listen. You may be surprised at what they share.

Both positive and negative states of mind contain a certain amount of turbulence. Negative minds contain energy which is self-destructive to the whole being. Positive minds may be involved in a certain amount of artificial "mood-making." They may be trying to manipulate their thinking and trying to see a negative experience as a positive one. When you are living in a world of the "positive" and the "negative," you are living in the world of duality. You are living in one world or the other and back and forth between them. If it is not one world, it is the other. A mind that lives in neither, is tranquil and non-judgmental, lives in the moment and is spontaneously alive. It is a mind that is able to flow with ease, while accepting each moment as it comes.

If you live without focus, "never enough time," and you experience physical restlessness and mental chatter, then daily meditation is a must. Meditating daily will help you to connect with your unconscious mind and help you to let go of being consumed with achieving, and/or criticizing and evaluating yourself. You will begin to see more and more clearly that now is the only time that there is. You will begin to find that each day your decisions are based in peace and love and you will begin to let go of what tomorrow may bring. You will love all that you are today.

In slowing everything down, you will begin to see aspects of yourself that you didn't know existed and you will truly understand what unconditional means.

If you want to try something a little different for a daily meditation or you want to mix it up a little, you might try a Mayan focused meditation. The Mayans had 13 tones of creation. They would focus on one of the tones each day, due to its significance for that day. If you focus appropriately, you may experience each day more fully. I might suggest that you select one of these "tones" and see what occurs for you when you gently focus on it. Do you experience feelings, see colors, experience energies or any other phenomenon? What difference do you experience from one to another?

The following is a list of the 13 tones:
- Unity
- Challenge
- Activation
- Definition
- Radiance
- Equality
- Attunement
- Intention
- Manifestation
- Liberation
- Cooperation
- Transcendence

Going Deeper~

~Take time to be still, quiet and/or meditate. Do it for your whole being, body, mind, emotions, and spirit. Agree with yourself to do it once or twice daily, for 5-20 minutes.

~ Practice letting go of all thoughts—can you do it more easily and quiet your mind for longer periods of time each day?

~ Are you comfortable sitting quietly and being still? How does it feel to "just be"?

5

Beginning the Process

People can change at any age. Where there is life,
there is possibility. Even ancient beliefs can be
overturned or replaced in a matter of moments.
~Barry Kaufman, ~*Happiness is a Choice*

The only thing that we are guaranteed in life is "change." Life is
filled with it. As part of change, we are always gently and not so
gently guided toward our destiny. It may be more enjoyable, if
we learn tools that will help us to easily stay on our path. Can we
learn to go with the flow routine? If we resist the direction that life
is guiding us, there may be a lesson there for us. This book will
offer you tools for your process of letting go into change. You can
enjoy the process that is occurring. Hopefully you will see it from
the vantage point of opportunity and infinite possibility. This is a
process of letting go of all that is not supportive of the Authentic
You! That means everything that doesn't support you.

We have the tools—the knowhow to make our life everything
that we could ever want, but often we are so busy thinking that
we "don't know," "don't deserve" or "aren't worthy" that we have
become blind to what is really true! Some of these thoughts may
be recognized by you, while others may be held deep within your
unconsciousness. Traumatic events in our childhood can sometimes
set us up for living our whole life as if these beliefs were really true.

For example, if you grew up in a family where a parent always
told you to be quiet, not to ask questions and they also told you and
insinuated that they knew best for you, you could in turn come to

believe that you "didn't know" much or at least you didn't know what was best for yourself.

So how do we remove the blinders, the old ways of being and begin really living?

We can begin the process of totally changing our lives by looking at the way we think, what we believe (maybe even what we eat!), and begin moving toward our heart's desire. Through this process you will understand who you are and what you are capable of.

Let's look at the relationship of health to our mind and body as we begin this process.

6

The Health of Our Mind and Body

Neglect of the mind-body link by technological medicine
is actually a brief aberration when viewed against the
whole history of the healing art. In traditional medicine
and in western practice from its beginning in the work
of Hippocrates, the need to operate through the patient's
mind has always been recognized. Until the nineteenth
century, medical writers rarely failed to note the influence
of grief, despair or discouragement on the onset or
outcome of illness, nor did they ignore the healing effects
of faith, confidence and peace of mind. Contentment
used to be considered a prerequisite for health.
~Bernard Siegel, MD, ~*Love, Medicine and Miracles*

Health is not merely the absence of disease, but is a state of dynamic being that represents far more. It is a state that embodies joy, wellness, peace of mind, gratitude, energy, healing, acceptance, self-confidence, vitality, and awareness. Our physical health reflects far more than what we feed ourselves physically. It represents what we feed ourselves on all levels—physically, mentally, emotionally and spiritually.

Our health is reflected in our attitudes, our thoughts and our physical presence, which in turn affects our physiological systems and in turn, each and every cell in our body. Each thought that we think, what we feel, believe and speak creates biochemical effects in our body. When we think and speak in anxious, distressed and negative ways, we affect our biochemical physiology which can in turn affect and create dis-ease. A mind that is ill-at-ease produces a dis-eased body.

> Fear is a marvelous motivator. It is never
> a solution. It is always the cause of any
> discomfort, of any pain, of any illness.
> ~*Emmanuel's Book II*

Many individuals are motivated by their fear, guilt, and negativity. They feel that if they weren't in that space, they couldn't act. They don't label it as such, but they choose their experiences from their base in fear, anger, anxiety and/or being a victim. They feel secure there, because they know nothing else. They have been taught well from their parents, family and society. It may feel safe and secure because they know this place so well, but they could instead direct their life forward because they enjoy creativity, have faith in themselves and in the process of life.

Many researchers and practitioners today have finally come to realize and acknowledge that eighty-five per cent or more of physical disease has a strong connection to the emotional and mental attitudes that a person carries. As the pace of life speeds up, and individuals pressure themselves increasingly, their nervous systems experience an overload and constant challenge to their health.

Within our amazing physical systems, the built-in emergency protective system called the "Fight or Flight" Response helps us to deal as effectively as possible with "real" stresses. This response is present to protect us from life threatening situations. When the fight or flight response kicks in, it prepares us, to literally, fight or run for our life and to flee from that real or imaginary "tiger." It's an automatic response that may be triggered again and again, whether we know it or not. It is a response that protects our life and health, but it may be triggered when we don't need to fight or run. We may judge many stimuli as threatening when they are not. Past programing and constant stress can have us unconsciously and automatically *reacting* when we could have consciously *responded* instead.

In order for us to react quickly to challenging situations, many systems shut down and normal activities in the body are placed on hold. The body is quickly prepared for physical exertion while metabolic functions are suppressed, the heartbeat and blood pressure increases, senses are heightened and the blood flow increases to the brain and major muscles.

Just look at how the *Fight or Flight* response affects our physiology and nervous system:

1) suppression of metabolic processes, 2) change in circulation patterns, (Blood channeled to the core rather than the extremities causing cold hands and feet as a result of constant real or imagined stress), 3) lowered immune function (including a lowered white blood cell count) and 4) an overworked stress response (adrenals, hormonal system, and the gastrointestinal tract are affected).

The *Fight or Flight* system can literally save our lives, but the problem today, is that this system is too often triggered inappropriately by situations which may be stressful but not life-threatening. Today, these life-threatening situations happen far less than imagined stresses which can occur from moment to moment. *Our bodies, mind and stress response system, however, cannot always distinguish between a hypothetical threat (which is imagined) and a real and genuine one.*

Our bodies can respond very effectively to stressful situations. In his initial work with the stress response and the body's ability to adapt to stressful situations, Hans Selye found that: 1) the adrenal cortex (our stress gland) became enlarged 2) there was atrophy and shrinkage of the thymus, spleen and lymph structures (immune system components), 3) almost total disappearance of the white blood cells occurred (immune system) and 4) bleeding ulcers occurred in the stomach and duodenal areas. If our bodies can potentially self-destruct when we over-react to stress, it is imperative that we decide to consciously choose creative (as opposed to destructive) responses to our life's challenges.

Research has actually proven that when we think negative thoughts, our cells can actually assimilate toxins in our systems, while on the other hand, when we think positive, loving and happy thoughts, our cells open to nutrients and welcome them in. With each action and thought that we choose, we either move toward life or away from it, toward creation or destruction, toward health or disease. We are either demonstrating that we want to live enthusiastically and be alive, or we are shutting down to life and moving toward destruction and death. (These are definitely not usually conscious choices but they do create self-fulfilling prophecies.) When we criticize ourselves and put ourselves down, or choose to feel guilty or angry, we in turn create discomfort and dis-ease in our body. According to the ease and zest for life that we hold—we create health and wellness or disease and illnesses in corresponding degrees.

> Physical ailments are always a sign of a resistance
> in the physical being; but with surrender to the
> Divine's Will and a complete trust in the working of
> the Grace, they are bound to disappear soon.
> (*unknown*)

Deepak Chopra has said that: *"We are the only creatures on earth that can change our biology by what we think and feel."* Amazing...what we can create! We are powerful! Our bodies do reflect everything that we think and feel. Our posture, the look on our face and every organ, tissue and cell reflect what we think and the beliefs that we hold and have held. We literally become what we think and believe. Look at people's posture... Someone who stands upright, back straight, eyes looking forward, shoulders back, and a spring in their step certainly will have a different kind of health, both emotionally and physically, than someone whose shoulders are forward, eyes looking down, back curved forward to support their head and no spring in their step. Who would you hire if you needed a worker?

Our body becomes a transformer of the energies of the mind—converting our beliefs and feelings into energy that feeds the body in different ways. Negative feelings and insecurities create dis-ease and a withdrawal from life and health. Emotions of grief, fear, anger, shame, and injury may dwell in our body from the first moment that they are experienced and stay with us for indefinite lengths of time (and possibly many lifetimes). These vibrations or electromagnetic frequencies then become lodged in areas that tend to hold those vibrational frequencies, possibly indefinitely.

> Modern medicine knows less than 10%
> of what your body knows instinctively.
> ~Deepak Chopra MD

When we are out of balance with the "flow" of life and we are holding vibrations of fear and negativity, we actually attract more of the same to us. ***What we focus on increases—what we fear and what we love is attracted to us.*** We actually attract everything that we need to perpetuate the state that we continue to affirm we are in. With negativity, we may hold it experience it and live it until we have had enough of it, and then hopefully we can finally make other choices! Have you ever had that happen when you just say to yourself: *enough!*

States of mind that individuals perpetuate could happen through affirming, "I don't know," "It's very hard," or "What a struggle!" As we continue to voice these thoughts, we are continuing their presence as truth for us. But as we become more and more aware of these defeating and destructive thoughts, we can let go of the old programming, consciously design and state what we want and align with more creative and beneficial choices. We can place our attention on our intention. What is it that you want to intend?

For example, instead of saying that something is "very hard to do," we could, for fun, actually say that it is, "no big deal" or even better…"easy to do," and then see the difference that it makes.

At the very least you might laugh and feel more relaxed about the outcome, while at the most, there may be a radical difference in both the process and outcome. We will actually feel very different when we change our thoughts about something as being very easy, as opposed to very hard. Try it now and feel the difference in your mind and body:

Pause for a moment, say the word "hard" to yourself and feel the essence of that word. Say it to describe something in your life. How do you feel when you say it to yourself? Then say the word "easy" and repeat the exercise. What do you notice as a difference between the two words? You can do this with any word or words. The words may mean something different to you than they do to someone else. Some words may impart for some people much more negativity than they do for others.

It does work—we *can* actually feel very different when we change our thoughts about something being very easy as opposed to very hard. We are far more likely to even smile or laugh when we say "it is easy." (even if we don't believe it)

When we say we "don't know" something, we actually limit our ability to be in touch with "our knowing." We may block ourselves to listening for and finding the answers that we seek. We create what we affirm. Recently I had a client that lost some keys and just couldn't find them. I told her to affirm that she "knew where they were." Within a day she found them in a place she would never have looked, but was *somehow* guided to look there. She felt it worked!

When we say that something is "a struggle," we believe and are affirming that what is occurring is "hard," "difficult," impossible," and a "problem." When choosing these words we are acknowledging that we are a victim of life, believing in struggle, and are powerless to change the circumstances and outcomes. These perceptions block us to seeing solutions, ease, and the many possibilities that we have the power to create.

Creatively changing how we perceive different stimuli may have dramatic and life altering results. Many individuals in my workshops have been amazed with the ease they experience in life when they change their mental and verbal dialogues and open themselves to new perceptions. Try it for yourself and have fun with the process. You will be rewarded for your efforts.

Our human bodies absorb what we emotionally and mentally experience in our thoughts and feelings. Many individuals are not aware of the constant emotional interplay between the mind and the body. The process is invisible to us, even though the emotions become trapped in different locations in the physical body. Vast amounts of feelings and information are stored in the subconscious and in turn our bodies. Everything that we have stressfully experienced throughout our lifetimes, from injuries to painful emotions, may become trapped internally.

Example: We spend the afternoon with someone that we dislike and with whom we feel discomfort. We leave late in the afternoon thinking, "What a pain in the neck!" Then we wonder why later that night our neck feels tense, stiff and painful. Whether we say to ourselves, "he's a pain in the neck!" or we merely decide to choose to be tense because of the situation, we are subtly programming tension and discomfort into our systems. We are reacting to the situation, feeling mental discomfort, then, in turn creating physical discomfort, which becomes statically internalized on a physical level. The following will give you more information.

In Louise Hay's book, *You Can Heal Your Life,* which was written many *years* ago, Louise gives numerous examples of "probable causes" for numerous illnesses. The following are a few examples:

Pain	Guilt, guilt always seeks punishment
Parasites	Giving power to others, letting them take over.
Asthma	Smother love, inability to breathe for oneself. Feeling stifled, suppressed.

Cataracts	Dark future, an inability to see ahead with joy.
Anxiety	Not trusting the flow and process of life.
Constipation	Refusing to release old ideas, stuck in the past.
Headaches	Self-criticism, fear, invalidating self.

In her book, Louise gives caring and supportive affirmations for each condition. These affirmations may help to reverse the unsupportive, unloving thinking and programming that is unconsciously chosen. It may originate from their parents or others but becomes internalized indefinitely.

Please take time to do the following exercise. It will help you to be more aware of how stressful stimuli affect you:

Sit quietly and comfortably in a relaxed and meditative state. Breathe deeply and release all tension. Breathe it out. Breathe it away. Relax your shoulders and allow your jaw to relax and your mouth to open slightly. Let all of the tension drain out of your body.

As you sit there, become aware of one situation that you feel uncomfortable with. Place it in your mind with all your attention focused totally on it. As you think about this situation become aware of what feelings or sensations you have in your body. Become more specific with your attention and find where in your body these sensations are located and describe them to yourself as best you can. What emotion, color, feeling is located in which areas? Be curious and really explore and see what you find. Our energetic feelings can really manifest as physical blocks, restriction, inflammation, toxicity and more. If you find any areas that need change, you may breathe the energy out or bring in white or colored light to heal those areas. You can create your own ritual of healing if you wish.

As you finish the exercise….bless yourself and surround yourself with protective white light and spiritual healing energy in whatever way feels appropriate for you.

What did you learn?

Our nature to succumb to stress or our willingness to be challenged by it, will strongly affect our future wellness. When we internalize negative feelings, overwhelming tension, depressing energy, and traumatic memories, they accumulate in our body and can adversely affect our health. Most importantly, it is important to acknowledge that *we are always doing "our best" in all circumstances.* We can support and honor ourselves, while believing in our power to find personal solutions.

In time, we may no longer react to situations and experiences and become anxious, stressed, tense or upset. If we trust in ourselves, accept what is occurring and create solutions, we will no longer live in negativity and fear and then create dis-ease. Stress and tension, or health and peace of mind—the choice is really ours!

One curious fact arises through my reading and research from Deepak Chopra. He says that, and this is very important, *the body's trillions of cells totally replace themselves over varying lengths of time.* The liver does it in 3 months, the brain in 6 weeks, the skin in 4 weeks and the stomach in 3 weeks. If the body is capable of totally renewing itself physically, on an ongoing basis, then how does disease and physical illness remain??? What is holding the disease in the organs, tissues and systems?? Is it our destructive belief systems? What do you think?

Our bodies are always striving toward balance and health despite what we do or don't do. We have within our physiology the means and bio-chemicals to create antibiotics, tranquilizers and anti-cancer drugs—all with the exact right dose and in perfect harmony with our body's own homeostatic systems. If we have this potential to renew, heal and be well, then what holds disease within us? If we replace 98% of all the atoms in our bodies within less than one year, why isn't there total renewal and health along with it? .....interesting.

If we hold the imprint of trauma, tension, injury and stress energetically, we may prevent the body's healing mechanisms from completely and thoroughly healing itself. As we continue to energetically hold the past and it becomes "stuck" in our physiology, it may need something dynamic to dislodge it. Some holistic measures to promote this type of healing include: homeopathy, energetic healing, regular exercise, massage and bodywork, juice fasting and detoxification and Ondamed Biofeedback. I use Ondamed therapy with my clients. It can quickly increase healing potential, detoxification, while reducing stress. Individuals don't realize how long these imprints remain in our energetic systems. They can remain indefinitely and progressively affect our health, through poor circulation, pain, stiffness, illness, and a myriad of other possibilities.

Health and Stress

All healing is a release from fear and suffering
~Course in Miracles

Since it is well known that up to eighty-five percent or more of dis-ease has emotional and mental origins, it is important to acknowledge that stress affects both our health and the quality of our wellbeing.

In Chinese and Oriental medicine, which is over 5000 years old, it is believed that there are external and internal causes of stress. Internal causes which are known as the "seven emotions" include: joy, anger, overconcentration, and obsession, worry, grief, fear, and shock. The 12 meridians or energy pathways are associated with different organ systems and each has specific emotional correspondence. Acupuncture practitioners believe that excessive emotions or inhibition of them have a detrimental physical effect.

For example, the corresponding emotion for the liver and gall bladder is anger, which could be expressed or inhibited, resulting in a stiff neck and shoulders, headaches or menstrual and menopausal problems. They also believe that excessive anger "exhausts the blood," in turn effecting energy, vitality, and blood distribution.

Joy or lack of joy is connected to the heart and circulation. Grief and worry, on the other hand, is believed to be collected in the lungs and large intestine. Symptoms might include bowel problems, fatigue, skin problems, colds, asthma or poor posture. Fear and fright is recognized as dwelling in the heart, kidneys and bladder. Symptoms may include bedwetting in children, urinary and circulatory problems and arthritis. Shock may first affect the heart and then be stored in the spleen causing fatigue, edema and anemia.

> Nowhere has the power of scientific materialism
> had more influence than in the medical system.
> Consequently, it should come as no surprise
> that health care, itself, is now gravely ill.
> ~Bruce H. Lipton Ph.D. & Steve Bhacrman,
> ~*Spontaneous Evolution*

"Fear at the present time is playing a great part in intensifying disease, and modern science has increased the reign of terror by spreading abroad to the general public its discoveries, which as yet are but half-truths.....there is a factor which science is unable to explain on physical grounds, and that is why some people become affected by disease whilst others escape, although both classes may be open to the same possibility of infection..... Fear, by its depressing effect on our mentality, thus causing disharmony in our physical and magnetic bodies, paves the way for invasion, and if bacteria and such physical means were the sure and only cause of disease, then indeed there might be but little encouragement not to be afraid. But when we realize that in the worst epidemics only a portion of those exposed to infection are attacked and that, ... the real cause of disease lies in our own personality and is within our control, then we have reason to go about without dread and fearless, knowing that the remedy lies within ourselves. We can put all fear...out of our minds, knowing that such anxiety merely renders us susceptible... and that we need anticipate illness no more than we dread being struck by lightning or hit by a fragment of a falling meteor."

~Edward Bach M.B.,D.P.H., ~*Heal Thyself* copyright 1931

The Mind and Healing

The root cause of most physical ailments is connected
with <u>not</u> living in accordance with one's inner guidance.
~Shakti Gawain, ~*Listening to Inner Wisdom,*
Unity Magazine May/June 2006

Lewis Thomas, who was president of *Memorial Sloan-Kettering Cancer Center* and professor of pathology and medicine at *Cornell University*, wrote an essay on warts and how hypnotic suggestion could cause them to disappear. Thomas wrote, "It is one of the great mystifications of science: Warts can be ordered off the skin by hypnotic suggestion." Our mind is very powerful in creating and changing many things. He further wrote, "There almost has to be a Person in charge, running matters of meticulous detail beyond anyone's comprehension, a skilled engineer and manager, a chief executive officer, the head of the whole place."

Healing can occur on all levels of our being when we make conscious choices, create healthy belief systems, get in touch with and let go of stored feelings, and adopt new attitudes, intentions, beliefs and ways of being. As we heal and change, we may we may feel the old and stored emotions that are released during the healing process. We can then choose to connect with the past experiences, judgments, angers, fears, and resentments and then we can release and heal the past. ***By feeling it, we are healing it.*** It may be important for most people to go to a qualified practitioner to help them with this process. I have worked with many individuals with Ondamed Biofeedback, Emotional Freedom Technique (EFT), Past Life Regression, Trager Bodywork, and other healing techniques. An individual may not always be able to do it by themselves, but they can get to the point of recognizing that they need help. EFT is very helpful, can be learned by anyone, and used in physical and emotional healing.

As our cells replace themselves every moment of the day, the only thing that remains permanent and deep within us, is our memories of various emotional experiences, and the pain, and feelings associated with those experiences. It is the painful memories connected with our programmed and conditioned reactions which cause disease states and physical ailments to seem permanent. But as we release and let go of the emotional pain and we eliminate the feelings connected with our memories, we have the opportunity to dissolve disease and to promote real healing. The memory may remain, but the dis-ease state and the pain can be dissolved and released!

Author Stevin Levine has said, "touch, or ..enter with mercy and awareness, those areas of ourselves from which we have withdrawn in anger and judgment." For healing to occur, we need to employ *merciful awareness* and unconditional acceptance of our pain, traumas and emotions. There is no judgment allowed. By feeling and focusing on physical and emotional sensations as they arise, we can heal stored emotions. By being there with these sensations and unconditionally loving ourselves, we can then watch them dissipate as we experience ourselves healing. (Try just loving yourself throughout each day. Look at yourself in the mirror and say, "I love you." That would be extremely beneficial for anyone just starting this process.)

If we can actually enter any area of pain as it arises and place our attention there, we can open our heart to healing ourselves and bring life back to stagnant, numb and lifeless areas. By breathing light into our dark and traumatized areas, by focusing on loving those areas, we can soften the tissues, improve circulation and promote healing.

As we change emotionally and release old beliefs and past hurts, we can finally enjoy really loving ourselves. As the old areas which have been numb and clogged begin to heal, we can actually feel layers of pain as these areas awaken to trusting and feeling. Bringing *merciful awareness* says, Steven Levine, "into our being, heals our pain and brings the sacred into the healing process." One sign of true healing is that people around you are "left with a sense of trust in the process." When we are in a space of love, healing, trust, faith in the Divine and peace of mind....people will be drawn to us and want to be around us because it feels so soothing. I have felt it in my own life. When I am in a creative and joyful place of personal integrity I feel that people are attracted to me even from a distance. The reverse is true as well. When I am in a negative space, I feel as if people disappear...

> Let your receptivity increase this year, to the extent of
> giving you the power to fully utilize the Force that
> is at work for restoring perfect good health in you.
> (*unknown*)

The following information has been used in "Life is an Opportunity" classes for handouts. I have included a few from each class. Please decide what works for you and what does not. All that is offered are possibilities for you to use grow and play with.

Visualization

Visualization is a tool which may be used for our benefit. Through this process we may consciously create desired outcomes in our life by sensing or seeing with our inner mental eyes. It is one of the best and easiest tools for personal evolution and change. In these exercises you want to focus using the right brain, creative infinity mode (leave the left brain and logical thinking behind). Step away from what you and others may think is possible and have fun with creating. It is really important not to focus on what you lack or don't have, but on what it would feel like to have your goal now. This tests your faith in what you cannot see and helps you to focus on what you want and do have. Your imagination is far more powerful than your willpower and fear. Every thought is recorded in the subconscious, so don't build up a mass of negative, fearful thoughts. Eliminate from your vocabulary: "I can't," "I don't,' and "I haven't," as well as all statements with negatives in them. Do these exercises with peace, confidence and faith. Be really clear about what you want. There are infinite possibilities and opportunities.

Aristotle said, *"The soul can't think without pictures."*

Visualization has been used for over 60,000 years by shamans and medicine men and is presently being used by businesses, schools, athletes, and individuals to create measurable results and goal achievement.

Visualization is a science with steps and guidelines that may be used for:
    Healing
    Creativity
    Performance
    Decreasing stress
    Increasing sales
    Increasing self-esteem
    Releasing roadblocks
    Creating change and new patterns

Our daydreams in a sense allow for unconscious creating. We can achieve quicker results if we are truly conscious, systemic and use great detail. Make it fun and enjoy the process! Thought>>picture>>>Action>>>>Manifestation.

The best manifestations come with the involvement of your heart. Use meaningful words and expressions. What does your heart desire? What would you love to experience? Allow for miracles.... They happen every day...

Really KNOW what you want, make it three dimensional and create it on all levels:
    Attention to it, and intend it
    See it
    Taste it
    Smell it
    Feel it
    Hear it
    Behave as if you have it

Use your visual, gustatory, olfactory, kinesthetic and auditory senses.

Our dreams are achieved when we tap into the deepest recesses of our mind and heart where our ability to create lies. Nature effortlessly thrives and continually creates from her unbounded potential…. Be like nature.

*Research has found that the more senses are engaged the denser the wiring of the brain becomes. (Up to ninety percent of the brain may be used.)

It is best to do it for no more than thirty seconds of visualization at a time. (If done without doubt, thirty seconds is enough. Some of my quickest manifestations have been when I did quick affirmations that were stated dynamically with certainty!)

There are morphic fields that are like clouds of group energy and they are filled with group beliefs…plug into the ones for creation and infinite possibilities. Use others for creativity and potential to raise your energy to higher levels. (Make sure you avoid the ones for loss, shame, lack, etc.)

When you are not consciously visualizing, *pay attention to what you focus on because the mind doesn't know the difference between what you want and what you don't want.* This is very important. Many individuals focus incessantly on what they are afraid of creating or having, not what they truly want! Over time eliminate your wasteful and fearful thoughts. Each time you notice them, replace them with something creative and beautiful!

> Your focus is your reality.
> ~Obi Wan Kenobi, ~*Stars Wars*

I have had fun with this process many times. One fun experience was when I was traveling out West with my sons. We were driving east from Northwest Canada and on the thruway in Ohio when I decided that I really wanted to eat at a buffet restaurant. The highway food is so bad, that I wanted more extensive choices. I probably drove another ½ hour and got off at an exit. I drove for a while but found nothing immediately. I decide that I would continue back toward the highway and then I saw a mall and shopping area where I decided to stop. We parked and stepped out of the car and I turned and looked behind me and there was a large sign "BUFFET." I was a little surprised. It was the most amazing one ever and was actually voted the BEST in all of the USA....shrimp cocktails, make your own ice cream sundaes and everything that you could imagine in between. I did the same thing in Florence, Florida when I felt like a Buffet. Try it sometime!

It doesn't have to take a lot of time. Just visualize what you want (free of doubt).

Fun visualizations:

1) An uplifting visualization is to visualize jumping into the sun. The sun's light is very healing. Visualize the power of the sun's energy flowing through every cell and clearing your energy of negativity, stress, trauma and whatever else you no longer need. Let go and be cleansed of the past. Have fun with this one!

2) How about jumping into an alternative universe which you create? There could be many fun scenarios with this one! Jump into a fun vacation, camping trip, exotic place....

3) How many different versions of yourself can you imagine? Really step outside the box to blow open those limits!

All that is required is to know this.
For you are the creator of your reality,
and life can show up no other way for you than that way
in which you think it will. You think it into being.
This is the first step in creation. God the Father is thought.
Your thought is the parent which gives birth to all things.
~Neale Donald Walsch, ~*Conversations With God, Book 1*

Affirmations

One key to personal joy and opportunity is to always focus your energy on what you do want! Affirmations work really well because you are focusing on what you want, not what you <u>don't</u> want.

Create affirmations with ease and joy:

~Be very clear, precise and to the point. If you need $5,000, what is it you really need it for? If you need a car, then ask for the car.

1) Use it to create what you want. Use a strong positive statement that something is already so, as if it is happening now.

2) When creating an affirmation, ask yourself: "Do I really want this goal?" Do I believe that it is possible for me to attain? Am I willing to accept this creative change in my life? When you create pictures along with the affirmations be sure to see them as if they are happening <u>now</u>.

3) See yourself achieving and being this goal. Enjoy the process while making any changes you need to. Modify and expand as needed.

4) Experience all the feelings that would be associated with achieving this desire. Tell yourself: "I deserve the very best in life and I deserve to have what I want and need. See your desire in vivid colorful pictures.

5) Ask for and create what you want, not the money to get what you want. See yourself smiling and having your heart's desires.

Be patient with yourself while you create. It may take up to 3 weeks to create new brain and energetic patterns so keep holding yourself and your thoughts in the highest of love.

There have been times when I have done simple affirmations that have really worked to shift my energy, creative process and perspective. I have just affirmed simple statements such as: "I can," "My life is magical," "Everything is easy," "I am so thankful" or "I am blessed." Make up your own or try these examples.

How to create wellness and stay well~

1) Do what brings you joy, fulfillment and supports your true worth. You are an amazing creation.
2) Nourish, support, love, and encourage yourself.
3) Release all negative emotions and forgive yourself. Let go of the old anger, resentment, fear and sadness.
4) Focus on what you truly want and visualize yourself there.
5) Let love and unconditional acceptance be the primary expression of your life.
6) Be involved in fun, loving, honest and intimate relationships. Heal wounds of the past.
7) Contribute to your community in some way.
8) Accept everything in your life as an opportunity for growth.
9) Hold profound gratitude.
10) Eat local and organic food.
11) Take life lightly and keep a sense of humor always.

Going Deeper~

~ What percentage of your thoughts are positive and creative? Negative? Neutral?

~ Are you aware of fearful thoughts that you have? What fears do you live with daily?

~ How well can you quiet and release your fears?

~ Are you a victim sometimes? You are being a victim if you feel hopeless or struggle...

~ Do you understand that your health is affected by your emotions?

When I was creating a course and workshop for teaching and supporting individuals to change their lives, my biggest challenge was in deciding where to start. There were so many possibilities, I wasn't sure how to put it together. After going through many personal changes I realized that the most important starting point was with our belief systems. We need to look at what we believe, what we have learned to believe and what we have perceived to be true.

So, let's look at how belief systems contribute to who we believe we are.

7

Belief Systems

My life experience has often been different from many people around me. I have always felt connected to Source/Great Spirit/ the Divine Universe, the unseen and guided by my intuition. It has often been reassuring. I have felt very blessed when I received, needed support. These gifts have kept me interested in exploring avenues that I may not have understood, such as heaven, reincarnation, spiritual philosophy, psychic healing, angels, "knowing," PTSD, and quite a variety of other interesting subjects.

I have felt fortunate that I came to understand that I could use my intuition to guide my intellect to the most appropriate healing possibilities and answers, as Einstein has verbalized:

The Intuitive Mind is a Sacred Gift
and the rational mind is a faithful servant
and has forgotten The Sacred Gift.

The intuitive approach worked well for me. I realized that the answers I received weren't always what I might have expected. I remember one time when I actually asked that a client do less in her life, rather than adding more supplements, therapies, etc. She actually said that she was relieved.

In listening to my intuition and my heart I was guided to live in natural and nontraditional ways. I chose to give birth to my babies at home, for example. There was no other way that I could do it and be true to myself. I pray, enjoy quiet time and meditation on the hill in my back yard each morning before I start my work day. Many of the personal choices I have made were not always logical, but based in my strong spiritual beliefs and connection to the Divine. This was how I had to live. I feel really blessed and grateful that I have been so connected to my heart and guided by the Universe.

When I was growing up my mother allowed me personal freedom that was free from her beliefs. Certainly I absorbed from her many unconscious beliefs, but she didn't consciously or constantly tell me "how I should live." I was very fortunate. The freedom she gave me was a blessing, but also provided challenges for me to explore while finding my way in the world.

When I meet new individuals, it often doesn't take me long to understand how they look at life, whether they experience it from a positive or negative viewpoint, a "cup is half empty" or "half full" vantage point. Often the first words that people say will give you an indication as to how they were brought up and how they see life.

Think about the times when you asked friends and family how they were doing. How many usually responded with a "not too bad" response? I have heard it as a fairly common response, especially around town—at the post office or supermarket. I feel that when individuals respond with a "not too bad" reply, that they measure their life in terms of "bad, worse and worst" as in things could be worse.

I am not suggesting that people deny or lie about what they are feeling, but many individuals could appreciate and focus on what they have rather than what they are lacking. When we look at the cup as half empty, we focus on what we don't have rather than what we do have. The words we use can determine the feelings that we create and hold. Depending on the words, we may continue to see what is lacking rather than what is "full," here, in this moment.

One day when I was at the dentist's office, something written on the bottom of a calendar caught my eye. It said:

> Yesterday is the past.
> Tomorrow is the future.
> But today is a gift.
> That's why it is called the Present.
> ~Bil Keane

If we don't learn to look at each moment as a "gift," then we may only see what isn't working, what is bad, what can only get worse, what is lacking, what we need, what we don't deserve, and what complaints we have. We will see what life brings to us through the eyes of negativity, lack and a "not deserving" mentality. We then live in a downward spiral, rather than seeing ongoing opportunities and continual enrichment.

> History is a reflection of the evolution and
> conflicts of the beliefs and belief systems created
> and extolled by fragments of consciousness.
> Every political movement, every religion, every
> psychology of mind, every interpretive science
> began with the expression of a single belief.
> ‑‑Harry Palmer, ~*Creativism*

There are at least 6 things we hold and utilize that continually affect who we are: our beliefs, attitudes, thoughts, feelings, choices and imagination. Let's start by looking at beliefs and see how they affect our lives.

We all hold many, many beliefs, of which, we are totally unaware. Everything we do, and everything that we think is governed by beliefs that we hold. We have held many beliefs for years, that we may have never have consciously chosen. We have been very well trained to think and act the way we do. Some individuals may call it "conditioned response" or "collective conditioning." The neurological patterning that we hold was created by beliefs of our family, friends and those around us. It is reinforced over time and then we behave in alignment with these belief patterns. Most individuals do not realize and understand the degree to which they are governed and ruled by what they believe. In essence, we have lost most of our "free will" to unconscious beliefs, causing us to see life in a mechanistic way that is fragmented and full of separation and competition. We have lost most of our ability to deeply connect with one another, to be self-determining and autonomous. (Hopefully this book will lead you to create and choose the best for yourself.) *The way we think and see the world has been produced by unrecognized cultural belief systems.* We have lost our connection to something very deep within us. *We are living in a trance of "the collective unconsciousness"* as Deepak Chopra might say.

> As the name implies, humanity is a life form defined
> by the trait of being *humane*. Throughout history there
> have been many exemplary humans who have lived
> by the humane values of compassion, philanthropy,
> kindness, benevolence, charity and generosity.....
> Today's civilization, by strict definition, more
> accurately represents inhumanity than humanity.
> ~Bruce H. Lipton Ph.D. & Steve
> Bhaerman, ~*Spontaneous Evolution*

I will give you an example of unconscious conditioning. I purchased an electric dog fence—one which has an electrically charged wire running beneath the ground. When a dog wears a battery powered collar and gets too close to the area of the buried electric wire, which is visibly marked by white flags placed above the ground along the wire, the dog will be warned by hearing a tone. If the dog continues closer to the flag the dog will receive a strong electric shock through the collar. This in turn usually causes the dog to yelp loudly and move away from the flags for safety. Once the dogs are trained over a two week period to keep their distance from the flags, they no longer need to wear the collars and the fence no longer needs to be plugged in. They have learned to believe that the area where the flags are, is a threat to their safety and so they stay clear. They have been conditioned over time to respond in a certain way. They are responding to an "imagined" threat that was once "real." (The electronic fence allows the dogs to be outside without supervision.)

Another example is similar to the previous one. A dog was attached to a chain in his yard every day. In time, the chain became dislodged at the fixed end and was not attached. The dog however didn't know this and continued indefinitely to stay within his normal range. This dog was conditioned to believe in certain limitation and it behaved accordingly despite the fact that its freedom was only a step away.

> A belief not only limits your imagining,
> but also limits your entire consciousness.
> ~Lynn Andrews, ~*The Woman of Wyrrd*

> And I have no beliefs.
> For to believe, is to limit my knowing.
> ~Lynn Andrews, ~*Shakkai*

We can look at belief systems as a mental framework or skeleton to which we keep adding our experiences, our judgments, and our perceptions. To support each belief, we may store data in our mental, emotional and physical bodies and in our body's computer, the mind as well. Whatever we program becomes a part of our software and "programming." Whether it is creative or destructive, it proceeds to create our reality.

Belief Systems (B.S.) affect us according to the different levels, intensities, and power that we give them. In his essay called *Creativism*, Harry Palmer mentioned some of the following about belief systems. Individuals can actually become crippled by their B.S. They may adhere to them so strongly that they lose their ability to observe, reason and be flexible (fear has a lot to do with this). Questioning others about their beliefs may cause aggressive reactions, manipulation and defensive behavior. They may verbalize something to the effect of: "You will be severely punished if you do that." (Aggressive threats to get you to refrain from doing something that you want to do.) "You make me angry." (as if you have the power to make others feel angry.)

On the other hand, there are large groups of beliefs that are widely accepted as fact or doctrine. They pass without question as common knowledge and as broadly held thoughts about what is true. It is the man-made logic that is often held behind the customs and common actions of groups of peoples and societies. If anyone questions any of these beliefs they are looked at as crazy, weird, unintelligent, strange and different rather than intelligent, autonomous or thinking individuals. *Those individuals who blindly follow the belief systems of their culture are always looking for support for their belief systems by appealing to the mental and emotional weaknesses and the insecurities of others.* They may say such things as, "Go to a professional who knows what you should do" or "Doctors know what is best for you." (as if you don't often know what is best for yourself) or "Sometimes you just have to do what you are told whether you like it or not." (Some individuals speak as if you have no intelligence or right to choose other than to surrender to others wishes).

Certainly, religion has fit into the category of belief systems. We have certainly watched it change over the centuries. We have seen reincarnation being spoken of in the Bible and then removed as individuals didn't want it there. Let's look at the following example:

In 869A.D. a pivotal point occurred in the history of religion and spirituality:

Pope Nicholas declared as of that time "the spirit doesn't exist anymore" ... and that "we are just mind and body." The Eighth Ecumenical Council decreed that what he said was true, so that from that time forward, spirit was to mean "strength of character" and nothing more.

But despite Pope Nicholas and his belief systems, "spirit" and spirituality have made a comeback! It hasn't been easy for everyone to deny the celestial light and the Spiritual-force that pervades all life. Many individuals have had enlightening experiences such as near death experiences, deja-vu happenings and a "sense of knowing' that leads them to believe in more than they can see or feel. There are many books available now on growth, energy healing, reincarnation and spirituality. Many classes, workshops and quite a variety of practitioners, are guiding individuals toward remembering and recovering their spiritual heritage. Through meditation, quiet contemplation, introspection and quieting the mind, individuals are reaching new and deeper levels of awareness.

Through these various means, individuals have moved from focus on an outer, superficial, material world where they feel separated and powerless, to awareness of living from an inner world, based in the heart, authenticity, and connection to the Divine.

The Heisenberg Uncertainty Principle

The Heisenberg Uncertainty Principle is very interesting to me. It concerns objective scientific study and double blind control experiments. Werner Heisenberg, a Nobel Prize winner, evolved a principle from information obtained from studying an electron. It states that one cannot look at a physical object without changing it. It means that objects and clients are changed when we observe them and that a researcher cannot stand apart from the research or research subject or project. Our words, actions, touching and presence affect everything around us. We are all affected by others in the same way. We are often feeling what others are thinking and feeling, whether we realize it or not. Sometimes we may not be able to distinguish between what is, "ours" and "theirs."

The last category that I wish to note is a fun and beneficial one if used appropriately. This is where our creativity can enhance our spiritual, mental and emotional growth in a way that really benefits us. *We can intentionally create our own belief systems* as we go through life. We can change them as we see fit or as the need arises. They don't have to be hard and inflexible realities, but may be flexible and adaptable to our evolution. Examples of these are: "I always make the best choices" or "Life teaches me what I need to know as I go along" or "I always have all the answers and help I need" or "I will figure it out, I always do" or "I am really, really lovable."

You can see from these examples how one could possibly utilize belief systems to justify their actions. Make sure that you don't fall into this trap, but have fun with your creative capacities. You can always explore your growth by trying different beliefs and seeing how they work.

Our beliefs and belief systems are based upon our upbringing:

1) The beliefs of our parents, family members, relatives, friends
2) Cultural and societal beliefs which are religious, national, political, local
3) What we see on television, hear on the radio and from the media
4) Misperceptions, fears, programming, trauma and past conditioning (all of which we may have totally and unconsciously accepted)

Most of us have grown up living in a web of collective conditioning. We never knew that it was there or that we could question it, we just totally accepted it. It is like an invisible fog that totally surrounds us and permeates our entire being—affecting everything about us, including our consciousness, choices, health and ability to see, perceive, reason and create.

Our younger years may contain many belief systems about how life "should be"…..
We may hold beliefs about:
Bringing up children—conservative, progressive, independent or none
Relationships—honesty, caring, communication, touching, intimacy
Pleasure and play—quality, quantity, freedom, joy, no time for it
Work experience—ease, struggle, balance with play, quality, passion
Time—being on time, being late, aging, worry about
Life—living with ease or struggle, meaning of life, passion for
Emotions & Feelings—Happiness, sadness, shame, anger, guilt, being right or wrong, good or bad, success or failure….
Love—unconditional, conditional, dependency, neediness, unlovable, lovable

Competition—its importance or lack of importance, need to
Money—success, failure, abundance, lack, worthiness, need
Gender Roles—male and female roles and identification
Our Culture—how to live, interact, eat, relate to others
Religion—Right or Wrong behavior, fear based, social
prejudices

What we have learned in each of these categories will determine
our beliefs and the quality of our life. Children often follow in their
parents footsteps, whether they intend to or not. It takes a great deal
of awareness to do otherwise.

Children who have grown up with negative, fearful parents
who consistently reacted to life with anger, frustration, guilt and
depression learned subconsciously from their parents to choose to
feel these feelings in connection with life and themselves. They were
subtly programmed to choose to feel unhappy and uncomfortable
with life and to believe that there was something wrong with them.

Many of these sabotage patterns were formed in the early years
between conception and 6 years old and came from the parents and
others in their environment. These were negative patterns that the
children didn't choose, but were downloaded so to speak from their
immediate environment. They were unconscious belief patterns and
emotions that were wired and locked in. They may have become
survival strategies, that were adopted and used when threatened, in
the unconscious belief that they would serve in times of stress. The
beliefs may have caused them to feel unloved, anxious, unimportant,
unintelligent, unlovable and separate.

Beliefs that some children grow up with might include:
"I never do anything right"
"I'm bad. I do everything wrong."
"I should be...." ("I'm not OK the way I am.")
"It is bad to express anger."
"It is good to express anger." (If the parents are constantly
witnessed being angry.)
"I should please others, so they will like me."

"I'll never amount to anything."

"I am unlovable"

"I don't know…"

Children who grow up with negative, fearful and limited learning experiences may have an inability to understand that their parents were doing their best at raising them, considering what the parents themselves learned growing up. As children grow, they will continue to treat themselves as others had treated them. For example they might punish, scold, devalue, and not love themselves—repeating again and again the verbal dialogue, criticism and judgments that their parents and others may have taught and instilled in them.

An amazing example of the 'absence' of social conditioning is sometimes seen in the mentally ill. *New Age magazine* reported in an article, *"Mentally Ill are Nicer"* that studies have found that the socially challenged are more socially responsible than their non-institutionalized neighbors. They further said that *Brain/ Mind Bulletin* reported that in a study conducted in Fairfield, Connecticut, mentally ill patients responded in a more altruistic way than normal subjects to a contrived emergency: An individual entered the classroom and appeared to fall and cry out in pain while the reactions of the observers were noted. Every psychiatric patient tested offered at least verbal expression of aid while twenty eight percent of controls said nothing. Aid was offered by seventy two percent of mental patients while only thirty two percent of the non-institutionalized offered assistance. Sixty per cent of mental patients assisted the accident victim while fewer than thirty percent of the others offered any help. Morale of the story: Brain/Mind suggests "When in trouble, call a "psychotic."

Sometimes when I am not centered in myself and grounded in my integrity, I see myself responding to others in ways that support their personal belief systems. In other words, while not operating from an integrated self, I am in a place that reflects others belief systems and what they believe and expect. I may respond to them with actions and words that they have grown to expect from others. For that reason, I truly want to stay centered so that I don't feed into others belief systems. I definitely want to choose to live in the present moment with personal integrity.

What beliefs did you grow up with?

The following is a list of some well-known ones:

> What will people think?
> Children should be seen and not heard.
> Work hard so you will have financial security.
> Real men don't cry or show emotions...
> There are starving people in the world....
> You have to pay the price.
> You can't have it all.
> Nothing lasts forever.
> College prepares us for our future.
> What you don't know won't hurt you.
> He is a pain in the neck.
> You are just getting older... (I tell my clients that I don't accept this belief.)
> Work now, play later.
> Self-Love is selfish.
> You can't teach an old dog, new tricks.
> We can't be happy if others are unhappy.
> ....never good enough.

The barrage of beliefs is endless in our culture. We hear and acquire them, day after day, year after year without awareness that we are actually choosing them.

Blame and the Victim Role

Barry Kaufman of *The Option Institute* talks in his lectures about three basic beliefs that society generally holds as true:

1) I have the power by what I say or do to cause you to be happy or unhappy.
2) Others have the power by what they say or do to cause me to be happy or unhappy.
3) I have no power over myself to make myself happy or unhappy.

Where do you believe that your power lies? ....within you? ....outside of you? ...with someone else? If you believe that others have power over you to make you feel one way or another, then the reverse would actually be true as well.... that you believe that you have the power over others to make them feel different feelings. Thinking in these terms gives one's power away and leaves you living as a victim and also possibly believing that you have power over other people's lives. As such, you may feel helpless and powerless to change your situation in any way. Usually all of this is done at a subconscious level of awareness. You may then feel guilty if you don't make the "right" choices in regards to yourself and others. Do you honestly think that your responsibility is to make others happy? Think about any ways in which you may do this.

If we give our power away and decide to place the control of our life in other's hands, then we will be at the whim of being controlled by them, whether they/we know it or not. The truth however, is that no one can control our feelings, our life or our future unless we give that power to them. If we did choose to let others have power over us what benefit would that serve?

When others tell us of their feelings (beliefs or judgments) about us, it will only affect us if we have similar beliefs about ourselves. Another person's judgments only tells us about them and what they are feeling, it has nothing to do with us and who we are.

> I knew that my heart and mind would always be
> tempted to feel anger, to find blame and hate. But I
> resolved that when the negative feelings came upon
> me, I wouldn't wait for them to grow or fester. I
> would always turn immediately to the Source of

> all true power: I would turn to God and let His
> love and forgiveness protect and save me.
> ~Immaculee Ilibagiza, ~*Left to Tell: Discovering*
> *God Amidst the Rwandan Holocaust*

If you want to learn about true forgiveness, please read Immaculee's book.

Others always have the best of intentions, even when they are angry, frustrated, and judgmental. Understand though, *we can never control others and what they do or what they think*. Our power lies within unconditionally accepting, loving, and programming ourselves, our feelings, our beliefs and our actions. We can do what we wish for ourselves and allow and give others the right to do the same. *We can choose to support and trust that we are both doing our best while letting ourselves and others be as we are. We can live with total and unconditional acceptance!* That doesn't mean that we are passive and want things to remain as they are but that we accept them as they are this moment. Then we have the opportunity to decide "what's next."

This is an important one: *We have always done and always do our best, based upon what we have known and learned up until that time.* Our parents did their best as well, based on what they had learned. They also believed, accepted and acted out what they had learned from their parents. All beliefs are passed on until someone starts breaking the pattern and starts changing and discarding the old useless beliefs and creates new ones. How long are you going to let the negative, dysfunctional and conditioned beliefs that run in your family continue?

The present time is a very important time to let go of your limiting beliefs so that you can move toward your full potential and all the possibilities that are now available to you. It is a time of great opportunity for beneficial change and personal and planetary evolution. Let's step up and be part of it!

We are the most powerful when we accept total responsibility for our lives, our feelings and our process without blaming others for what happens to us. As we support ourselves and others to be and choose what they wish, we can understand that all that happens is for our highest good, their highest good and the present evolutionary shift.

When we blame others for what happens to us, whether it is our parents, political figures, employers or friends, *we are choosing the "victim" role.* We are affirming that we are powerless over life's situations, and that things just "happen" to us. We may feel we have no control over our lives and that we are just a victim of fate, chance and bad luck. Victims always choose the role of powerlessness and insecurity and blaming others for being responsible for what is happening to them. These are individuals that are always wishing that life would be different, that the world would be different. They believe strongly that others control their fate and their life and that they have little or no power over their life. They may often say to themselves or others:

"It is hopeless, there is nothing that I can do."
"Nothing good ever happens in my life."
"It is your fault that this happened."
"You did this to me."
"I don't deserve..."
"I shouldn't even try...."
"It just is what it is..."
"That poor person......"

The ego or fearful, controlling aspect of our nature wants to live blaming others for things it thinks it can't control. When the ego feels that life is uncertain and threatening, it wants to be in control of everything so badly, that it creates the opposite effect of "things feeling out of control." The (unhealthy) ego, "The course in Miracles" says, is based in guilt and fear and would have us believe that the cause of conflict, discomfort, frustration and guilt and all that happens to us is based *outside* ourselves. All of our feelings, however, including fear, anger and negativity lie within us. We internalize them and there is truly never any real justification for any of these feelings. ***We can experience life free of negative emotions if we are conscious and aware of our choices in each moment.*** Each experience just is… we don't have to always have to describe it negatively. That may be a long stretch for you, but once you travel this path, you will understand it better.

> Our reality is held in place by agreements with space, time and mind. Magic, medicine and the creative impulse are the means by which we can renegotiate one or more of these agreements.
> ~Martin Keogh. ~*Hope Beneath Our Feet*
> ~Kaylynn Sullivan TwoTrees, ~*Indigenous Mind* (essay)

Our real power is visible when we choose our beliefs and create our life with intention, passion and mindfulness. Electing to be responsible for whom we are and all that happens to us is a platform of power, a foundation for strength. When we choose to be responsible for whom we are and what we feel, we can operate with integrity. We are no longer a victim. We release the victim role.

When we say, "When you did this, I felt or I chose to feel," we are affirming our power to control our own feelings and letting go of victimhood and blame. In letting go of blaming others we help them to open to truly listen to us talk about our feelings. In turn the communication helps us to work toward resolution. In choosing our feelings and beliefs we become more responsible for determining our lives. In time we begin to see more clearly how creative each thought and choice can be.

If we are frustrated, angry or upset with a person or a circumstance, we are choosing to be a victim. We are thinking to ourselves that something happened to us, and it was beyond our control or ability to cope with. This is an important one because it happens so frequently and shows us how often we give away our power and feel helpless as a victim. We can always at least determine how we choose to feel, what we will choose to do next and create a possible solution.

If I have a challenge with someone and I need to speak with them about it, I know that the best thing that I can do is not to "confront" them in any way, but connect with and accept them and ask for their help. If I have a confrontational energy about me, I know that a meeting will not work to resolve anything. I understand that I have to be free of all animosity and resentment or our connection will be destructive not creative. In this type of situation I have learned that if I enlist their help with my challenge, the meeting will go well. They feel as if they are important in the process and that I need their support, knowledge and wisdom to resolve the experience. I may even start the meeting saying that I have something to connect with them about and I hope they can listen and help me to better understand what is going on. I have had great results with this approach.

The beliefs that we hold and the conclusions that we draw from them can sometimes be erroneous or untrue. Each thought, each belief we hold can leave us feeling connected or separated, powerful or disempowered, or unlimited or limited. Each thought we think can become and remain true for us. Our minds cannot differentiate between what we want and don't want, believe or don't believe. We will find what we think about, seek and believe. We create self-fulfilling prophecies through our words and thoughts, even if we don't totally believe or recognize all that we are thinking! *We are and we become what we tell ourselves we are. We become the thoughts that we think about all day long.*

We are always making decisions as to how we want to feel, based on all the beliefs that we hold. We are exactly what, on some level, we are choosing to be. We have the opportunity to create ourselves as we wish. As we begin to choose our beliefs, we see that we are completely and totally responsible for whom we are. We see that in changing our beliefs, our feelings and behavior change as well. If we want to create a new reality for ourselves, we can't use the old beliefs. We need new beliefs to create anew.

If we believe that life is difficult, a struggle and that we are a victim, we will create and make it that way, and through our beliefs it becomes true. Many of our beliefs are so deeply embedded in our unconscious that we aren't even aware that we hold and believe them! Then we reinforce them again and again.

At one time, I was totally unaware that I was living with beliefs in financial limitation. Living as a single parent with 3 growing boys, I was often challenged to meet their needs and my own as well. I believed subconsciously that I could not earn a living that would meet our needs and wants and also provide for personal vacations as well. It was out of the question! I believed that I needed a man in my life, who would share the housing and food expenses of daily living, as well as all or half the expenses of vacation travel. I didn't believe that I could do it for myself or by myself. Thankfully, as time passed I was given opportunities to see that I did not need to continue believing in what I could not do, but could focus on what I wanted to create instead. The latter was certainly more rewarding than the former.

As I consciously let go of many beliefs in financial limitation, in no time at all, my vacations surpassed what I had believed was possible. Within 1 ½ years, I took a 3 week vacation across the US with 2 of my sons, went with a group to the Yucatan in Mexico to see ancient pyramids in Mayan country, traveled to Alaska to go hiking and sea-kayaking and went to a Naturopathic Convention in Aspen, Colorado, where I had some time daily for hiking in the mountains. Previously I had not believed enough in myself to think that these types of trips were possible. I believed what many other single moms in my position probably believed, that I couldn't do it on my own, by myself! It felt really great to let go of those limiting beliefs and begin to create what I really wanted in my life.

Look at these negative beliefs that are wide-spread in our culture:

"You have to work hard and struggle to get anywhere in life." (belief in struggle)

"I don't have any friends." (Might be said when one is feeling lonely and others are busy- probably not true)

"I can't…..." (Limits your ability to create solutions and focuses on negativity, impossibility and limitation)

"This is the way my life is, it's hard, I never have enough and it always will be this way." (this contributes to being stuck, may be rooted in fear of change)

OR

Life flows abundantly—I provide all I want for myself. The universe is always there to help me when I need it. (Create an affirmation that works for your belief system)

My life is full of endless possibilities. I feel my connection with harmony and all life. There is Divine Harmony in every aspect of my life.

I believe that everything is possible for me. There are unlimited resources to fulfill all my dreams!

There are limitless possibilities in all situations.

As my life changes, new opportunities always arise.

Based on our beliefs, we choose struggle or ease, and then, based on that choice we choose either to be joyful or unhappy. It is all determined by what we choose to believe. There are many voices that we can listen to. On the whole, most individuals have no neutral thoughts, but many creative or destructive ones, often more destructive ones.

If we think and see in limited ways, we will find life to be limited. Unfulfilled dreams can be blocked by our subconscious beliefs, resistance to change and ineffective action.

But … *if we believe and live a life as if there are limitless possibilities and infinite solutions, we will live with options and choices far beyond what we ever thought was possible.*

Rules for Being

1) You will receive only one vehicle (in which you reside) for this lifetime. Please appreciate it for all it provides for you. You

would be wise to love and cherish it and treat it as a sacred work of art. *How are you doing so far?*

2) The life that you are given is an opportunity to celebrate. You are now in the "School of Life and Opportunity." *Are you awake, asleep, a participant or a victim?*

3) There are no failures, errors or mistakes. Each experience offers choices. Our personal power and evolution are determined by what we choose and learn. *Have you chosen well so far?*

4) Lessons may be repeated in a myriad of ways until we awaken and thrive in those circumstances. You may stay in some classes or grades longer than you would like. *Have you had to repeat many lessons again and again?*

5) Life is a continual learning and evolving experience. There is always change. Wow, how wonderful! *Have you enjoyed it so far?*

6) You will experience the same lessons wherever you are. You can't escape, so open your arms and welcome and celebrate each one that comes. *How does that feel?*

7) Others may offer us a reflection of ourselves. What we don't like in others may offer us some insight about ourselves and the opportunity to unconditionally accept ourselves and others. (It is sometimes easier just to love everyone.) We don't always have to look in the mirror to "see." *Are there some reflections that you need to surround with love?*

8) We have the opportunity to be the "creator" or "co-creator" of our lives. We have many tools, unlimited possibilities and enough experience to create more than we could have dreamt was possible. *What is it you want to create?*

9) Answers to our questions can be found in stillness, silence and just Being. We can find the guidance that we need if we trust that we can. Reach out to the Universe, Source or God for unlimited support. *Have you given yourself the opportunity of silence and stillness recently?*

(adapted and changed from Dr. Cherie Carter-Scott's "The Ten Rules of Being Human")

Words

You must speak straight so that the words may
go as sunlight into our hearts.
~Chief Cochise

The words that we use every moment are not only powerful, but creative too. They create our reality and our future, whether we state them in our mind, or out loud. Words may create confusion, misunderstanding or clarity in our thinking and perception. If we label what we are feeling with words that are not accurate, it can affect how we feel. If we say, "I did it wrong," we may not necessarily be describing the truth which might actually be, "I did my best and did it as well as I could at that time," or "I made what I felt was the best choice at that time." Our words really affect our feelings and judgments. *Our words are far more powerful than we ever imagined.* We are continually creating self-fulfilling prophecies through the words that we use to describe what we are thinking, feeling and doing.

From now on I will ask you to *very carefully choose the words that you use.* Make sure that they describe your experience as accurately as possible. Take the time you need and be thoughtful about each word. Eliminate such words as "good," "bad," "right," and "wrong." They really don't accurately describe our experiences. Be specific and have fun selecting the words.

I find words so interesting. I really listen to the words that people use and take them as each person's truth. So if I ask you how you are doing and you say "not too bad," I may assume that you measure your life on "bad, worse, worst." And to the contrary if you were to say "pretty good," I might assume you measured your life's activities and your days by "good, better, best," in a sense. Saying "pretty good" still doesn't let me know much about your life. Those words are very general and are usually said without much thought.

The words we use can really portray our feelings whether we know it or not. ***The words we use can actually determine how we feel as well.***

If you say "bad"...how does it leave you feeling? How about the word "good"...does that have a different effect? The words we use can affect how we feel every minute and then how we move forward in life. The challenge with using "good" and "bad" is that if something was good and then it is no longer....then you will be using the word bad. This in turn dictates how you feel. If you use neither word, but describe more accurately your experience, then you may not feel "badly" when things have changed. But, remember, the words we use, often dictate how we then feel whether we realize it or not.

This good/bad continuum is called duality. It is like a trap. It doesn't serve us and contributes to the dualistic and polarized world that we live in. Just changing our words and thoughts can help to lessen its grasp on us. We will talk more about this throughout the book.

Play around with the words that you use, just for fun and see how you feel and what results occur.

Sometimes words are also misleading. I always thought the word cynic was about a negative person and outlook. I was very surprised when I looked it up one day. Here is what I found:

"Cynic: a member of a school of ancient Greek philosophers who held virtue to be the only good and stressed independence from worldly needs and pleasures: they became critical of materialistic social values."

Is that a different meaning than you would have expected? It is interesting that social values could affect our belief systems, because someone or some group believed a certain way and dictated their beliefs to others.

I am by nature a dealer in words, and words are
the most powerful drug known to humanity.
~Rudyard Kipling (1865—1936)

When editing the final draft of this book which has been in process for over 30 years, I realized that many of the words had to be changed and upgraded to the present evolutionary period of time. Life has changed, evolved and is moving at a rather rapid pace. With the present awakening and new meaning in life, our consciousness is moving from the logical head centered approach to a feeling and heart centered life and evolution. It has been interesting to shift my work and keep thinking about what words I presently want to use and speak in relation to the information that I am sharing.

Remember that words are either disempowering or empowering. Choose carefully!

Internal Dialogues

We may have accepted what others believe and feel is true and formed conclusions about ourselves based on their beliefs. In our childhood, an internal dialogue may start as an unconscious reaction to what others told us....

Children were told:	Children conclude:
"I know better than you, do what I say."	"I am stupid, I don't know anything."
"Be quiet."	"People don't want to hear what I have to say."
"You make me angry."	"I have the power to make others angry."
"If you loved me you would do the dishes."	If I don't do what my mother wants, it means that I don't love her."

"Take this medicine if you want to get well."	"Healing comes from external forces, I have no power over my body to heal.....my body cannot heal by itself."

As we grow older, messages may change, yet remain the same.

Others say to us....	We conclude.....
"If you really loved me you would do what I want you to do."	"I have to do what others want to show that I care."
"You make me mad."	"I have the power to create what others feel."
"As you get older expect poor health."	"I have no control over my life...certain things are inevitable." Aging contributes to poor health.
"Can't you ever do it right?"	"There is something wrong with the way I am. I am a failure at everything. I can't do anything right."

We not only learn beliefs from those around us, we create them too based on our reactions to others and others reactions to us. But what others believe and need, tells us only about them, their beliefs and conditioning and their feelings about their life. What we decide to own, live and empower tells us about who we are and what we choose to believe.

Being conscious of what we focus on and empower is the key to our freedom, creativity and present and future life.

Beliefs to release~

"Dress warmly, or you'll catch a cold."
"Everyone has to pay their dues"
"There is something wrong with who I am."
"I am powerless......"
"I am not in touch with my needs."
"We have to take the good with the bad"
"I cannot change. This is the way I am"
"You can't have your cake and eat it too."
"Sadness and worry means that I care."
"If I feel guilty, I won't do it again."
"We should do certain things in life."
"Try hard if you want to succeed."
"I have a problem"
'I can't'
"I don't know"
"That makes me….."
"That is killing me"
"What a pain in the ….."
"My past dictates my future"

These expressions can disempower and weaken us both physically and emotionally and dictate the quality of our life. Choose words carefully when you speak. Eliminate destructive sayings.

No one can make you feel sad, frustrated, rejected, depressed or joyful unless you give that power to them. As long as you place your feelings in other people's hands…you allow yourself knowingly or unknowingly to be controlled by them. They may not even realize the power that you have given to them.

Believing in any one or more of these beliefs sets you up for being a "victim." If you believe that life is unfair and you live in a constant struggle, feeling hopeless all the time, then you are choosing to be a "victim."

The only way that others' judgments can impact us is if it connects with a belief that we have about ourselves. Another person's judgment has nothing to do with us unless we have similar beliefs and it "strikes a chord." Others beliefs are about them and their life. You don't have to make it about you. The more you realize and heal your past, the less your present will be negatively affected by others. We can never truly control what others do or what they think of us. We gain personal power when we release trying to do so and refuse to blame anyone.

We always have the best of intentions…always….based on all that we have lived and experienced. We certainly can evolve and do better at another time as we learn how to.

Through holding integrity we can support others to choose to be and do as they like. Through unconditional acceptance we can lovingly allow others the freedom to be what they want to be. When we choose unconditional love, integrity and inner peace, we support others to make their best choices as well.

We can create our own belief systems, trust our choices and know ourselves better than anyone else does!

Ask Yourself:
1) Do you believe that you are stuck with the way you are and that you can't change?
2) Do you understand that choosing struggle, feeling helpless and being a victim gives away your power?
3) Do you want to release your old ways of being? Do you believe that you can do that?
4) Are you aware of any long-held beliefs that you do want to change?
5) Are you aware that you may hold beliefs that prevent you from having everything that you could ever want?
6) This is an important one!!!! Do you really want to do the things that you feel you "should," "have to" or "ought to" do? (Do you just feel pressured by yourself or others to do these things?) Take a break! Do what you want for a change.
7) Can you gladly follow your intuition and sense of knowing? If not, why?

8) Are you ever afraid to just be yourself? Why?

9) What is the difference between your wants and needs?

10) When you love yourself do you know what you want?

Many beliefs often don't always get us what we want. If we keep doing what we always have, we will continue to create the same old stuff.

In order to change the result, we have to eliminate the cause and change or alter our beliefs, behaviors, and perceptions. As we reconstruct our thinking patterns, we become a powerful being and a contributor to the collective consciousness evolution. We can deliberately choose new beliefs, habits and intentions. When we have intentions and goals, our motivation releases dopamine when we take action toward our goal. But if we endured failure in the past, our memory banks ((right pre-frontal cortex) may bring the fears we felt in the past to the forefront. We may then get obsessed with negative possibilities, lack of confidence and uncertainty. If however, we decide that we can achieve what we want…the "I can do it" mode, we access the left pre-frontal cortex of the brain. If we stay in the "I can" mode when we set our new goals, we will recognize the old negative patterns when they arise. We can then decide to release the old painful memory (consciously or maybe through EFT) and retrain the brain and with a new "normal" as we create new thinking patterns.

> All experience is an arch to build upon
> ~Henry Brooks Adams

Listening to your Heart

Steve Jobs was an entrepreneur, inventor and cofounder and chairman of Apple Inc. He was the cofounder of Pixar and on the Board of Directors for the Walt Disney Company. Jobs was widely recognized as a pioneer of the personal computer revolution and described as a legendary futurist as well as the "Father of the Digital Revolution." He was adopted at birth, and though he disliked formal schooling, was eligible to skip 2 grades in elementary school. His parents sent him to college, though they couldn't really afford it, but Jobs was bored and dropped out of school after 6 months. He continued his schooling by auditing classes that he was interested in. One of these classes was calligraphy. He believed that if he hadn't chosen to drop out of school and take that calligraphy class, the typefaces for Mac applications would have been vastly different. He realized that following his heart and intuition was one of his all-time smartest decisions.

We can't always know or understand our choices when our intuition guides us. Sometimes it is days, months or years later before we realize why we chose to do something out of the ordinary. Following our heart is creative, not logical like following our mind. In following our heart we are free of the dualistic world. We are free to be creative. Opportunities can arise by our stepping out of the norm and following the inner voice that guides us toward our highest and best possibilities. The intuitive voice will often speak softly and subtly and may not always grab or hold our attention. In choosing to listen to this voice we will hear the wisdom and truth that it has to share. This voice may be our Higher Self or Source guiding us toward possibilities that may be beyond our "wildest dreams."

When Steve Jobs spoke at the Stanford University graduation ceremony in June of 2005 he shared the following:

> You have to trust in something, your gut, destiny,
> life, karma, whatever. Believing that the dots will
> connect down the road will give you the confidence to
> follow your heart. Even when it leads you off the well-
> worn path and that will make all the difference...
> you have got to find what you love.

I know that many opportunities are possible (affirmations)~

My beliefs and understandings guide me and support my joy.
I can decide to create what I really want.
I can be motivated by gratitude, love, acceptance and my heart.
Being present in each moment is a key to unlocking my creativity.
Through choice, I can be creative, powerful and responsible for my life.
Every choice I make can support my feeling harmoniously alive.
I can respect, honor and appreciate myself and all that I know.
I am always my own best authority!!!!!
Being deeply connected to my spiritual self supports a loving, joyous and unlimited future.

~In changing and creating my beliefs and choices and operating from my heart, I create my life. I can always change how I feel, what I perceive and how I experience life. Through my new heart-felt beliefs and the creative process, I create what I want for myself and share it with the world. Life is wonderful!

Going Deeper ~

~Identify family beliefs that you still have and are finally ready to let go of. Are there some that you truly want to keep?

~Try on some new and radically different beliefs. Enjoy this process. There are no limits! (For example: Money comes to me no matter what I am doing. I am in the most perfect relationship ever. I take vacations in exotic and amazing places.) Begin reprogramming your personal computer (your brain).

~Enjoy listening to others and sometimes only just do that.

As we stop searching for how to change our lives and we release the old and well-worn beliefs in the process of change we touch and recognize the being underneath all the superficial values. As we enjoy the courage to surrender to the deepest truth of who we are we release all that contributes to the separation from our true self. In turn we connect more freely with our inner knowing. By connecting with our heart in this process we discover truths that were only whispered to us before. Maybe we just needed to live from our heart in the first place. In the heart is where we find safety, peace and the love that we have been searching for.

8

Letting Go of Judgments and Becoming Free

O Great Spirit, help me never judge another
until I have walked two weeks in their moccasins.
~Edwin Laughing Fox

In my early 30's, I started questioning and learning philosophies that I am sharing in this book. I found Barry Kaufman's books about his autistic son and the *Option Process Program* had a profound and lasting impact on me. Barry talked about miraculous healings that occurred when individuals chose *to live without conditions, judgments and expectations.* I was in disbelief. How could anyone live without them? I started exploring the subject, ways of being and how I could change. I took it on as a challenge that I would do. As I began to understand how we create our own unhappiness and poor health, I realized that I would like to live my life differently. I was already half way there. My mother was very unconditionally accepting, loving and non-judgmental. She certainly had fears and judgments that were part of her generation, but she was definitely very exceptional in her own right. (She actually breast-fed me for 3 months, which was very unfashionable at that time.) I was very blessed to have her as my mom. Her example definitely benefited my children who enjoyed my unconditional love and acceptance.

Let's explore what it means to live with and without judgment…

If all people in the world stopped judging this very moment, our world would be a very different place. This means that you couldn't judge people that looked or lived differently than you... politically, culturally, ethically, morally, etc. There would be no prejudice. You might be wondering, "How can I live without judging, when it is necessary for me to do this in order to make the best decisions and choices and to protect myself?"

I will explain what I mean.

I have mentioned before, that we are always doing our best in each and every situation and in each particular moment according to what we have learned and been taught up until that time. That doesn't mean that we might not do things differently as we learn more and as we grow and evolve. It just means that *we are always doing our best* in that and every particular moment.

With that in mind, understand that we have the best of intentions when we think that we have to use judgments as instruments to defend, protect, care for and support ourselves and those that we love. When we use judgments we may believe that we have to be able to distinguish and choose between *polarities* or opposing forces and energies such as:

Right and wrong
Good and bad
What is possible and impossible
What to do and not to do
What to love and what to fear
What will lead to success or lead to failure
Who to love and who not to love
Who to trust and who not to trust
What to believe in and what not to believe in

We judge in order to make the best decisions and choose the "right" actions. Our judgments though, can be based upon many things that negatively affect our perception and ability to truly "see." *Judgments can be based upon our ingrained beliefs, negative self-esteem, trauma, fears, limits we believe in, conditioning, failures, rejection, abandonment and loss.* Together these types of experiences create filters, which are like glasses or lenses through which we see the world. They color our perceptions and create our judgments. For example, once someone has continually failed at certain efforts, they expect that failure will happen again and again and they may even play a part in creating the circumstances around which failure is created….. a self-fulfilling prophecy becomes created.

When we live with the dualities of "right" and "wrong" and other similar judgments, we continue to live in the world of duality and opposition. We believe we are good or bad, right or wrong, etc. It can be great on one end of the spectrum, but we are constantly bouncing back and forth between the two. To avoid this way of living, we have to avoid this way of talking and thinking and totally avoid the dualistic words that put us in this position. What a relief! No more duality! Try it, you might be surprised.

Keep coming back to your heart. What would your heart say?

Whatever is occurring, is just what is occurring, it doesn't create our reaction or response. We do. We create our responses and reactions according to our past experiences, beliefs, conditioning and all that we have felt, judged and accumulated!

Dualities are part of the world that we are finally leaving behind. They have outlived their usefulness. We have learned the hard way what needing to be right is all about. We are moving from competition to connection and separateness to community. We are moving from contrasts and winner/loser mentality to balance and focus on the whole… a Divine state. I am so ready. The world of duality wants someone to be "right" and someone to be "wrong." In that world, there is war, opposing forces, armies, Democrats and Republicans and constant opposition, someone always needing to be right and in power. How can we ever create a world of love if we participate and believe in the old scenario? As we release the past and make more conscious choices, we shall create a new life vibration for ourselves and the planet.

One of the founding visions for America was transformation and a better future for humanity. As a multicultural society, we have explored space, computer technology, human potential and the "new age". Present movements are elevating new leaders from the bottom up like Barak Obama our first African-American President and now like Senator Wendy Davis of Texas and recently Senator Elizabeth Warren. Warren champions social and economic issues and Wendy Davis has literally "stood up" for women's rights. Both are working for society as a whole and not the political institutions. They are a welcome sight on the horizon.

The "populism" movement is occurring now because leaders are opening people's eyes to what is going on in all frames of life...."what isn't working." People are finally waking up to social injustice and the need to work together for a better future for us all. President Obama has been honest enough in saying that inequality is "the defining challenge of our time."

> Man did not weave the web of life,
> he is merely a strand in it.
> Whatever he does to the web, he does to himself.
> ~Chief Seattle

In writing this book, there were many delays. I started and stopped working on it many times. Sometimes while being a single mom, I just didn't have time. Other times I doubted that anyone would want to buy and read my book. More recently I was ready to finally send it in to the publishing company within a week, but a week turned into two weeks and then a month and then two months. I decided to let go of immediate deadlines because it just wasn't ready. There were more personal stories to be added, editing to be done and changes to be made. The "rerouting" was all part of my growth and evolution as a child of the universe, a child still learning about the Divine Providence. Timing is important and things aren't ready "till they are ready." During this process of writing my book, I have gone deeper into my own healing process, learned more about myself, and released more self-judgment. I was finally deeply committed to this project, where previously I wasn't. I was proud to tell others that I have written my first book. I was confident and sharing word about this endeavor. I was excited to be a first time author. I was growing and evolving still. It is still an ongoing process.

But, let's get back to looking at judgments. We sometimes forget that we are capable of a wide variety of reactions or responses to whatever is occurring, whether it is a bounced check, a loss, rejection or a failure, TV news, someone's anger, injuries or accidents. Our judgments and perceptions can lead us in many directions.

> There is nothing either good or bad,
> but thinking makes it so.
> ~William Shakespeare, ~*Hamlet*

What we see in others (that we don't like) and that we judge, may be what we see in ourselves (that we don't like) and judge. It can be both a mirror and an opportunity. We may not like who others are and what they do, but it is not up to us to change or judge them. Why try, that would be wasted effort. They may be just giving us an opportunity to see things in ourselves that need changing. ***The beauty and the blessing is that we can only change ourselves!***

> Your brother is the mirror in which
> you see your self-image.

I love Barry Kaufman's work and books, and all that he has done to help individuals and groups. He and his wife's work is truly miraculous! He always has something uplifting to say in all circumstances:

> I think it's possible to see good
> in even the worst events and situations.
> ~Barry Neil Kaufman

Yes, we could look for the blessing and benefit in each experience, but we have to make it a choice and priority to do so. I wonder what we would find if we chose to do that. There is always much more to each circumstance than meets the eye.

One time I asked a Vietnam War veteran if he needed anything less than the war to become a more peaceful person. He affirmed that nothing else would have had the impact on him that the war did. He was now very much for creating a more peaceful world due to that experience.

When we look at our experiences and judge them as: "bad," "awful," "hard," "a mistake" or "unfortunate," we may not only lose sight of whether the experience is bad, we could subconsciously think and believe that we are bad as well. We may not clearly differentiate in our minds, whether it is a bad experience or that everything is bad, including ourselves. If we refrain from judging the experience, we won't become involved in this whole ripple of negativity and in turn, separate ourselves from and move away from what is happening. At the same time that we see things as "bad," we may choose negative emotions and begin to sabotage our life and health by further making choices that continue this downward spiral. Many people do it again and again without even seeing what they are doing. What we may see as bad, unfortunate or a mistake is only an experience. If we awaken and see it as a stepping stone toward our heart's desire, we will enjoy a very different experience.

As we change the way we think and experience life, it is important to refrain from judging our discomforts and unhappy states of mind. If we can bless these times and thank them for the lessons that we have learned, then we can move on much more quickly. It will free us to more easily move toward all that we want. As we go through changes, we may feel worse before we feel better. Try not to judge that everything that you are feeling from the present moment is bad. It may be old feelings that are coming up to be released. Bless them and then let them go...

My dog Simon was certainly one of my growing experiences. He was a "love" in my life, but also one of my bigger challenges. I believe Simon, had previously been physically abused by a male. I picked Simon out at the humane society when he was 2 years old. He looked so sweet in his very small cage. As he became part of our family, I noticed that, not only was he afraid of going down the cellar stairs, but he was also very afraid of and wouldn't go near some men. He would run away from them no matter how friendly they were or how many times he had seen them.

Simon was part golden and part Samoyed. He was a big white fluffy teddy bear and as gentle as could be, at 90 pounds. He would rarely if ever confront another dog or ever growl. He would even be protective of cats and kittens. He would look right in your eyes and be very present with you. But Simon was very strong and, of course, he had an uninhibited wild streak in him being Samoyed. At the end of an 8 mile hike, he would want to keep walking and at first I had to catch him to get him into the car. That wasn't always so easy. I finally knew to bring snacks and a leash to corral him. He was so strong that walking him on a leash was almost impossible. He would walk me, not the other way around. He might pull me into snow banks, when I had my office clothes and shoes on. Going out the back door I might almost miss the 3 steps once he started running. I finally put up a wire fence so he could be outside and not on a leash, and somehow he would climb over it. Then I put in an electric dog fence and he would understand if it wasn't plugged in and he would make a run for it. The first time I realized that he knew the electric fence wasn't plugged in, it was too late. By the time I ran out there he was nowhere in sight! There were many times I wanted to take him back to the rescue services. I had had enough…..

As a single mother of 3 boys I had my arms full with being a Naturopahtic Doctor, going back to school at UNH, teaching yoga and ski racing. Simon was putting me over the edge. (I was choosing to let that be true!). I kept saying to myself as he pulled me into snow banks, "This is an opportunity!" When he ate whole birthday cakes off the table or food off the counter (He was very big and tall), I kept saying "What an opportunity!" When he chewed up containers of homeopathic remedies….I said "How wonderful!" (I think he was looking for a remedy). I can certainly understand in retrospect that he wasn't doing anything *to me* but was doing "his best" with the circumstances. I am sure that he had extreme PTSD because of the abuse. I had enough of my own challenges so his behavior was sometimes more than I thought I could handle. His behavior was probably related to survival mode plus the new found freedom that he now had. He was such a love…..

The challenges continued on but I never gave him back. Thank God! He was a truly amazing dog. I was so glad when he got older and I could outrun him! That was a happy day. He didn't try very hard to get away after that.

One time when I did a long hike with the dogs on Mount Washington, there were so many rocks that Simon finally stopped walking about 2 miles from the end of the trail. His feet were beginning to bleed. He had done many hikes before that, but not on ground so rocky. So four of us carried him down (he weighed 90 pounds). People joined in and helped carrying the stretcher I made out of clothing and sticks. Simon just laid there as happy as a clam! He really taught me a lot. We can have great challenges that bring amazing experiences, blessings and healings. I really loved that dog! He was a blessing in my life.

Laughter

When I was a Fine Arts major at Syracuse University, I used to travel on weekends to Boston and New York City. One evening while I was in Boston I decided to go with some friends, to a lecture presentation at Boston University. I was unfamiliar with the featured speaker, but decided to go along. It turned out to be one of those life-changing moments. The speaker was Ram Dass, a well-known spiritual guru at that time. I don't remember exactly what he said, but I never forgot the essence of who he was and how he presented. To my great surprise, here was a spiritual teacher with a sense of humor. I was very surprised. I just didn't expect that you could mix humor with religion. I had thought that religion was serious business and there was no room for irreverence. I was pleasantly pleased to have that belief system demolished. My new one was laughter and spirituality unite!

Blessed are we who laugh at ourselves,
for we shall never cease to be amused.
(*unknown*)

There was little laughter around me when I was growing up. My family never laughed….freely or uproariously. Everything was serious, reserved, and quiet in my household. My father preferred that we not speak at the dinner table, "seen not heard" syndrome. We didn't make jokes or act light heartedly. I don't think we knew how to. There was a real absence of the kind of spontaneous laughter that kids love. There were certainly no demonstrations of it by my parents. As I grew older, I realized that laughter was one of the more important, missing and necessary aspects of my life. I desperately needed to find some light-hearted and uproarious laughter for myself. So, I decided to spend time with friends and individuals who had a great sense of humor, and an ability to take life lightly. I needed to surround myself with laughter and silliness of being in the moment. I was loved the energy of spontaneous joy, laughter and light-hearted people.

A few times when my boys were young, I noticed that I couldn't laugh. I would actually stop myself from really letting go and laughing. One time occurred at the playground at my sons' school. I felt as if the world would fall apart and I would lose control of my life, if I were to let go and laugh. I actually stopped myself from laughing and from enjoying a fun and light-hearted moment. It felt like I was stopping myself from stepping into an alternate reality. I just didn't know how to feel safe doing it. Where did that come from?

Another time, I did a little better, but there was still so much room for improvement. I was having dinner with my sons, when they finished eating and were throwing a ball back and forth. Before I knew it, the ball landed in the spaghetti sauce and the sauce landed on me. They thought that was pretty funny, but seemed afraid to laugh. I was a little upset, and trying to be serious and express that seriousness, but realized the real humor in the situation and then we all laughed. It was delayed but I did a lot better than I had in previous situations. At least I saw my choices and picked the best one.... to be in the moment with laughter! It *was* pretty funny!

Laughter is very beneficial and therapeutic for us.... Babies know it. They may laugh more than 300 times a day, whereas an adult may only laugh fewer than 20 times a day. Wow!

Research has actually proven the beneficial physiological effects of laughter and humor. (As if we didn't know it was good for us.) Research was done at *Bowling Green State University* and they found that laughter does many things including:
~ Reduces muscle tension and pain
~ Stimulates endorphins and the cardiovascular system
~ Stimulates and activates most of the major physiological systems
~ Decreases cortisol (stress hormone) secretion
~ Stimulates the immune system
~ Relaxes arteries
~ It is like internal jogging
~ One minute of laughter = 10 minutes on the rowing machine
~ It is highly contagious

Let us all make sure that we laugh as much as we possibly can! Starting now...... Did I make you smile? Or laugh?

As we learn to reprogram our minds and change the words that we use to describe our experience, it is important to begin saying what we really mean and to use words that contribute to creating what it is that we really want in our lives.

Instead of using the words "good" and "bad," look at selecting words that accurately describe your experience. For example, if you were in a minor car accident, you might have formerly described it as "bad," but as you open yourself to perceiving life in new and non-judgmental ways, maybe you would describe it as something that rerouted your day, slowed you down or offered you the opportunity to meet someone new. As we broaden our perspectives, we can play and have fun with words, ideas and experiences and learn to consciously choose what we think and say.

When individuals come to my workshops and lectures, I often invite them to begin to look at life differently especially when some forms of stress, an accident or unexpected challenge occurs. I suggest that individuals have some affirmation to use at those times, so that they don't fall into old habits of assuming that certain things are just "bad." Examples of possible words or phrases are: "Wow!" "How interesting!" "Just what I wanted!" and "What an Opportunity!"

After the first meeting of one of my "Life is an Opportunity" classes, one of the participants was driving home when she suddenly found herself involved in a car accident. Since she had just left the class with my suggestions clearly on her mind, she said to herself, "What an Opportunity!" as she was getting out of the car. To her surprise, she soon had a laugh. She found out that she had run into someone else who had just finished taking my class. She reported at the next class that they both had quite a laugh.

Certainly it is better to choose to feel light-hearted as opposed to grim or negative when the unexpected occurs.

It is interesting to note how some words are so frequently used without a thought or conscious choosing. Words like "good," "bad," "right," "wrong,' "problem," and "can't," do not clearly share what one's experience is. These words are used commonly and unconsciously. As we begin to consciously choose, be more responsible and awake in our life, we find that we can replace these words with ones of truer meaning.

As we become clearer, we begin to describe formerly negative experiences with more creative and interesting terms, such as "unique," "unusual," "an opportunity," "unexpected," "a stepping stone," or "challenging." As we begin to see differently and begin to let go of jumping to conclusions and judging, we realize that we are responding to life with joy, enthusiasm, greater peace of mind, and passion. We may learn to unconditionally accept what is occurring (that doesn't mean we love it or want it to continue, it just means that we are present with it now). We begin to move toward life, experiencing it as a continual upward spiral of growth and opportunities.

I would like to share one experience that I had with a friend's judgments. After a few years of saying that she wanted to take my "Life is an Opportunity" workshop, she finally did join one. Three weeks into the workshop, I could feel a judgmental essence about her, I was feeling judged! Within a week, an opportunity arose to share my feelings and ask her what she was feeling. Her response surprised me. She said that she was "judging herself in relationship to me, but not judging me." This was an awakening moment for me in that I realized that judgment in any form is felt by others. We may not always be able to tell who is being judged! Judgment in any form produces an uncomfortable effect. This means that if we are even judging ourselves, others could feel discomfort if they are in our vicinity.

> When the judging mind is clearly noted, its fragile
> nature can be observed. We see opinions forming
> and melting away like snowflakes. We see that each
> comment is like a bubble. When awareness touches its
> insubstantiality, its essential emptiness, becomes readily
> apparent. The likes and dislikes of the judging mind are
> just old karma and conditioning running off. But if we
> compulsively react to these preferences, if we identify
> with them, they become the cause of new karma.
> ~Stephen Levine, ~*A Gradual Awakening*

Many individuals anticipate certain experiences and outcomes based upon their judgments about themselves, their lives and their self-worth. Every day, again and again, they reinforce their judgments by living up to what they believe their self-worth to be. Depending upon their self-worth and self-image, they reinforce their beliefs, both consciously and unconsciously. All that they believe, expect, and anticipate becomes actual self-fulfilling prophecies. If we continually rush to judge life, we remain stuck in fear and limitation, and distance ourselves from endless opportunities. Feeling stuck, in turn, creates feelings of discomfort, being a victim, and wishing that life were different. If we continue to judge situations, individuals and possibilities, we limit our creativity, challenge what we want and hamper our ability to just "be."

As soon as we judge, we give power and feelings to that judgment and distance to the experience. We have chosen it on some level, without realizing that these conclusions, interpretations, and perceptions, that we have freely chosen, could be based upon past experiences, and reactive, fearful or erroneous thinking. On the other hand, if we don't judge or label experiences, we won't create our future from reactionary feelings. Our thoughts create our feelings about each experience. If we change our thoughts, our labels and descriptions, our feelings will change. If we eliminate and let go of the negative thoughts, the negative and fearful feelings will be gone. If we are just present with the experience without reservation and with unconditional acceptance we have made a tremendous step! We don't have to always label experiences from a judgmental place.

It is important to remember that we are always doing our best in all circumstances. Even when we use judgments, we do have the best of intentions of utilizing them as a means for supporting and safeguarding ourselves as well as those that we love. Please, don't judge yourself for judging. Continue just to be present in your heart with unconditional love.

In being aware of our thoughts, we can release judgment and choose to be non-judgmental. We then allow ourselves to see the hidden opportunities as they arise. We can choose to feel that what happens is somehow a meaningful experience and that it is wonderful just to be alive. We soon realize, that we can learn to trust ourselves, the universe, and each experience to bring us just what we need each moment of the day. We can move effortlessly through our day, inspired to use our potential to create divine harmony in all that we do.

Ourselves and Others

Resistance to change becomes painful.
~Becky Mulkern ND

One of my favorite quotes that I would often read in class in my "Life is an Opportunity" course is the following one from Barry Kaufman's book *Happiness is a Choice*:

> We could begin by judging everything as good and then grow into letting go of judgments completely. The stock market crashes and I lose my equity. How wonderful! What an opportunity not to rely on my investments! My wife announces she wants to leave me. Perfect! I can trust this will be best for her, the children and me. My employer fires me without notice. How interesting! This can be my chance to re-evaluate who I am and what I really want. My child blames me for making her unhappy. Wow! What a fascinating idea! Her statement challenges me to question who is responsible for our personal happiness; my search for an answer can only enrich me. If we let go of judgments of people and events as bad, we usher in a time of miracles and wonder. We will find what we seek!

As we walk the path of life, it is important that we understand that *we can really only work on ourselves and our growth, but not others.* Each relationship that comes along is really perfect for us, and very appropriate for our growth at that particular moment. Life always brings with it opportunities for beneficial change, greater love, freedom, and power. In viewing life as an opportunity, we can decide to *honor the differences we see in others, rather than focusing on their deficiencies and/or how we would change them.*

When we are challenged with others actions, feeling "how can they act that way?" we need to remember that *we are all in the school of life together.* Some individuals may be in a post-graduate course, while some may be stuck in second grade, repeating it numerous times. We can choose to be patient with others inability to be what "we" want them to be. We are wasting our time in continuing to judge them, because it will only cause us frustration and anger. We have to accept that this may be the furthest that they evolve in this life time or that they are moving at a slower pace than we are. Otherwise we are really wasting our time and energy. Letting go of expectations and just loving others as they are is really the healthiest practice.

How evolved are we really, if we are a postgraduate degree student and we are judging a second grader? That may help you to lessen the need to judge....

Sometimes challenges occur when your biological family, is not the family that you would have preferred. Certainly there are many lessons there. Maybe you feel many discomforts including: no loving connection, they don't "get you," they don't ask how you are or seem to care, you feel separate....or you are the different one in the family. You may try again and again to have it different, but it never happens. Many individuals have felt this. If this applies to you, you may find peace of mind by deciding to accept everyone as they are and stop judging them. You may decide that your real family doesn't have to be your biological one. That may give you the peace of mind that you are looking for. Just because you are related, doesn't mean that you have to be experience more than that. Over time you may become closer to them, but the key to your happiness may be in releasing your need for them to be different. You can just love them as they are. Maybe your real family is comprised of sons and daughters and friends. You may all be very closely connected and you can be thankful for that.

We are the most powerful when we control our own actions and we understand that everything outside of us is really a mirror reflection of who we are and what we feel, think and believe. Everything in our environment actually reflects back to us who we are and believe we are. It is to our advantage and beneficial to our evolution not to blame and judge others but to gratefully and consciously accept them. Through this choice we hold our power and integrity intact. We remain powerful by changing _our_ beliefs, feelings and actions and refraining from wanting to change others.

If we feel discomfort at times in social experiences it may be because we feel an impact if others are judging us, and it resonates with a deep seated negative belief that we actually have about ourselves. We can remain comfortable and free if we remember and remind ourselves that others judgments say nothing about us, they merely tell us what the speaker or thinker judges to be true (which of course doesn't mean that it is necessarily true!).

Remember, we cannot be responsible for others, only ourselves. We can never control what others think, so why try??! If we judge others and try to control what they think and do, we are immediately creating separation between us. The more you try to change others, the more they will want to remain the same. Isn't that how you react to others when someone wants to try to change you?? If they don't like the way you are, you certainly aren't going to change for them, are you? We can change ourselves though, if we feel it is in our best interests.

If we choose to let others judgments affect us, then we are not only choosing to be a powerless victim, but we are also allowing ourselves to be controlled by others. Others have no power over us to make us guilty, sad, angry or otherwise, unless we give them that power. If we don't like the way others treat us, it is important to remember that we get treated in life: 1) according to the way we teach others to treat us and 2) according to the way we treat ourselves (and others). We may get back what we give out. What do you think might happen if you unconditionally love yourself? It is worth a try... there is no loosing with this one...

One of my favorite stories that illustrate what happens when we are judgmental is Leo Tolstoy's, *The Three Hermits—An Old Legend Current in the Volga District*. It is only about 8—9 pages and well worth the reading. If you have time please read it!

(In a nutshell, this is my short version. Hundreds of years ago two clergymen decided to visit two elderly hermits on an island. They rowed a boat to get there. On the way back after the visit, the clergymen talked between themselves about how needy, deprived and unfortunate the hermits were and how little they seemed to know. As they are rowing back to the mainland they saw something in the distance coming toward them and they soon realized that it was one of the hermits and he was walking on the water. The clergy had forgotten something and the hermit wanted to return it to them. Moral: It is easy to make assumptions about others without knowing the truth.)

Judgments and Health

*What you focus on increases…..*what do you want to choose?

When we injure ourselves unexpectedly, falling or stubbing our toe, or hitting our "crazy bone" the first thing that many often do is swear, get angry and send negative energy to ourselves and the whole experience. We wonder why such a thing could ever happen to us. How could we have done this? We may feel a victim of the experience, blame ourselves and feel that things should have been different. Why, however, instead don't we bless ourselves when we need it most? Have we become conditioned to react this way?

We can carry this over to others as well. If others are involved in something that is very challenging or "hard" for them, we can also see them as a victim and say, "Oh that poor person." We are affirming that they are powerless and helpless in the situation. This certainly doesn't empower them or send them beneficial energy. We are just reinforcing their powerlessness.

There are other circumstances that fall in the same category. Wars, climatic destruction, accidents and injuries, catastrophes and health issues could fall in this category. It is more beneficial to send love, prayers and best wishes to others than pity or reassurance that they are victims. If we buy into the victim mentality we help no one including ourselves. Why would we want to harbor the energy of pity or "that poor person?" There is always the potential to learn lessons within all circumstances and crises may provide blessings and opportunities. Sometimes, we, humans, are motivated to learn through our challenges what we need to.

Even Nelson Mandela who spent 27 years in prison, never appeared to look at himself as a powerless victim. He had courage, perseverance and great patience. He achieved greatness because of this. We can understand him better by looking at his favorite poem *Invictus* by William Ernest Henley. The following lines sustained him through those 27 years:

> It matters not how strait the gate,
> How charged with punishments the scroll,
> I am the master of my fate:
> I am the captain of my soul.

Many individuals are unaware of their conditioning, beliefs and judgments concerning pain. Often when people are in a painful state, they surround themselves with "why is this happening to me?... judgment, rejection, anger and blame. There is usually an effort made to escape, deny or ignore what is occurring. When however, we judge what is occurring as bad or unfortunate, we leave a place of energetic dis-ease within us that is not healed or whole. This place holds discomfort of the past and brings it into the future. When individuals experience pain and hurt, whether it is physical or emotional, they usually feel upset and angry about the situation and then they may get angry about being angry. These judgments may further perpetuate the situation and negativity. This progression contributes to disharmonious energy getting lodged within us as forms of emotional tension and negative vibration.

Why are we unable to see the larger picture and have compassion for ourselves when we need it most? We have all been taught to react this way...especially boys and men.

We can avoid this chain of events that starts with our minds and ends with dis-ease in our bodies, by choosing to live with a non-judgmental attitude, to trust life and embrace each situation fully and completely. Even when the old mind tapes return and we see ourselves judging, we can gently remind ourselves that we have a choice to live without fear, judgments and negativity.

It is important to understand that *in "feeling it, we are healing it."* We can choose to feel (in our mind & body) our old, long-held, uncomfortable emotions, name them, accept them and let them go. A great healing exercise is to think about an old painful experience and place your elbows on a table and hold your forehead. There are neurovascular holding points over your eyes (about 1 inch above) that help to redirect the energy from the reactive part of your brain to the healing and active part of your brain. Hold these points and think about any painful experiences, feel them in your body, and continue until you take a deep breath or feel that you are finished. It works very well to dislodge and release old trauma. You may feel a pulsing that stops when the process is complete.

So, next time you stub your toe or trip and fall, take time to bless and love yourself and offer healing energy to those parts of yourself that need it most!

Right, wrong, good or bad

Why do we kill people
who kill people
to show that
killing people is wrong?
~Holly Near

Within each culture are sets of laws, rules, beliefs, and judgments about what is "right and wrong." Some of these may have been set up as guidelines for individuals that may not have known "right" and appropriate action. Some rules may have been set up to deter "wrong" action. Others may have been adopted by individuals or groups who have felt that they knew what was best for others to follow. Many of these "laws" and ways of being have been followed without question. But in actuality there are many rules/laws, about right and wrong, that are not followed across all cultures. If you say, "what about killing?" then remember there are many exceptions to the rule of "Thou shalt not kill." Here are some examples:

In some aboriginal cultures, human flesh may be a food staple. In our culture, some individuals ask for "mercy killing" to end their life of un-ending pain, and for some individuals "euthanasia" is condoned or may be a "lifesaver".

In India, killing of cows is forbidden, while in many nations, beef is a staple in their diet. Monks in Tibet feel that they should watch every step so as not to step on an insect and kill it, while in industrialized nations chemicals are made and sold for eliminating many insects and weeds in the environment. Some individuals kill "weeds" in their lawn and gardens while they plant others and promote their growth.

On the other hand, vegetarians may prefer not to eat meat because an animal would be killed. But they would choose to eat plants that are killed instead. Some individuals say that plants feel as much pain as animals do.

Individuals say that killing is bad or wrong even though so many individuals do it so often in so many ways with so little respect for life. It almost seems as if some cultures make up rules to fit their belief systems.... "we can kill this, but we can't kill that." And then each person has a different view of what that should mean. Who is really making up all these rules and which ones should we follow or believe?

The words "good" and "bad" are used commonly to express personal judgments made by many individuals. We judge someone as "good" when they do what we would like them to do and "bad" when they don't conform to our control or wants. We call them "good" when they measure up to certain ideals that we have in mind and "bad" when they don't measure up to our beliefs about how they "should" act in appropriate ways. And we may change these judgments occasionally when we favor one person over another. We are constantly varying the system with which we judge and measure others as to whether we believe they are "good" or 'bad."

Guilt

You have a problem if
you believe you have a problem.
~Becky Mulkern ND

When we let go of suffering, we can be joyful. Suffering blocks our opportunities. Suffering is born of feeling that we are a victim.

Meditation is a beneficial tool that brings us back to our center and senses and allows us to recognize what the mind often spends its time doing. We cannot change what is occurring in our mind if we don't recognize it. With meditation, quieting the mind and being, we return to the present moment. We can then witness our mind and its sometimes anxious, fearful and erratic nature.

One of the biggest wastes of our time and energy is guilt. What do we gain from it? Nothing. What use is it? No use. Why would we stay in that place? Because we think we should. Why would anyone want to punish themselves? Does it serve a purpose? Not really. We think it somehow serves us and prevents us from repeating a behavior. We can change this thinking and remember that we are always doing our "best" in all circumstances at all times. We always do as well as we can, given the circumstances and given all that we have learned up until that time.

It is sure that those who hold grievances will suffer guilt,
as it is certain that those who forgive will find peace.
~*The Course in Miracles*

Guilt is freely chosen, but sometimes chosen unconsciously more than consciously. Many individuals may feel that guilt will motivate them in one direction or another and prevent them from repeating a negative way of being. Individuals may believe that guilt will keep them on track, so they do not do something "bad" or "wrong" again and again. There is certainly no guarantee that guilt would prevent you from repeating any particular behavior. The old saying: *"What you focus on increases,"* would lead us to believe that if we continually focus on our failures, we might create more of them.

> Misery as a human experience comes from judging
> ourselves, other people and events as bad or terrible
> for us. We can say quite accurately that we have
> "thought" ourselves into unhappiness with our
> judgments, and we can think ourselves back out
> by examining them and letting them go.
> ~Barry Kaufman

We can choose to be motivated by love, instead of fear, to do our best in each circumstance, then there are more creative possibilities available to us. If we are afraid we may move toward unknown and unwanted possibilities. If, on the other hand, we hold love in our hearts, we are more relaxed, clear, self-supporting and ready for whatever the future holds for us. From this space we are more likely to create and make choices that support us and those around us. If our choices don't seem to support those around us, they still may be beneficial for them whether they realize it or not. What works in our best interests may also spur others to make their best choices.

Many individuals become challenged when they make promises that they can't keep. It is a big lesson! Do you often make promises that you can't carry through on? Could you refrain from making them? If a promise is one that you *don't* want to make, it might be better not to. If you think you want people to make promises to you, you may need to reevaluate that. Are you setting yourself up for disappointment? Sometimes we may not feel that we can do what others want or need. That is OK. It may not be as good for them as they think.

When others are angry at us they may want us to feel bad or guilty about what they may consider our shortcomings. But if we support ourselves, we can allow and respect their right to be angry and let it be theirs and not our issue too. If we feel guilty, it may be striking old cords of "feeling wrong" from our past that have not yet been healed. If we don't do what others expect, are we responsible for their feelings of unhappiness, disappointment and frustration? Because we don't do what others want and expect, that doesn't mean that we are somehow wrong or bad. It just means that we may have had our own personal priorities or needs. If we don't trust and support ourselves unconditionally, we may end up not only being manipulated, but feeling guilty and wrong. We can support ourselves when we make our best choices and do our best. Each action that we choose, can present us with the opportunity to learn lessons, find new opportunities and be our Authentic Self. We have to look for these possibilities and take advantage of them. If we operate out of guilt, we are less effective at all that we do. We will be unable to see and create what is possible for our future.

Failure and Success

It's a psychological law
that we tend to get what we expect.
~Norman Vincent Peale

Today, many individuals spend little or no time with play or leisure. The heavy emphasis is placed on work, achievement and success. In the work place and with competitive sports, heavy emphasis is placed on success and failure as a way to measure not only achievement, but self-worth and personal value. This paradigm of failure becomes very real when you equate it with someone's self-worth. We are not what we do. We are not our job, or our title or our position in life. Our value and personal self-worth comes from *who* we are, not what we do. It doesn't come from what we achieve or do, or what we win or lose. We are and we become what we believe about ourselves. We can become anything we want if we have faith, operate from our heart, and support, appreciate and love ourselves.

Some individuals live with such fear of failure that they actually don't try in the first place or they quit before they can fail (or succeed). Due to fear of failure many individuals may not even attempt to pursue things that they really want because they feel it is better not to even attempt what they may want, because they might fail. This approach provides many missed opportunities.

British author John Creasey demonstrated that continued effort and belief in oneself does pay off. Believe it or not, his manuscripts were actually rejected 753 times before he began publishing his 564 books. Baseball has another great example of how unlimited effort pays off. Babe Ruth, struck out 1330 times in order to accumulate 714 home runs.

If you look at Abraham Lincoln's history of effort, you see a man who never quit and continued persevering despite all seeming failures and what appeared as odds against him. This was a man who was born into poverty and who lost his mother at an early age. He didn't get into law school when he first applied and his fiancée died before he could marry her. Though he lost 8 elections, failed in two business endeavors, and experienced one nervous breakdown, Lincoln demonstrated his determination and integrity by going on to become one of our greatest presidents ever. Lincoln never seemed to reinforce the idea that he had a problem or a defeat, but continued to show his personal power and his ability to continue to create for himself whatever his goals and dreams defined. We might never have had such a great role model as president if he had given up and allowed himself to be consumed with failure.

- ~ Basketball star Michael Jordan was cut from his high school team the first time that he tried out.

- ~ Henry Ford went bankrupt multiple times before he got Ford Motor Company off the ground.

~ Walt Disney was fired from a newspaper that he was working for because he had "no original ideas."

~ Bill Gates quit college.

~ Albert Einstein didn't do well in school and was judged a "misfit" and "would never amount to anything."

~ Steven Speilberg dropped out of Junior High School when he was placed in a class for the learning disabled.

Many of our most powerful creators didn't do well in the "system" because they were such powerful creators. The system often tries to make everyone the same and doesn't seem to appreciate our differences. Gifted individuals who don't want to be held back, have a certain amount of determination. They don't want to be told that they were "doing it wrong." If you are interested in more uplifting stories, look up *true inspiring stories* on the internet.

Failure doesn't have to be fatal, but failure to change your fear of failure can certainly be destructive. If individuals can see as Lincoln must have that each new experience is a lesson, a stepping stone or a rerouting experience then they can move ahead in life with ease and celebration. He certainly allowed life to work to his advantage. All of his challenges allowed him to build personal strength and endurance.

Some individuals are so afraid of failing that they cause themselves health threatening anxiety. I had a friend in college who was extremely intelligent and diligent. All her life she had achieved all "A's" in school. At the point that I knew her, she was so afraid that she might not continue to achieve these grades that she was literally a "nervous wreck." Her hands even shook with fear! She was such a bundle of nerves that she could not hold her hands still. She appeared to equate failure with getting anything less than an "A'.

In high school, my oldest son always did well and achieved high honors. He definitely always pushed himself to achieve, because he had a high interest and curiosity in learning. I was glad to see him back off on his studies one day and pressure himself less, play a little more and take life more lightly.

I had an experience where I was glad that my endeavor didn't work out as I had originally intended. It felt as if it "failed" at first, until I realized that I was relieved that it didn't reach the goal I originally intended. It was a rerouting experience and I was very thankful as I discovered that everything was working out for the best. For 3 years I had been gathering groups of people, practitioners and speakers together for a holistic weekend. I would spend half a year in preparation and planning. It was a lot of work and concern. That year, the signup response was so poor that I cancelled the gathering. I was actually very relieved not to have to plan them any longer. The cycle was complete and it was time to move on to other new endeavors. The cycle could possibly have ended sooner if I listened to my desire to move on.

> Failing is among life's least pleasant experiences,
> but nothing else is as essential to success.
> ~Marisa Taylor, ~*In praise of FAILURE,*
> ODE Magazine Oct. 2008

If we eliminate the word "failure" from our vocabulary and use other words, our experience could be quite different. We could say: "I was rerouted," "I have an opportunity to try something different," "I am glad that cycle is finished," "Wow, I learned so much about myself through this experience," etc. There are certainly lessons that can enrich our life experience.

Many individuals chase success as a way to achieve happiness …. the "I will be happy when…" syndrome, in which you are always chasing the next goal and the next. In truth this creative process should be reversed. The happier we are, the more success we achieve and then the more continued success and happiness we will enjoy. When we are joyful we create more dopamine in the brain and this actually turns on the learning centers in the brain. In turn we become better and more creative in all that we do. That, in turn, creates more joy. Success isn't about hard work and effort. Effort and force block our passion and potential. Forced action creates tension and resistance. True success comes from Divine purpose, joy, inspiration and dynamic creative energy. When we are inspired and joyful, everything is effortless. Wow! The moral is, start with joy.

Studies have found that successful people love what they do and want to fill their lives with more of it. They are very self-reliant individuals who choose to be responsible for *everything* that they create in their lives. They understand that they are the source of their success or lack of success. They acknowledge the answers that lie within them as well as their determination to create greater opportunities. They are stimulated by creating solutions for their challenges. They are free of blame and excuses. In continually teaching and accepting themselves, they connect with their heart and soul, and develop their abilities to perform in outstanding ways. They are definitely inspired by life and loving what they do.

Over the years, many individuals have found their career and work to feel meaningless, boring, and unfulfilling. People seem to be gradually shifting emphasis toward more life affirming pursuits. This leads one to question, "What is real success?" and "what do I really want?" Values are changing for family, fun and pleasure. As individuals search for spiritual connection, they are questioning what is really important for them. Individuals want meaning and enjoyment in their lives. Maybe through our quest to follow our heart and understand our definition of success and failure, we will decide to eliminate those these terms and associated goals. We shall follow our passion.

What would happen if we let go of needing to achieve success in our lives and we decided to do what we love and move confidently toward creating our dreams. (Would we need to measure results in terms of success and failure?) As we do what we love, find and follow our passion, we may realize that we are achieving all we could ever have wanted without focusing on success. Maybe success will no longer be the goal. Maybe there will be no goal, just living our dreams.

Non-judgment creates silence in the mind.
~Deepak Chopra

One of the favorite things that I have created for this course is the following list. When I was teaching individuals about the power of their words I found it invaluable. I wanted them to pay attention to the meaning of what they were saying. I would often ask them if they could use different words to express a thought or feeling, especially when they described something as "good" or "bad." Often, I wasn't sure what they really meant. When they gave me another word, it often related a radically different meaning than what they were previously expressing. For example, they may have said "My day was bad," but when I asked them to give me another word to describe their day, they sometimes said that "Many unexpected things occurred." They then realized that maybe that wasn't so bad after all. We really have to watch how we describe our experiences, because depending on the words that we use it can have an effect on how we feel. Certainly, "bad" has a very different feeling than "unexpected" may. What is interesting is that two different people could say that "unexpected" events occurred during the day and depending on their past history, for one of them it might have been great and for the other it may have raised anxiety, even if the experiences were similar. Our history, past trauma, and stresses can determine to a large part how we feel and act with each experience.

Labels and Judgments that Create Destructive & Constructive Spirals

Be thoughtful about the words you choose because they create the feelings that you feel and the future that you live.

Here is a fun list for you to play with:

Disempowering, destructive	*Empowering, creative*
~survivor	>really living, doing well, thriver
~don't know	>know, learning
~dysfunctional	>learning, healthy
~need	>prefer, want
~sorry	>(some individuals apologize for everything) Release apology, you are doing your best.
~but	(release using but)
~wrong	>did my best
~right	>OK, well, marvelously, my way
~foolish	>silly, vulnerable
~not too bad	>pretty amazing
~bad	>doing my best, feeling sick, tired, etc.
~no problem	>I am happy to do it, thanks for the opportunity
~try	>I will do it
~can't remember	>can recall, am remembering
~hard	>It's easy
~tough	>challenging, easy
~hate	>prefer….
~work at it	>I'll do it, create it.
~must	>choose
~can't	>can, I don't want to
~ought to	>want to, don't want to
~should	>choose, don't want to, have other choices to make

~risk	>choice
~problem	>challenge
~quit	>changed direction
~never	>prefer…
~impossible	>I'll think about it, possible, I'll do it
~mistake	>opportunity, stepping stone, lesson
~guilty	>did my best
~failed, failure	>did my best, learned, moved on
~don't have time	>have plenty of time, don't want to do it
~battle, struggle	>challenge, a process, I can…
~bad luck	>interesting, a rerouting experience
~it is what it is	>Sometimes we are rerouted, things are changing
~sacrifice	>blessing (try that one on)

See if you can think of words to place in the blanks on the right side~

_____   _____

~not good enough	
~chance	
~waste	
~uncontrollable	
~neurotic	>responding without fear
~working hard	>moving with ease, letting it happen, enjoying
~If you can't beat them join them	

~killing two birds with one
  stone

~Woe is me

~such a crime

~what's the worst thing that
  could happen?

~addiction   >enjoying food, being
                                      conscious

~fall apart for no reason   >feel my pain, feeling my
                                      sadness

~scares the hell out of me

~feeling sorry for myself   >feeling, going within

~I can't stop   >I choose something
                                      different

~so worried something will
  happen

~gets me in trouble

~ain't that a shame

~bother

~vicious cycle   >hmmm…looks familiar

~deathly afraid

~burden

~you aren't supposed to…

~things upset me   >I am challenged >I can feel
                                      my feelings

~beyond my control

~life's just tough

~hard one to break   >how can I break this… I can

~no one will think the worst
  of me

~prolonging the agony   >wow, this is painful

~never enough   >always more than enough

There may be times when a word or saying in the left hand column is appropriate. Please use it then.

On the whole, eliminate the words on the left side column from your vocabulary. These terms and phrases usually create destructive spirals. When we utilize these words and phrases, we are directing our attention toward fear and failure, hardship and obstacles. To replace them, use the examples given and/or find other more appropriate descriptive and creative words. Add your own words to the list. As you eliminate the negative and conditioned responses and dialogues you can begin to speak more accurately and honestly. Always think about what you want to create, not what you fear. Have fun with this very creative process!

It always seems impossible until its done.
·Nelson Mandala

Beliefs to release:

~Everyone pays their dues.
~Life always has its good and bad, ups and downs.
~I can't feel good all the time.
~My feelings are beyond my control.
~At certain times I may be unhappy if others are unhappy.
~I have no power to change my life.

Ask Yourself~

~Do you live as a powerless or powerful person?
~Do you feel that you can change what needs to be changed?
~Are you afraid of change?
~Do you have beliefs that support you to follow your dreams?
~Can you just be yourself and enjoy my life?

Understand~

~Our perceptions and beliefs can serve us and contribute to our well-being and opportunities.

~If you continue to do what you always have done, you will continue to receive what you always have received!

~You can live without being motivated by fear or pain.

~This moment is all that there is... You can just enjoy each moment.

~Beliefs are what you freely choose and live by.

~What you are is what you choose to be...

~You can be responsible for your life through being creative, conscious and powerful.

~By creating your beliefs, you can change your feelings, your life and what the future holds for you.

Going Deeper~

~Meditate each day for 20 minutes. As you learn to let go of all thoughts, try doing it for longer and longer periods of time. Are you comfortable with yourself when you are still and quiet?

~What are your beliefs about success and failure?

~Is success something that you need?

~Is your life dependent on your achieving certain successes?

~Are there words you can use to replace the terms 1) success and failure?

~Look at the Labels that you use. Eliminate the ones on the "Negative Spiral List." Add to this list if you like.

~Be aware of the times that you are judging yourself and others. What fears are motivating your judging? Do you ever judge that you are "bad" or that you do things "wrong"? When you notice self-criticism, immediately shift, change the words that you are using and say and intend what you want to happen. You can do it!

> Darkness cannot drive out darkness;
> only light can do that.
> Hate cannot drive out hate;
> only love can do that.
> ~Dr. Martin Luther King Jr.

9

Our Choices Can Empower Us

The following is one of my favorite handouts from my course. It is written by Portia Nelson (1980):

1) I walk, down the street.
> There is a deep hole in the sidewalk.
> I fall in.
> I am lost...I am hopeless.
> It isn't my fault.
> It takes forever to find a way out.

2) I walk down the same street.
> There is a deep hole in the sidewalk.
> I pretend I don't see it.
> I fall in again.
> I can't believe I am in the same place.
> But, it isn't my fault.
> It still takes a long time to get out.

3) I walk down the same street.
> There is a deep hole in the sidewalk.
> I see it is there.
> I still fall in....it's a habit.
> My eyes are open.
> I know where I am.
> It is my fault.
> I get out immediately.

4) I walk down the same street.
   There is a deep hole in the sidewalk.
   I walk around it.

5) I walk down another street.

The Choices in Life in Five Short Chapters

1) ~*Unconscious and unaware*: You are struggling and unaware that you are alive but mentally unconscious. You are involved in a completely dysfunctional, limited and/or destructive way of life. You are asleep!

2) ~*Unconscious and aware*: You are becoming aware of your behavior and way of life, but are stuck, limited and unable to change. You feel stable where you are. You don't want to change.

3) ~*Unconscious and capable*: You can catch your behaviors and change. At first you catch it a while after you do it but with conscious practice, the window is shortened until you can stop yourself before you do the old behavior and substitute the new behavior. You are beginning to see the Light. Hooray!

4) ~*Conscious and capable*: You are enjoying new behavior without thinking about it. You are still unaware of all the possibilities that are available to you. Life is starting to feel more harmonious every day. You feel like you are starting to live in the flow. You are enjoying the changes.

5) ~*Optimal Creative Consciousness:* You flow with the universal force. You are in harmony with yourself and your choices. There is a creative power, energy and feeling of passion in all that you do. You are awake to life, love and being yourself. You celebrate who you are and what you are capable of creating. Congratulations!

During stages 2 and 3 you must stay awake and develop your ability to see what you are doing. By releasing that part of you that gets caught in the drama you feel more conscious. You begin training yourself to respond in a new way and to create your life differently. This stage doesn't last forever, if you stay awake. Soon it will become easier and joyful. Most personal belief systems are held in place by negative emotions and fear. You may unconsciously choose to fit in so you don't have to feel the rejection, uncertainty and hopelessness when others judge and/or reject you. As you are willing to see and feel your emotions, you can bless them for their lessons, and clear them from your psyche. This allows you to consciously make healthier choices.

Wouldn't it be great if we could see our life clearly and change our reactions when they were repetitive, defeating and not serving us? We can decide to be consciously aware of the present moment in order to serve both our present and future life and mental and physical wellness. *How we react or respond to what is going on in our life is the only element that we can control. With trust in our process, we can feel that everything happens for a reason. We can choose to be content with the ups and downs of life as it is unfolding.* We can be an observer sometimes and curiously watch the show!

What if as we grew up our parents had given us free range to make all or most of our own choices? What if they had let us choose our favorite foods, when we wanted to do homework or what sports we wanted to play? What if we could choose to go to college or not, or whether we wanted to study this or that? What if…? For most of you that may not have been an option. Our parents may not have trusted that we knew what was best for ourselves. But how else would we gain wisdom and experience if we weren't given the opportunity? If we had learned to make choices at an early age, and more naturally and responsibly made choices as we got older, would our life have been different? Did your parents ever say to you: "I trust that you can make healthy and appropriate choices for yourself?"

There are thousands of choices continually present every day. Many individuals don't understand that. (Do you?) Many people think that they can do this or that, but don't see the many other options that might not be quite so visible. Life isn't always so black and white. There are many shades of green, blue and pink!

Every day we make thousands of decisions and choices that affect our life and our future. Each choice can affect whether we live in "the flow" or not. Our choices affect whether we live in chaos and struggle or peace and harmony. We can discontinue negativity, worry and judging (since it never gets us where we want to go anyway) and choose peace of mind, unconditional acceptance and love. *We can choose to make no one wrong or to have it "our way." We can decide to be joyful rather than right.* We will receive a far greater return for the energy that we expend when we choose love and joy in each situation, rather than being right or righteous. Each choice is extremely creative, so why not *live by choice instead of chance.*

> Each time a man stands up for an ideal or acts to
> improve the lots of others, or strikes out against
> injustice, he sends forth a tiny ripple of hope, and
> crossing each other from a million different centers,
> those ripples build a current which can sweep down
> the mightiest walls of oppression and resistance.
> ~Robert Kennedy 1925—1968
> *U.S. Attorney General from New York,*
> *Assassinated during presidential campaign*

One time I was walking with my youngest son along a river and waterfall. I had a limited amount of time because I needed to return to work. When I was ready to turn around, but my son didn't want to and was refusing to. I decided not to argue and let him have his way in that moment. I think he took four to five steps and said "OK, let's go back now." He seemed to feel good that he had a chance to be in charge and I was grateful that it didn't turn into an argument.

My middle son was my biggest challenge throughout my boys' youth. One time he had called me on the phone and I asked him to return home immediately. It was important to me that he do so right away. I asked him to return home and he refused. I asked him a few more times, but he still refused. I decided that I didn't want to argue, manipulate or threaten him so that I could have "my way," so I said that I would call him back in a while. I hung up. I had no idea what I would do next, but I liked none of the first options that I thought about. In about 30 seconds, my son called me back and said that he was coming home! (He can be very strong willed, so I was amazed!) Again, my choice to be unconditional benefited us both. I didn't have to force or threaten him or work my will. I just wanted to love him and that was all. We both had what we wanted without my reacting to him or my being disrespectful.

When we live without fear in the flow of life, we make healthy choices and feel the ease and freedom to just be ourselves. It feels as if we are always in the "right place at the right time." Some people might say that we are living in Divine Harmony, being Divinely Guided and part of the Divine Plan. As we learn to feel this flow and make choices that keep us in harmony, *we learn that it is really far easier to go with the flow rather than against. If we are not in the flow, we will feel struggle and fear, increased effort, and the need to control life.* When I feel powerless or that my life is a struggle, I know that I need to *change either what I doing or thinking or both.* I am allowing myself to be a victim without realizing it. If we are living in the flow, we observe and see the natural order of the universe in all that is occurring. We can flow through each experience and not plow through it!

One valuable exercise that I used for quite a while came from "The Course in Miracles." It was invaluable to me as I was raising 3 young, energetic, very strong willed boys. The Course had daily/weekly lessons that were phrases such as: "I choose the joy of God instead of pain," "I am spirit," "Let me be still and listen to the truth," "I am sustained by the love of God," "I am entitled to miracles" or "Light, and joy and peace abide in me." The Course would recommend that you repeat and use a saying for however long seemed appropriate for you.

The one that I found helpful and fun to use was Lesson 34, "I could see peace instead of this." It worked so well. I could walk into a room full of boys arguing and not getting along, and say to myself *"I can see peace instead of this."* In no time at all we might be rolling on the floor laughing. If I had felt the circumstance had been bad or wrong, or that I "should" fix it, I could have been pulled into the mayhem. I wasn't, once I used that phrase. I easily made choices that supported being in the universal flow and harmony. You can even substitute another word for peace (like joy, ease, etc.) and it could work equally well. Please try it for yourself and see what happens.

If we try to resist change and don't accept what is occurring, we will create discomfort and resistance in our life. We have to be careful, aware and conscious of when our mind judges that any change that is occurring is "bad" or inappropriate in some way. It may not be. We might assume that what is happening is moving us in the wrong direction, when in actuality it may be an amazing process of evolutionary growth and change for us. We could remain stuck and static there, rather than moving forward. If, however, we let go of assumptions and expectations, and truly see what is going on, we can then have the clarity to create and select changes that direct and connect us with our creative flow. It is easier to remain in the flow when we are unconditionally accepting and we making inner changes, especially changes in our perception and state of mind. As we recognize that *we are a spiritual being who is living through a human experience,* we can lighten up and focus on releasing old worn out, limiting habits, and play with all possible options and possibilities. If we truly support and know who we are, the bottom line is that we realize we don't want to waste time analyzing or judging things that don't serve us or lie in our best interests.

> Our problems cannot be dissolved in the same state
> of consciousness in which we are creating them.
> ~ Albert Einstein

When we think of what we want to attract, *we could just open our arms and welcome the unexpected, knowing that we deserve what is truly ours.* In doing that, try to engage and raise your energy to vibrate with what you want as your desired outcome.

Listening

If you talk to a man in a language he understands,
that goes to his head.
If you talk to him in his language,
that goes to his heart.
~Nelson Mandela

"Be seen not heard!" How many of us have lived with this philosophy? I did. I grew up in a household where this was expressed. My father always wanted us to be quiet at the dinner table. He preferred that we didn't talk, so it was a pretty quiet dinner....boring, numbing and dysfunctional! He would get angry pretty easily, so we knew to suppress our need to talk. I was always pretty quiet and shy growing up. I wonder if there is any connection.

Listening is a conscious experience. By listening with unconditional acceptance and warmth, we encourage others to freely express their thoughts and feelings. As they feel safe and are encouraged to think freely and find their own solutions, we are more likely to hear their underlying concerns, not just what they are saying. It may be helpful if the speaker acknowledges their words and reflects their thoughts, meanings and feelings back to them. For example you might say: "Sounds like..." or "Do you mean..." or "How do you feel about that?" *Over ninety percent of the interaction should be based in unconditional acceptance and compassionate support...leaving judgment and expectations elsewhere.* Questions are really a gift that helps the speaker to discover beliefs that underlie discomforts and assumptions that the other person holds.

Every individual matters.
Every individual has a role to play.
Every individual makes a difference.
~Jane Goodall

How many individuals are truly listened to? Most listeners are thinking about what they are going to say as soon as the other person finishes speaking. How could they really be listening? They may even interrupt the speaker before he/she is finished. As we are listening, can our thoughts and actions be free of our ideas and attachment to outcomes? Can we be truly present and listening?

When I studied Social Work at the University of New Hampshire, one of the most interesting classes was "group work." I found what occurred fascinating. We participated in groups of 12 students and would take turns leading the discussion. The first time around, it occurred that 3 students did most of the talking and monopolized most of the time. They were "talkers." They did not allow other individuals an opportunity to speak. You would have to cut one of them off in order to speak. Many individuals would not prefer to do that. In the second group meeting, we were asked to allow everyone equal opportunity to speak. What a difference in the dynamics of the group. Interestingly enough, the individuals who weren't apt to cut someone off in order to speak, didn't talk for long. They were to the point and had profound and interesting things to say. Reserved people unfortunately aren't often given time to speak when others dominate the conversation. They are the ones that I want to listen to.

I learned so much from this example, that now at the beginning of group workshops that I lead, I always tell individuals that I hope that they can be respectful of everyone in the group having an equal opportunity to speak. I have actually interrupted individuals who have gone "on and on" and asked that they finish their dialogue so that others could speak as well. One individual would laugh when I caught her.

I have known individuals who have decided not to speak for a while because they wanted to practice listening. That would be an interesting experience for most people. We could all practice listening more.

John Francis PhD, who is called the *Planetwalker* decided one day that he would not talk for a day, but would practice listening. He so enjoyed the day that he stretched it into a week, a month, a year and ultimately reached 17 years before he spoke again. Wow! If you see videos of him before and after that period, there is a really marked difference in his appearance. He now expresses a peaceful loving way about himself. He was definitely a rebel who followed his heart and his beliefs. He is now a teacher of evolutionary ways. I heard him speak at the Marion Institute's annual *Connecting for Change, Bioneers Conference* in New Bedford, Massachusetts. His book is called *Planetwalker.* Look at his videos online.

The most important avenue for listening involves what we constantly say to ourselves. The inner dialogue that we hold with ourselves can be sabotaging and disempowering or nurturing, creative and loving. How can we achieve and be all that we are capable of if we are beating ourselves up? Let's choose love and unconditional acceptance for ourselves in all circumstances. We can do it and intend to do it.

Feelings
(This is a key part of this whole opportunity process)

Feelings connect us to our Higher and intuitive self. Through our feelings, we can more easily recognize that part of ourselves that is outside of the logical, material, and fearful mind. We connect to a deeper realm of life and ourselves. We feel our connection to all that is. We then release the need to be anything other than that which we are.

How you enjoy each moment of your life depends not only on your relationship to yourself, but your relationship to your feelings (emotions and body sensations) as well. This is tied into recognizing your personal freedom to make choices and to feel OK about what you choose to feel about those choices. How do you feel with your anger? Do you feel angry, guilty, frustrated or even

OK about it? Do you get angry about being angry? *It isn't about the anger, but your relationship to the anger that is important. The judgments about your feelings can be more problematic than the feelings themselves.*

Anger is the weak persons imitation of strength.
(unknown)

This is very important—*when you have negative feelings about your feelings, it prevents you from processing and letting go of the original feelings when you are ready to move on.* You become stuck with your negative feelings about your feelings!! What good is that? Be gentle and kind to yourself. You deserve it.

Through releasing judgment, being aware, and experiencing what is occurring while you are unconditionally accepting it, you improve your relationship with yourself and your feelings. You don't have to love what is going on, just see and accept it in this moment.

Sometimes when we are feeling anxiety, it may not be solely our feelings. We are intimately connected to others and sensitive to those around us, so we may pick up feelings and energies that do not belong to us. Certainly when there are challenging economic times, environmental trauma, and physical hardship, many individuals are feeling anxiety and stress. We may all feel and connect with this challenging energy, without realizing that this energy is someone else's or even the feelings of society as a whole. Perhaps some is ours and some belongs to others. Relax, be conscious and check in to see what you think.

Cutting Cords

When used at appropriate times, this is a very beneficial exercise. I have used it often and recommended that clients use it when they have been in unhealthy interactions with other individuals. If you have a negative interaction with someone, and afterward feel really agitated, depressed, angry or unsettled then this would be a great exercise for you. It could also be used daily to clear unwanted negative influences and energies:

Sit quietly, breathe, relax and attain a conscious meditative state. Take a few minutes just to be.

Scan you're your body to see if you can detect any (psychic) energy cords connecting others to you. They could be any size... from a thin cord to a large pipe. There is no appropriate way for everyone to do this. You may sense them, but not see them. There could be one or more. These cords may be draining your energy or bringing negative emotions to you. You may be feeling another person's anger and negative feelings. What you are feeling that is disruptive to your psyche may not be yours....but you are feeling it because you are truly connected to them.

Once you find these cords, note how many and where they are. Then you want to take an implement to disconnect them or cut them from connecting to your body. You may use imaginary scissors, a saw, a chain saw or a laser beam. Whatever appeals to you is perfect. Once you cut them, let the cord return to its origin and the fill in the cut area with healing white light energy. There is no appropriate way to do this, only your way. After that, surround your being with a cocoon (egg shaped) of white light, healing and protective energy. Program this cocoon to repel any negative energy and let in only love and beneficial feelings. You could even place mirrors on the outside of the energy cocoon that face out and repel and negative energy. Add any other ritual that feels appropriate. Don't forget to use this one when it is needed. It works very well.

You can use this process to disconnect old cords that may have been connected to you for years. Old partners, friends, workers or enemies that are no longer around could still be draining your energy. Life can be challenging enough without dragging along others with us! Wish them well disconnected.

If we hold a high energetic force of 500 (love), as Dr. David Hawkins mentioned in his book *Power vs Force*, others with a lower force like anger (150) may connect with us energetically as a means of healing their anger and trauma. They will absorb our beneficial energy. Neither of us may know this is going on, but it may be. If you experience feelings which are out of proportion to the situation check to see if they all belong to you. Ask yourself intuitively. See if you receive a simple "yes" or "no" to your questions. If you have a response that says that these feelings are not all yours, then ask what percentage are yours and what percentage belongs to others. Just understanding this can be very enlightening. You may feel a difference in your psyche just in asking these questions. If you hold loving integrity, you may not even feel others fearful or challenging energy. The key is in holding our integrity.

In writing about this, I became conscious of understanding a fear in my own life that I thought was mine. I now believe that this fear also stems from someone close to me and is from the greater world as well. It is fear of "not having." We may all feel it and interpret it differently than the another person. Here is an example....what if someone that you are close to has an intense fear of not having you in their life, and you have a fear of not having enough money to pay bills. The energy level of "not having" might be similar for either scenario I would guess, but the intensity of that emotion might vary. We may then experience more intensity of this fearful emotion because it is really a combination of both theirs and ours. Initially we may misinterpret it as solely our fear.

If we want to have a healing and healthy relationship with our feelings, we have to be open and increase our awareness to them. We can feel the feelings, without judging them. As we understand our feelings, we can refrain from undermining ourselves or negatively affecting our sense of well-being. Feel your emotions without ignoring, suppressing or stuffing them. Some of these feelings may not feel very good, and that is OK. *You can have an underlying sense of well-being, no matter what you are experiencing.* Wow!

Try this. When you are feeling distressed or negative feelings....
stop, breathe, let go of everything but the moment and just be still.
Let go of everything else. Can you feel that underlying health ...the
internal peace, the stillness, the space between the thoughts.... This
is where your well-being lies. Feel this space....

The choice for wellness is up to you. It is possible and already present within you. Celebrate the wellness you feel!

Enjoying Each Experience with an Open Heart

Write down a list of feelings and emotions that you feel at different times (at least 5 - 10). Enjoy writing a wide variety of examples. After you have completed the list you may wish to go back and identify which make you feel at ease and which don't. With each sensation do the following:

1) Bring the feeling into your awareness. Feel, sense, accept and enjoy the feeling. You are always enjoying different feelings at different times in different ways. Certainly a wink and a hug is different than a challenging interaction or communication. Find and identify any form of pleasure that is present in that emotion. You may be surprised.

2) Notice there are some that you feel that are not exclusively bad, wrong or discomforting. Maybe you can be grateful that it does feel good in some ways. Feel the gratitude. (sadness or grief may fall in this category)

3) Be grateful that you can feel and be sensitive. (Many people are so closed down they feel little or nothing.)

4) Instead of thinking that some of these feelings should feel a certain way, realize that the way it feels right now is appropriate.

5) Surround yourself and your experience with unconditional love. You are whole and complete.

6) One part of you may feel that everything is OK just the way it is. How does that feel to you?

7) Be aware that you could see these feelings as an instrument of God's love/the Universe's love and support for you. All feelings have something to teach us. What can you learn from this feeling?

> The only question is; does this path have a heart?
> If it does, then it is a good path.
> If it doesn't, then it is of no use.
> ~Carlos Casteneda

Allow yourself to be non-judgmental and unconditionally accepting with each feeling on your list. Be aware of what you feel and be willing to experience whatever comes to you. This type of experience may be new for you. Don't change anything that comes up, but just experience what arises. Feel unconditional acceptance of yourself with whatever feelings come up. When you come to a place of resolution with each of the words, thank and bless yourself.

This type of exercise may help you to better identify and enjoy feelings that you didn't enjoy before. The most appropriate time to do it may be right after meditation, deep relaxation or prayer. Deep breathing before, during and after the exercise could help you to stay more in the moment, and be more accepting and less judgmental as well.

As you practice exercises of this type, you will slowly become less judgmental about everything from your thoughts and your feelings, to what is happening in your life. Each moment presents opportunities to evolve and become all that is possible for us. This is true whether we feel blessed or not.

We can decide to make the most of each moment when we look at our choices, release our judgments and honor our feelings. *As we fully live each moment without judging anything as bad or wrong, we can allow each moment to unfold as it is supposed to. (This is a great one to remember!)*

Transforming stress

Question: Am I struggling with certain issues in my life? (Remember: I can either change what I am doing or what I am thinking or I can also change both.

The first and most important step is to recognize the areas where I am struggling, feeling powerless and opposing the flow of life.

Creative Action Plan:

Areas where I am struggling or feeling powerless are:

....

To begin creating shift and change:

1) I can begin.........
2) I can change.......
3) I can release....
4) I can stop....
5) I will continue..............
6) The first steps toward change are..........
7) Areas of support........
8) Areas that negatively affect progress........
9) I can support myself in these areas.........
10) If I change what I am doing.........
11) Individuals who support me.......
12) Areas for daily intention & affirmations.......
13) Challenging areas that I need to let go of judgmental and self-sabotaging attitudes........

When an experience or stimuli occurs in our lives, *we have thousands of choices as to how we may "respond" (acceptance) or "react" (fear).* If you consciously choose an action, you would generally you choose to respond. Within the possibilities of response, there are thousands of possibilities! Think about it. You don't have to do just "this" or "that." Certainly, operating out of the old paradigm, you could tremble, have a panic attack, feel boxed in, become extremely tense, go into a cold sweat, become angry, or all of the above. (Wow, that sounds like too much work and no fun!) Or you could change your habits and reactions, choosing to stand on your head, laugh and say "this is an opportunity." Mix it up. Try something different, just for fun. *Break up the old patterns and begin a new life and paradigm. The choice is yours. It may be easier than you think.*

Years ago I started playing around with the word "risk." Risk had meant to me, doing new things that I feared doing. I was afraid of the possible unknown outcome. Growing up I was protected and really didn't explore beyond the safety of my immediate environment, so with new experiences that I hadn't had before, I was unsure I even wanted to try. I became brave and I decided that I would risk doing certain things and see what happened. I was delightfully surprised. Everything that I risked doing, turned out to be better than I expected. Wow! So from that point on I decided that I would call it a "choice" rather than a "risk." The unknown felt less scary. In doing these new and different things I decided that in the process I would totally and wholeheartedly support my decisions. It worked just as well or better. "Risk" had fear behind it and "choice" had all possibilities, love and myself supporting it. I was sold. I stopped using the word risk and began choosing what I wanted and unconditionally accepted myself in the process.

For me the experiences that stand out, are in relationship to men that I was interested in. I was terribly shy and often would hold back feelings and thoughts about fun possibilities. In deciding to support myself through "choices," I decided to suggest things that were "totally "out of the question" previously. One example, occurred on the coast of Maine when a male friend and I rowed out to a very small island during the day. I thought it would be fun to stay overnight on the island and previously I would never, ever have mentioned it. Everything came together, we stayed and it was quite an adventure.

During this process of shift and change, I rewrote the following saying that used the word "risk" and replaced it with the word "choose." I replaced other (negative) words as well in the second version. (The original verse is written first.) Here is the end result:

To laugh is to risk appearing a fool,
To weep is to risk appearing sentimental.
To reach out to another is to risk involvement,
To expose feelings is to risk exposing your true self.
To place your ideas and dreams before
a crowd is to risk their loss.
To love is to risk not being loved in return,
To live is to risk dying,
To hope is to risk despair,
To try is to risk failure.
But risks must be taken because the
greatest hazard in life is to risk nothing.
The person who risks nothing, does
nothing, has nothing, is nothing.
~William Arthur Ward

To Laugh is to Choose to Be Joyful

To laugh is to choose to be joyful.
To weep is to choose to be sensitive.
To reach out for another is to choose to be vulnerable.
To expose our feelings is to choose to be true to oneself.
To place our ideas and dreams before the crowd is to
choose to inspire others.

To love is to choose to be unconditionally
caring and accepting.
To really live is to choose to live without fear
and risk just existing.

To hope and trust is to choose to believe
in all that is possible.
To stand by your choices means that you totally support
yourself and you let go of fear and
fearing failure.

But choose we must because our greatest challenge
is to be awake and let go of fear.
The man, the woman, who exists half asleep in fear,
chooses nothing, has nothing and is nothing.
Choice brings profound opportunities that we could only
have previously dreamt of. Through choice, we awake to
the awesome wonders, opportunities and miracles of life.
We become our Authentic Self.
--Becky Mulkern ND

Which version do you prefer?

We can also look at the words choice and discipline. Many people feel they have to discipline themselves to do things, like exercise or eat healthy, etc. But discipline will never work very well, because it will demand that you push yourself to do something that you probably don't want to do and/or that others may expect you to do. Choosing on the other hand involves doing something that you really want to do and support yourself in the process. So choose without reservation what you want in every moment, and if you can't feel light and inspired with the choice, consider not doing it. Unconditionally support yourself in every choice.

The following is an exercise that may help you to heal deep level emotional, mental, and spiritual traumas. Take time to do it in a quiet environment.

Healing the Inner Child Exercise

(I learned this exercise years ago from Jody & David Hodges—(Copyright 1987) in a *Holistic Attunement training*)

Please select an emotion from the following list that you would like to work with. You may select it in any way that feels appropriate:

Humble	Cheerful	Calm
Communicative	Secure	Successful
Reliable	Supportive	Joyful
Hopeful	Approved	Goodness
Content	Pleasant	Harmonious
Appreciated	Satisfied	Clarity
Understood	Enlightened	Steadfast
Peaceful	Confident	Fulfilled
Loved	Faithful	Divine
Whole	Authentic	Unconditional

Sit in a quiet place and do the following:

Ask your Inner Self to offer yourself the feeling of the experience of......... (your word)

Ask the Inner Self to take this (emotion) back in time and to offer it to your younger self and to assist that younger self in growing up maintaining full access to this emotion whenever and wherever it was needed.

Ask your Inner Self to take this resource...(your word) back in time to the being that you were just before the traumatic/stressful incident or sequence began to occur, and to assist that being that you were in going through that original experience differently, holding on effortlessly and naturally to that part of yourself in feeling....(your emotion) Ask your Inner Self to carry this resource forward in time, everywhere that it is needed.

In essence, you are asking your Inner Self for a healing, and asking that the healing be extended throughout time, past present and future. Also ask that a healing be offered to anyone else involved in this pattern in whatever form and time frame that is most useful for them.

Ask your Inner Self to erase the cellular memory of the fear and pain associated with those memories to the extent that it is useful to your total being to do so.

(This exercise is taken from a class that I took over 30 years ago)

> Choice: Setting intentions may set things in motion on the
> subconscious plane, but for true
> change, intentions must also be
> reflected in our daily conscious choices.
> By accepting the implication
> within *Spontaneous Evolution* that
> we are all cellular souls in an
> evolving super organism called humanity, we need to ask,
> "What daily choices can I personally
> make to reinforce this emergent worldview?"
> ~Bruce H. Lipton Ph.D. & Steve Bhaerman,
> ~*Spontaneous Evolution*~

Going Deeper~

~Make thoughtful and creative choices. Create new and unusual ones than you might not normally make. Enjoy the process.

~Live in the moment. Just "be." Slow everything down. Be as aware of each moment as you possibly can be.

~Continue to pay attention to the words that you use to describe your thoughts, feelings and experience. Reword negative spirals when appropriate or when it would lend to more clarity, creativity and self-support. Create uplifting spirals.

~Look at your belief systems continually. Let go of and transform the ones that you no longer need and create new ones, just for fun.

~Be aware of any tension, stress or discomfort that arises when you are judging and/ or reacting to challenges. Consciously let go and breathe. Respond to life with ease, creativity, joy and gratitude.

10

Unconditional Acceptance is the Key to Peace of Mind

> Unconditional acceptance and letting
> go is one of the easiest,
> yet possibly one of the most challenging choices
> that we can ever make!
> ~Becky Mulkern ND

Unconditional acceptance is one of the key concepts in this book. It is a very powerful place to be. If we can all live from this place, the world will change rapidly!

Being in an unconditionally accepting state is truly one of letting go and being present in the moment. It is not a passive state, but a state of true presence. *You are the most invincible when you are allowing yourself to be the most vulnerable.* You may think that this would be a weakened state, but if you truly accept yourself and all that you are, then being vulnerable and open to life would truly just be your state of being! In actuality you would no longer describe it as a state of vulnerability....because you would feel strength and power in truly being your Authentic Self.

When we live in a state of unconditional acceptance, we live in the moment....totally. We are here, present and safe. We see and know what is going on around us. We are aware of everything.... from how we are feeling, to the details, colors, life around us, and our sensitivity to our surroundings.

Recently I read a short comment made by Helen Keller that really impacted me. I will share it with you. A friend of Helen's had gone out for a walk and when she returned, Helen asked her what she saw on her walk. Helen always wanted to experience the world through other people. Helen was very disappointed when her friend said "Nothing in particular." Helen was very surprised that her friend had seen nothing of interest that she could share. I am sure Helen was wondering if her friend was even aware of her surrounding environment or was she lost, deep in thought and unaware of her surroundings. Since reading this, every morning when I go for a walk, I think about what in my personal experience that I would share with Helen. This morning I might have shared how the early morning sun felt on my face, the rosy color of the alpenglow on the mountains, the fluorescent fall colored leaves on the staghorn sumac bush or the red and green colors of the oak tree sprouts on the sandy beach by the river. There is so much to see and share if we are aware of what surrounds us. (I have seen this story a number of places. One was in *The Atlantic Monthly, Three Days to See.*)

I hope you will think of Helen Keller sometimes on your walks or trips. What would you share with her?

When we judge that our life experience or other people should be different, we are not accepting them as they are. We want them to change. We need them to change. We can truly only change ourselves. It is as if we are trying to be in charge of the universe and wanting it to be different, as if it isn't OK the way it is. ***But it is not up to us to change anyone, but to unconditionally accept them as they are.*** There is perfection in where people are. We just have to be able to see it and acknowledge it. It is as perfect for us as it is for them. When we operate from the ego, righteousness and/or fear, we are not in a space of unconditional acceptance. From the point of unconditional acceptance we may see the perfection that is present.

When you live in a state of heart-felt unconditional acceptance and being, resistance and fear dissolve. You have heard of the saying ***"what you resist persists,"***.... resistance is fear. If we surrender and live with acceptance, we will truly know peace of mind. Lack of acceptance creates disharmony, struggle, anxiety and lack of presence. When we don't accept, we are literally "against" something. *Our power and passion increases when we are "for" life, not against it. Stand for what you want, not against its opposite!* For example, stand for peace, not against war. Stand for health not against cancer or diabetes. Keep your focus on what you want to create. This is the way of the evolutionary change. Let us unite in what we stand for.

When we resist and push against anything, we actually give strength to and empower the cause we are fighting against. If we declare a "war" on drugs, poverty, obesity, or war, we energetically add to the strength of what we want to eliminate.

> We might say that you have this upside down
> and backwards. It is time that humanity realizes
> that as vibrational beings you call forth into your
> reality what you place your focus and attention
> upon. If your focus is on opposition to some action
> or controversy you are actually feeding the very
> thing you would desire to change or improve.
> ~Peggy Black and the 'team', ~*Upside Down and
> Backwards* from humanitysteam.org 10/30/2013

Think about how many people support and stand for non-violence. They certainly care about peace, but they haven't yet understood yet the energetic quality of speaking of non-violence instead of what they are "for." We want to stand energetically for peace, harmony, communication or love instead. Just think about how different these feel. Think about "non-violence" and then think about "peace." What difference do you feel? It feels so different to be for something as opposed to it. This is a powerful one.

Everyone has heard of the therapeutic effects of pets. Research scientists have actually proven that having a pet actually has specific and measurable effects on both a person's body and mind. Just the presence of an animal can: 1) increase a sick person's survival rates,

2) lower the heart rate, 3) calm disturbed children, and 4) promote conversation in non-communicative people.

It is easy to understand why these effects are present. Animals are not complicated. They are non-judgmental, accepting and present. They provide an opportunity for physical contact. In studies where they measured the effects on the elderly, they found the elderly smiled more, were more alert, less aggressive and more tolerant when an animal was present. How wonderful, therapeutic, and uncomplicated. Let's hope that more individuals can share their pet's example of unconditional acceptance.

When individuals live their life aligned with fear, they may consciously or unconsciously believe that suffering is a necessary part of life. They become a victim of struggle, hardship, aging and dis-ease. *Those who constantly choose to identify with fear are always pursuing life, and not living it.* They battle their over-active mind and life, while they believe that worry is a necessary ingredient for keeping control over their life. They believe that without worry, they would be a victim in life. They even believe that worry somehow helps them get what they want while at the same time, they may have many excuses for not getting what they want.

As soon as we decide and accept that we are not perfect in this moment, we enter the realm of fear. We become bound by the illusions of fear when we believe that they are real. But we can exhale and let go of any illusion that says to us that we are not perfect now in this moment. We can let our outworn beliefs, our past and our history die. We can choose to be reborn to seeing our history differently. As we let go of all the old beliefs, we can then see that our past helped us to evolve and to see the truth inside of us. We shall find our true selves as align with our hearts, our perfection and Infinite Intelligence/Source/God. We will know then that we are extraordinary and free!

> You can be in heaven (Oneness with All) and not know
> it. Indeed, most of you are. This can be changed, but not

by something you are doing. It can only be changed by something that you are being. This is what is meant by the statement, "There is nothing you have to do." There is nothing to do but be. And there is nothing to be, but One.
~Neale Donald Walsch, ~*Communion With God*

Our personal truth is powerful. Freedom is an experience of our spiritual consciousness and our Authentic Mind. No one person and nothing outside of ourselves can free us. Thinking cannot set us free. The real truth of who we are lies beyond our heart and in transcending what we believe we are. In order to know our boundless consciousness and the nature of our true self, we have to connect with the spiritual aspects of our being. (Whatever that means to you)

Everything in our life continually changes and is capable of change. *Change is the only thing that we are guaranteed.* Through our infinite capacity to choose, we can create evolutionary change in each and every moment of our lives. What frees us to be, to see our choices and to choose, is acceptance. *By operating from a space of unconditional acceptance, we are more capable of using all our resources that were previously consumed and frozen by fear.* We gain incredible clarity that allows us to see, think and act in very creative and boundless ways. We realize the infinite choices that are available to us. As we cease the battle with our mind, we operate from our hearts and simply allow miracles and wonders to unfold. As we let go of fear and release previously held limitations and beliefs that say "we have no choices," we begin to see options and choices far beyond what we ever thought was possible.

The first peace, which is the most important, is that which comes within the souls of people when they realize their relationship, their oneness, with the universe and all its powers, and when they realize that at the center of the universe dwells the Great Spirit, and that this center is really everywhere, it is within each of us.
~Black Elk

When we refuse to accept others and we judge them from the vantage point of fear and anticipation of their next actions, we actually can determine their response by freezing them into their history. People will respond in manners that we expect. We may not even realize that we are doing it, but any expectations that we have of others can manifest itself before our eyes. *We can create what we focus on and fear. When we accept ourselves and others as we are now, this moment, we allow for all to be in flux, in change, reborn and truly alive.* Through acceptance of each moment, we can know ourselves deeply. Through unconditional acceptance, we can honor our strengths and see and accept ways in which we may not feel strong. We can open our arms and meet what is before us, while we release, bless and let go of what is moving away from us. We can live a fluid and dynamic life experience.

All suffering can be recognized, blessed and transformed through unconditional acceptance and love. It can never be healed through fear. As we release and refrain from living in fear, we experience our feelings while being present for ourselves. We can choose to feel blessed and joyful as we understand and support the fact that we are always doing our best!

We can also support others to be and do what they choose to be and do. Through acceptance we give others the freedom to be what they want to be.

If I ask you which of your friends you feel the most comfortable with, I would assume that the individuals you select are non-judgmental and unconditionally accepting. There is a big difference between those who live this way and those who don't. There is a grace and comfort in being with them and a feeling that you could tell them anything and you would not be judged. How wonderful! Usually there aren't many friends in anyone's circle who are like this.

This is why in being unconditionally accepting to ourselves we become an example to others. Holding unconditional acceptance for ourselves is a way of truly loving and caring for ourselves.

Meanings & Feelings of Unconditional Acceptance

Unconditional acceptance is the primary aspect of my "Life is an Opportunity" course. As we accept what is before us, we relax, breathe and more easily focus on creating the solutions that we need. In my class, I asked individuals to share what "acceptance" meant to them and the following are some of their responses:

Unconditional love	a freeing experience
Non-judgmental	comfortable
Not seeking or needing approval	contentment/silence
The way I am—it's OK	door to the world of choice
Relief, freedom, loving self	being here, focusing
Being yourself	perfection
No fear	It doesn't matter
We are responsible for our own feelings	connecting with our worth
Everything is alright!	value, spiritual self
a blank slate	intimacy

I also asked the participants in the class, "What can you say to yourself to get yourself into a space of unconditional acceptance?" These are some of their responses:

It doesn't matter!	Take a deep breath
Life just goes on…	Relax, I'm OK
It's their life…	I am doing my best
Be a listener not a talker	Chill out!
I can see peace instead of this	I let go
Nip the negative in the bud	It is not my business
Body awareness and calm	I release
I trust in myself	I let go of control

Holding Unconditional Acceptance in your Heart creates

1) Acceptance of each unfolding moment, all of it, with both its rewards and challenges and all it brings.
2) Conscious focus on the process that is in front of us.
3) Letting go of fears and knowing that we are safe.
4) Living in the present moment, here and now.
5) Releasing thinking or analyzing, while experiencing the present moment. Enjoying your intuition and creativity.
6) Using visualization and imagination to see/project/intend what you want.
7) *Letting life change you.*

With acceptance we allow life to change us, gently and easily. We need less and do less to modify life because we experience an inner shift of consciousness and perception. Miracles occur with this change of perception. When we try to change life inappropriately, we may meet pain, resistance and struggle. We can then choose to come back to unconditional acceptance and love for ourselves.

Forgiveness

Forgiveness means giving up all hope
for a better past.
~Lily Tomlin

When I think about the regret that individuals may hold about the past, I say to myself. "Get over it"…look to the future and create it differently next time. Create it in alignment with your true self and Divine Harmony. The past is gone. Learn the lessons of that time and see the many opportunities for creating your future differently. Focus on what you are grateful for now and understand the power you have to create your future differently.

Forgiveness was something that I always questioned, though I never really thought a lot about it. In time I understood why I felt unsure with the idea. I noticed many individuals when they were upset, they believed that others had done something "wrong" to them. They decided though, that they would forgive them. It was the labeling of something "wrong," that caught my attention and didn't feel quite appropriate. Certainly if we believe that others are wrong, we are being a "victim." In teaching my "Life is an Opportunity" classes, I emphasized over and over again that in every situation, we are always doing our personal best, according to the knowledge, experience and upbringing that we have. I believe that in each and every situation we do our best at that particular time. If that is true, then how can we still label what others did as "wrong" or "bad"… when in actuality that may not be true, if they are doing their personal "best?"

If we feel that someone did something wrong to us, we might say that we forgive them but we could still be holding onto negative feelings of "they were wrong," while still holding resentment, anger and/or judgment. We can continue to allow the experience to hold power over us due to our perception and attitude. When we forgive, release the past and let go, we allow energies to transform and we free ourselves from tension and constriction even to our heart. We can release the emotional pain and still hold and bless the memories and experience for what it has taught us.

Can we accept that they were doing their best? Can we nourish ourselves and send nourishment out to others in the Universe? I feel that the key to really letting go and releasing the past is to accept that everyone did their best in each situation. Everyone is given opportunities to grow and learn. If we release criticism, judgment and feeling "wronged," we in turn actually have nothing to forgive. If we feel that we have something to forgive, then we can look at the experience and decide how we want to proceed. If we do not process, accept and forgive if we need to, we may hold onto feelings that create ill health in ourselves over the long term. The experience may hurt us far more than anyone else.

Nelson Mandela knew the power of forgiveness better than most. He immediately forgave all of the people that imprisoned him including his jailers and the politicians that were responsible. Years later he even had tea with Betsie Verwoerd, the widow of Hendrik Verwoerd, the architect of apartheid. He knew that love was the greatest power in the universe and he practiced it with people of all belief systems. He even invited his prison wardens to his inauguration as the first democratic President of South Africa. Mandela always treated everyone with respect while embracing their common humanity no matter what their station in life was.

> Always forgive your enemies—
> nothing annoys them so much.
> ~Oscar Wilde

Another extraordinary book about forgiveness is in *Left to Tell* by Immaculee Ilibagiza. This is a story about the 1994 Rwandan genocide and Immaculee's survival by spending 91 days in a pastor's cramped bathroom with seven other women. Her story of embracing prayer, holding deeply to her connection to God and living with unconditional love, is a true story of forgiveness. She talks about her faith and the hope that inspired her to later speak with those who killed her family. She provides an example of the power of forgiveness in the truest sense.

Years ago I had a client with Lou Gehrig's disease and one day she was telling me a story about high school and an incident with a young man. Then she said, "and I never forgave him!" Wow....the way she said it almost knocked me over. Her energy felt so intensely powerful that I understood how anger, resentment and negative feelings might cause or contribute to chronic dis-ease. She actually seemed to feel good that she still held onto her blame. She seemed proud of her anger.

Unconditional acceptance is the key to living without judgment, blame, resentment, guilt and anger. It doesn't mean that we condone others actions, it just means that we accept what has occurred, so hopefully, we can move on. Unconditional acceptance is very much like unconditional love. If we unconditionally accept an experience, then we are really surrounding it with love.

If we wish to really release the past, rituals can work well as an instrument for change. In we doing some type of ritual with a past trauma and emotional pain, we must first accept the experience as a teacher for us. Then we can surround it with love and bless it. Next we may release and transform our pain to love, while we still holding on to the memory. The memory may then be of an experience that allowed us to grow and evolve. With this process we release judgment, blame and being a victim and we take full responsibility for our role in the situation. We may actually mentally thank the others involved in this situation, for the lessons we gained. We support ourselves for doing as well as we did. We understand that at another time we can create other possibilities. We can be thankful for the new opportunities that have been created.

As we unconditionally accept this moment, we place attention inward and we utilize love to access our relationship to ourselves and others. We base ourselves in integrity and wholeness, rather than in thinking and judging.

> You will know that forgiveness has begun when you recall
> those who hurt you and feel the power to wish them well.
> ~Lewis B. Smedes

If you feel that there is some situation that you just cannot forgive and release, question whether you are in any way saying that you are right and they are wrong? If we hold onto anger, remorse, resentment, sadness or guilt, we keep ourselves based in negativity and we halt the flow of spiritual energy and love through our whole being. Our anger and negativity hurts only ourselves. Old unresolved feelings hold us back from everything that we truly want.

Some issues that are aligned to issues of love and forgiveness include:

1) Times when you felt unloved by individuals who may have "hurt" you.
2) Times where you offered love but it was rejected.
3) Times when those who loved you were manipulating you.

In a ritual of forgiveness/unconditional acceptance, you may wish to say something to this effect:

I accept that you did your best in this situation, and I accept that I did my best in this situation. I accept the fact that we both came together to learn and grow through this experience. We may not have been able to see very clearly at the time, but as we move on from the situation we may both have more insight and understanding of the ways in which it was beneficial for us. I know that it was a stepping stone in my process of growth, and I know that I have already learned many things from it. I have learned.......... In the future I know that in similar circumstances I will respond differently. This may include the following actions or possibilities...

> World peace must develop from inner peace.
> Peace is not just mere absence of violence.
> Peace is, I think, the manifestation of human compassion.
> ~His Holiness the 14th Dalai Lama

As we release ourselves from being what we think we "should" be and what others may want us to be, we see the opportunity to just be authentic. Feel the freedom of being your authentic self.

Exercise:

Relax, breathe deeply and connect with a state of Being (whatever that is to you). Breathe slowly and release any tension that you might be feeling.

In your mind, visit a person and a place in time that may still need resolution. You may need to speak to someone (in your mind) from the present or past. There is something that you have left unsaid. There may be one or more experiences that occurred where you didn't speak your mind or truth when you may have wanted to. Now is your opportunity to resolve in your mind what may need saying. Be thoughtful about the words that you choose. Take time to say what you need to.

Words left unspoken can cause you pain and dis-ease. This exercise is for you...you can't change someone else. Saying what you need to may help you to release the past and move on.

When you are finished, bless both of you, give thanks for the opportunity and take a few more deep breathes.

Open your eyes when you are ready.

Trauma

> You cannot grow spiritually unless you are
> prepared to change. Those changes may come in
> small ways to begin with, but as you move further
> and further into the new, they will become more
> drastic and vital. Sometimes it needs a complete
> upheaval to bring about a new way of life.
> ~Eileen Caddy, ~*Flight into Freedom and Beyond*

Sometimes trauma is helpful and necessary to initiate and create significant shift and change in our lives. Can you identify and be thankful for the beneficial changes that occurred in your life through trauma and challenge? Can you identify how many traumas you have experienced?

Being reactive to certain situations is a sign of the "imprint of trauma' in your psyche. Trauma lives in our beings, long after the traumatic experiences have occurred. When an experience arises that is similar to previous challenging events, it may trigger deep subconscious memories of pain, anxiety, and trauma. We can react in the present, to triggers from both the present and past. Previous stress that is not healed can live deep in our being. Layers of these stresses build up and contribute to a reactive and hyper alert quality in our nature. There are true causes for anxiety, reactivity, hyper alertness, and quick to anger, it is not just the "way you are." It can be healed and released. Acknowledging it is the first step.

I will give you an example of this. One of my clients has two dogs. One young dog, let's call him Charlie, that she accepted from a family member was very hyperactive. Most people would assume that this was the dog's nature. The funny thing was that Charlie liked to drink coffee if it was on the coffee table. He would not drink water, tea or juice or anything else, but the coffee, if it was there. He wouldn't spill it either. That gave me an idea. Since I had given her some remedies for stress, and one nervous system remedy had coffee in it (which is used for poor sleep and hyperactivity), I recommended that she put some drops of this remedy and *Rescue Remedy* in the dogs' water. The first day that she did it, both dogs slept and "chilled" most of the day. She was amazed. After that, Charlie would then go over to coffee on the coffee table, smell it and then go to the drinking water. Both dogs began drinking much more water too. Formerly when she got home from work, Charlie was all over her, jumping up etc. After the introduction of the remedies, he waited when she got home until she came over to him. Wow! He was truly a mellower dog. She was amazed at the difference. Evidently, Charlie had experienced some trauma and his hyperactivity was a result. The remedies were especially for addressing these issues, so they worked well to our surprise.

We don't have to be stuck with and endure physical, emotional and mental imbalances. There are many possibilities for healing and beneficial change. Just see a Naturopathic Doctor for guidance and some natural remedies. You may see some dramatic changes, just as Charlie did.

In the years before completing this book, I experienced 5 major traumas before I realized that I had PTSD (Post Traumatic Stress Syndrome). I hadn't understood the impact of my traumatic experiences from previous years, until I began to heal and look back at my symptoms, traumas, and challenges. I had always carried on no matter what happened to me. I was good at it, because there seemed to be no other options. Finally I realized that I had to start addressing and healing my own deep physical, mental, emotional and spiritual health issues. One of the traumas and challenges that affected my health was a car accident. A few years later, I experienced a ski accident, broke my leg and ended up with hip replacement and a titanium femur. Even now I am still in recovery from that injury. There was deep emotional trauma, injury and physical trauma to the leg's flexor muscles and further traumatization from the surgery. It was my first surgery. It took me a while to realize how deeply and in how many ways this experience impacted me. I always had a perfect, very strong and dependable body. Then it felt no longer true. Initially my balance was challenged. I couldn't hike as fast without leg spasms and I couldn't bike or ski for 2 years. I continued to realize even years later, how traumatic this experience had been both physically and emotionally. It gave me great insight into PTSD, its effects, symptoms and treatment. I was humbled by the experience.

> We are routinely pressured into adjusting too quickly
> in the aftermath of an overwhelming situation.
> ~Peter A. Levine, ~*Waking the Tiger*

During the time after the car accident, my niece recommended that I look at the book *Waking the Tiger - Healing Trauma* by Peter A. Levine. What was most interesting about this book was a list of 100 symptoms of trauma. After the car accident, I saw that I was experiencing 25 out of 100! Wow! I couldn't deny that impact on my being. Many symptoms, last quite a while before they diminish, others are gone within a few weeks or months. Take a look at this book if you have experienced any major traumas.

As I listened to my body after the accident, I learned what I could do without traumatizing or stressing my body further. I could actually cross country ski within 6 weeks after breaking my leg. It was gentle enough and was an easy fluid movement, so that was great. I could hike in the spring with poles and push myself up mountains. I needed to be out in nature and I could be. It was my church, my refuge and my connection to the divine universe and what was real to me.

After experiencing all these major stresses and traumas, I realized that I couldn't even smile anymore... I was just barely holding on to my life...just going through the motions. I began addressing and healing the different traumas (I have an Ondamed Biofeedback system for traumas and promoting healing). I actually began to practice smiling, until it became more and more part of my every day. I practiced often. At first it was really challenging because it felt so superficial. I just wasn't feeling joyful. I kept on practicing until finally I could feel a difference in my psyche. It seemed to work! It was simple yet it made a big impact. It brought me back to the moment where I could be thankful and joyful. Smiling and laughing actually does change the physiology. If you pay attention you can feel the difference in your being. I was happy to enjoy smiling again and not just pretend!

Trauma can occur and stay in the body indefinitely due to its emotional, mental, physical and spiritual impact. Most of what is stored occurs on a subconscious level. Some of the following circumstances contribute to internalized emotional and physical trauma:

Relationship challenges and losses
Economic Hardship
Abuse of any type (physical, mental, emotional)
Abandonment/rejection or neglect
Loss or death of those you love
Prolonged & Daily Stresses
Negative & Self-defeating attitudes
Losses
Disease & prolonged illness
Unhealthy relationships
Numbed & Pain-filled feelings
Fears
Accidents and Injuries

We are not always aware that we have experienced trauma. I have seen clients lie on my massage table ready for a massage, supposedly relaxing, but their fists are clenched, and they aren't even aware of it. I believe that there are many more individuals with PTSD than are truly recognized.

Releasing and transforming trauma is important for us to be able to and move on to higher levels of health, consciousness, joy and spiritual evolution. Trauma prevents us from reaching our potentials because we are like a dear in headlights….immobilized and dysfunctional. Being in alpha brain wave state can help to promote healing of traumas in a much shorter time. When traumas are experienced and the fight or flight response is initiated it doesn't always just turn off again. It remains on indefinitely, preventing us from accessing the healing that we need to bring us back into balance and health. Canadian Dr. James Heart Ph.D. a neurologist, physicist and psychology researcher works with a variety of trauma and PTSD clients and heals them through placing them in the alpha state to release stress and deep trauma issues. When living with trauma, it is much harder to access the alpha state which actually helps to heal the trauma. There are a number of ways to access the alpha state including meditation, Ondamed biofeedback (which I use with clients) and Dr. Heart's approach to name a few. Please explore these if you have experienced significant trauma in your life.

Numbing

Many individuals unconsciously suppress their feelings as a way of protecting themselves and dealing with life's many stresses. These experiences may include overwhelming pain and injury, feelings of inadequacy, shame, guilt, rejection, abuse, and negative emotions. Numbing our feelings may protect us against what has occurred and is occurring in our life. This is a process of doing our best to take care of ourselves no matter what comes up for us. In some circumstances we may have good reasons for wanting to feel numb, especially if we are trying to carry out our day to day responsibilities and/or we may need to protect ourselves from unbearable emotional pain. Numbing ourselves could become progressive and addictive over time; becoming a habitual or continual response and phenomenon. *If we are aware of our actions, we might choose to respond differently and change this reaction to a response before it becomes unhealthy.* Unfortunately in this state of numbness we aren't always aware of what we are doing. Numbness keeps us from feeling anything.

I was in a car accident over 11 years ago. My car was unexpectedly hit from behind with a very hard impact. There were 3 impacts in a matter of seconds that I didn't see coming. My car was hit in the rear left bumper, within a moment the opposite side of the car hit a tree and then I hit my head on the inside of the car door. I realized that I had a 1" gash on the side of my head and that the whole left side of my face felt different and like it had sagged. I didn't feel anything else immediately except for shock that this had happened and come out of nowhere. Over time I realized that I experienced trauma throughout my whole being from that sudden, unexpected event. The intense impact created a huge shift and release in my psyche that I could no longer ignore.

In the aftermath, I remember feeling a sense of numbness that I hadn't felt before. All I could say, again and again was "I feel so numb." Looking back, I felt that the sudden injury dislodged deep numbness that I had held and lived with for years. The numbness had covered up my deep emotional pain. I had endured so much pain in my life that I didn't want to feel, look back at or try to recall any of it. I had no idea how much was there or what to do with it either. So, over the years, I continued to ignore and suppress my feelings, add to the baggage and somehow think that I was safe from it all. That wasn't true. That was the beginning of really unwinding feelings that needed to be healed and released. Our process can go on for an indefinite period of time, depending on how traumatic the events are and how long the feelings have been suppressed.

My father was barely present physically or emotionally. That may have been one factor that caused me to shut down emotionally, be out of touch with and suppress my feelings and in turn feel numb. My father never interacted with me in any meaningful or loving way. I felt no love or connection to him. A psychic once asked me if I had a father. She couldn't see any sign of him in my life. He was never there except as a financial provider. He provided us a beautiful home and nice clothes, etc. This lack of interaction with my father, contributed to a pattern that proceeded to happen throughout my life. I was always in relationships with men who couldn't be there for me. They were just like him… present physically but not emotionally. I would think that I was getting closer to changing that, and then it would happen again and again. I have learned that I had to be there for myself and then maybe I will attract a man who can be there for me. I am still in that process… I hope that I can heal that challenge in this lifetime. I think I am very close.

By being present in the moment, we can more readily feel our feelings and understand them. We then can choose and/or create another response that serves us and promotes our healing and wellbeing. *We must understand that we will be healthier, experiencing our feelings and processing them, than we are stuffing them.* Through this process, we can understand that by unconditionally loving and accepting ourselves right now, we can heal those parts of ourselves that fear experiencing our feelings.

When you begin a healing process, take time to sense any numb areas within yourself (physically or emotionally). Be compassionate, unconditionally loving and understanding. Focus on one or more areas where the numbness is most obvious and breathe in and out of those areas. Don't intellectualize, just be present to the process. Be gentle and patient and continue to do this process over time, repeating the process when you can. It probably took a long time for you to come to this place. It make take a while to release and free yourself of the old, dead, hurt, angry, unloved and shut down parts of yourself. As you heal, allow yourself to wake up and experience life anew. As you consciously trust in this process you will grow and evolve into a being that can experience feelings without turning off. The feelings don't have to good or bad…they are just your feelings. You can accept your feelings and experiences and then choose what you wish to do next. There is no rush…take your time. Holding unconditional acceptance, as you feel and open to your experience, is key. Continue to breathe and just be, as you feel your feelings. Then, take time to decide your next step.

Breathing can be a key activity to prevent the numbing from taking place. *Breathe deeply as soon as you feel yourself beginning to react to any experience….* This prevents the stress and trauma from settling into the system. If you know or feel that an experience might be stressful, begin deep breathing before it gets to that point and breathe deeply right through the experience.

> If the breather keeps breathing, the continuing
> flows of energy will wash through and open the
> patterns of contraction, bringing lightness where
> there was density, softening and relaxing the hard,
> painful places in the person's experience and turning
> old emotional hurt into radiant, loving joy.
> ~Michael Sky, ~*Breathing*

If you are unsure how often you may have chosen to numb yourself, the following is a list so that you may be more aware of your life's experiences:

Do you often have low energy, not enjoy life, have very few close friends, rarely feel loving toward others, cry very infrequently, rarely feel sad, watch TV daily, sick often, challenged to express anger or love, little or no exercising, nothing in life excites you, poor sleep, depressed often, drink and smoke often, unloved as a child, don't feel good about yourself, unaware of your body and your feelings, rarely feeling love or grief and not satisfied by meals. That could be a short list, but it gives you a sense of what happens when you numb yourself. It can be healed and changed through your awareness.

Emotional Healing Crisis

Many gentle therapies, including meditation, acupuncture, massage, yoga and relaxation may trigger emotional healing. Sometimes as the body lets go and relaxes, feelings that have been stuffed and/or trauma that has been deeply held and experienced, may release. It is not our choice. The wisdom of the body releases old emotions and feelings as is appropriate. Tension and fear can hold emotions in, so any type of relaxation can sometimes spur their release. These emotional experiences could be rare in a therapeutic setting. I have been fortunate because I have experienced many physical and emotional healings over years. These healing processes have arisen at odd times throughout my life.

One time, I was given a free acupuncture session by a very qualified practitioner. During the session I experienced quite a release of old sadness, tears and emotion from a previous marriage. I cried hard for over 45 minutes. I have always been open to healing experiences, so I welcomed this opportunity to let go of some old baggage. The more old emotions that we can release, the more present and available we will be to each new moment. Old fear and trauma create energetic layers through which we experience life. In this way, we do not always see with fresh eyes or hear with fresh ears. All of our experiences are colored by our past if we hold onto trauma, whether it is a conscious or unconscious holding. I have had many opportunities to work with myself and clients in healing past life pain, unresolved stress, and repressed emotions and trauma. The release of old, stagnant, long held energy and emotions creates a huge and beneficial shift in physical and emotional illness and disease. Release of old traumas should be a welcome opportunity.

There were times in my yoga class when individuals relaxed so deeply that they would start crying as they touched and connected with old traumas in their psyche. They would quietly leave the room to process. Tension from your diaphragm to our throat may signify a need to release grief, while a tense face, neck and shoulders may relate to feelings of fear. Tension in the back could relate to stored anger. If a person is open to release and heal old stressors, it may come more quickly for them than another person who is reluctant to change. Most people have little understanding of how much trauma and unresolved emotions they carry. If a catharsis comes, they may be totally unaware that it is a healing process and not a disease process. Signs of emotional release may range from a single sigh, to tears, shaking, anger, and depression or emotional or verbal release. Don't judge what is happening, just feel it, release it, bless it and let it go. You may wish to write in a journal or create a type of healing ritual around your experiences. Celebrate each step that brings you closer to being your true and Authentic self.

> Truth is stranger than fiction, but this is because fiction
> is obligated to stick to probability. Truth is not.
> ~Mark Twain

My Unusual Healing Process

On Saturday, March 27th 1999, I hiked up (and back country skied back from) the Gulf of Slides on Mt. Washington in New Hampshire. There are no ski lifts here, so I was hiking and carrying my skis. It was a healthy and energizing day. I always enjoy focusing on taking care of myself, so I had taken my vitamins and herbs that morning and had brought more to take with a healthy lunch that I had prepared. I had even put some remedies in my drinking water that I felt would be appropriate and energizing for any kind of physical stress and activity.

It was a beautiful, sunny, crystal clear spring day. I hiked in about 2 ½ miles or more, left my pack and carried my skis and up a steep gulley. I skied a few runs and then relaxed, had lunch, and then skied down. The exercise was nothing out of the ordinary for me. The whole trip only took about 4 hours.

That evening I went to a dance in Portland, Maine with a friend. By the second half of the dance, my left leg was really bothering me and it seemed to get worse as the night proceeded. I had to sit down and keep it elevated on the chair in front of me. When I returned home, there was so much pain that I felt as if I was going to pass out, as I walking up the stairs to go to sleep. The lights felt as if they were dimming. I was experiencing nausea and felt like I might faint. Was I was going into shock because of the severity of the pain?

Sunday morning I found it very difficult to walk, sit down or stand up without experiencing pain. Going up and down stairs involved going one step at a time. Bending down was impossible. I had trouble loading wood into the woodstove. I felt very disabled by the pain that I was experiencing from my left hip to my knee. I took herbs, vitamins, homeopathic remedies and applied topical salves to the affected area. I took remedies that were specific to the symptoms and pain that I was experiencing, including comfrey, in a homeopathic form for the connective tissue and bones.

Monday, my leg felt a great deal better. Walking up and down stairs was much easier, but I still didn't feel like I could run any marathon. It was still very painful to sit or stand.

Tuesday there was improvement, but there was still pain with movement and when lying on my side. I continued with remedies and external applications.

Wednesday I felt well enough to ski all day in a modified way. I still had trouble bending my knee and so I had to keep my leg straighter than normal. (I had to be outside and moving and it was gentle enough for me to do that.)

That night at my monthly "Guided Self-Healing" class in Massachusetts, I shared my story of the past week's experience, because I felt that the pain and discomfort was not the result of injury, but was a healing crisis or healing change. The course instructor asked if I had practiced any the healing work from the course with my pain, and I responded that I hadn't yet. He suggested that maybe I should explore this avenue of healing. I realized that he may have understood something about my experience that I hadn't yet grasped. I decided that I would explore this direction when I returned home. No sooner had I made this decision when visions came to my mind of a male peasant with a wooden leg in a rough woven tan garment.

Since I was in class and wanted to pay attention to the class, I stopped the vision and was sure that I would return to this later *when I returned home. I was pretty uncomfortable at the meeting and kept continually shifting my position.*

On the way home, before I had hardly reached the highway, visions began returning and I realized that I needed to go with it and work with the healing that was occurring.

It progressed easily, since I was used to doing creative visualizations. I had not ever done anything as profound as this before. The vision returned. I could see myself as a male peasant in my 40's in 14ᵗʰ century England. I felt myself experiencing nausea, shock, pain and a recent amputation of my leg. It had been cut off by authorities who did not like me voicing my strong ethical and moral beliefs. I also felt the emotional aftermath of the amputation and feelings of "not wanting to live," depression, being "disabled" and being nursed back to health by a gentle and caring woman. It was a slow healing process and it felt as if I was never wholly alive after that experience. I continued to feel disabled, and carried it forward into other lifetimes.

As I deeply experienced my feeling and previous experience, the pain began diminishing and just about went away. Over the next few days there was a little pain and further change and healing that occurred.

When I returned home that night after class, I felt compelled and guided to look up comfrey (symphtum) in the Materia Medica (Homeopathic). I was curious why it seemed so appropriate for my healing process. I was very shocked and surprised with what I read.... "for deep injuries to the tissues and wounds to the bone as well as <u>amputation</u>! Wow, it seemed that I wasn't losing my mind. I really did experience trauma in my past. I knew that comfrey was great for healing broken tissues and bones, but I didn't know about amputation. It felt as if in reading this, I was affirmed and that my visions and experiences of deep healing over that past week were confirmed by the Universe.

Thursday was a great day. I skied all day without pain or discomfort.

Many changes occurred in my life through this healing process. I realized that I was healing my own emotional feelings of disability and depression. After that experience I can see that I was much more able to speak out for my beliefs, feel my wholeness and direct myself toward creating and fulfilling my dreams. Life felt more dynamic!

One reason I like to share this experience is that I believe that sometimes individuals may go into a healing experience without knowing it. They may interrupt it by taking pharmaceuticals or do something else that would interrupt the energetic healing process. ***Not all symptoms that occur in our life is disease or a negative experience. Sometimes it can be a healing process, especially when it comes "out of the blue" and we have been feeling great.*** It can come as an emotional release of anger, depression, sadness or pain in the body. If it doesn't seem to make sense...it could be a deep healing process. Celebrate these experiences, and go through the process in a healthy way, because there is an opportunity to become free of past blocks and limitation. This is the path to wholeness.

Power vs. Force

Force must always be justified,
whereas power requires no justification.
~David Hawkins MD, ~*Power vs. Force*

In the book "Power vs. Force" by David R. Hawkins, MD., Ph.D., correlations are made between power and force that bring me to revisit thoughts of love and fear again. Power, I believe, is based in presence and unconditional love. The need for force is based specifically in fear and the absence of love.

When we look at what happens when individuals operate out of one or the other and we can look deeper and see the underpinnings and origins of both. Power is noble, meaningful, dignified, uplifts, operates on principle and supports the significance of life itself.

Force operates from a totally different energy. I don't even want to say an opposite place, because it is really the lack of love, consciousness and Being that creates the need for force. When individuals operate from a place of force, they automatically create opposition, reaction, separation and defensiveness. They are pushing "against" something and it has to be constantly fed because of its insatiable appetite. They are creating polarization win/loose scenarios, enemies, conflict and a need for constant defense, proof and support. It is an extremely destructive and self-centered mode of operation that when supposedly satisfied and goals are met, leaves one feeling empty and meaningless.

> Why obtain through force,
> what can easily be created through love?

Power is a calm and still energy that is itself complete and self-evident. It makes no demands and has no needs. It is constructive and supportive, giving energy to life by endlessly motivating it with meaning, value and selflessness. True power comes from our connection to the Divine and Infinite Intelligence. We are patient with life and allow the universe to direct us in our highest ways. Power comes from our being able to wait for outcomes without forcing them.

> True power, then, emanates from consciousness itself;
> what we see is a visible manifestation of the invisible.
> ~David Hawkins MD, ~*Power vs Force*

I had a number of experiences with my sons where I was able to see the impact of power versus force. One time I was with my youngest son and we were walking with friends along a waterfall when I realized that I had to return to work. I told my son that we needed to turn around and return home. He refused and said that he wanted to keep walking. I continued to try to persuade and pursue him, but he was stubborn and would not turn around. I decided not to argue and let him have his way in that moment. I said to him that I would continue in his direction. I think he took 4—5 steps and said "OK, let's go back now." He was totally happy after he had some say in the process. I was happy too and surprised. There was no use of force or need for argument and we both won!

If you want peace,
you must give up the idea of conflict
entirely and for all time.
~The Course of Miracles

I never punished my boys, but would ask them "Why did you do what you did?" This would give them the opportunity to explore for themselves what they were doing without it getting muddled with "you are bad and wrong." My middle son certainly tested me to the limits many times. But it was all worth it and I just loved him no matter what he did. He shared with me in his college years, "Mom, if you hadn't been there for me, just loving me, I wouldn't have made it." Unconditional love and acceptance is the key to raising healthy children and experiencing healthy relationships with others as well as ourselves.

Intuition

The Intuitive Mind is a Sacred Gift
and the rational mind is a faithful servant
and has forgotten the Sacred Gift.
~Albert Einstein

Intuition is one of the more valuable qualities that we can honor. Not only will it guide us in directions of our highest good and Divine harmony, it can answer questions that elude us. Only by being in a space of peace, serenity and acceptance can we listen to this inner voice that sometimes whispers or speaks very softly. To listen we have to eliminate the constant chatter and mental thinking that pervades and directs most minds.

One of life's most precious gifts to us is our own sense of inner knowing and wisdom. This gift cannot be replaced with values, judgments or opinions that we have gathered second hand.

When I graduated from Naturopathic school I felt that I had knowledge about many therapies for a wide variety of diseases and health issues, but I also realized that there was still so much that I just didn't know. I was overwhelmed. I soon realized that my best possible answers to the many possibilities available for each individual client, was in working with my intuition. My intuition has always been very astute and had always served me well. I spent much time acknowledging, developing and experimenting with it too. I realized that when working with clients I had answers that my intellectual mind would not provide....something as simple as: *it would be better for someone to do _less_ rather than for me to give them more to do*, or *it would be better for them to do x, y and z, but not more vitamins or herbs.*

The only real valuable thing is intuition.
~Albert Einstein

One of my favorite books that I have read is *Blink—The Power of Thinking without Thinking* by Malcolm Gladwell. He speaks of how the intuitive mind is actually smarter than the intellectual mind and gives examples in relation to the arts, medicine, science, the military and in general life. He redefines how we look at how we think without thinking, and talks about the choices that are made in the blink of an eye when people follow their instincts. In following their intuition, individuals usually come up with better results than those who think things through logically and come up with errors and/or poor results. His book will change the way you make your decisions. It is very supportive to those who have always been intuitive thinkers.

> We believe that we are always better off gathering as much information as possible and spending as much time as possible in deliberation. We really only trust

conscious decision making. But there are moments,
particularly in times of stress, when haste does not make
waste, when our snap judgments and first impressions
can offer a much better means of making sense of the
world. The first task of *Blink* is to convince you of a
simple fact: decisions made very quickly can be every bit
as good as decisions made cautiously and deliberately.
~Malcolm Gladwell, ~*Blink*

Certainly meditation is beneficial for connecting with our intuition. Being in nature also brings us back to presence, truth and our spiritual connection to life. These two practices are truly important on a daily basis. Once we attain regularity in these, we may more easily acknowledge the intuition when it does arrive. Often, there are many missed opportunities. We can ignore messages, because not only does the intuition speak softly, we may also doubt its accuracy and truth. We can rationalize the importance of other avenues of operation. But later, we may say… "I should have listened."

Assumptions (belief systems) shared by many individuals Please release:

1) The mind and body are separate and disconnected from one another.
2) A materialistic scientific way of looking at ourselves is of primary importance. Consciousness is not very important. It is scientifically proven. We are primarily physical machines that have learned to think.
3) Human awareness experiences (near-death, auras, etc.) can be explained through science.
4) Our present scientific way of seeing the world is true and accurate. We see and experience life as it really is.

5) We are nothing more than a body and a personality with thoughts and memories.
6) Time is real, we cannot escape the effects of time.
7) Struggle and being a victim is a real part of being a human. We are victims of life, death, aging and disease.
8) Technology will save the world. I don't have to do anything.
9) Aging is normal- it affects everyone in the same way.
10) Aging causes suffering, both physically and emotionally.

Can you think of more assumptions that people believe? Many are based in cultural, scientific, societal and religious beliefs. Some of these assumptions come from "Ageless Body Timeless Mind" by Deepak Chopra.

From the Course in Miracles

~On Anger:
   ~ Anger cannot occur unless you believe that you have been attacked, that your attack is justified in return and that you are in no way responsible for it.
   ~ All anger is nothing more than an attempt to make someone feel guilty.

~On Growth:
   ~ Teach no one that he/she is what you would not want to be. Your brother is the mirror in which you see the image of yourself.
   ~ Only you can deprive yourself from anything.....this realization…. is truly the beginning of the dawn of light.
   ~ I am alone in nothing. Everything I think or say or do teaches all the universe.
   ~ *Miracles are natural. When they do not occur, something has gone wrong.*
   ~ When a mind has only light it knows only light, its own radiance shines all around it and extends out into

the darkness of other minds, transforming them into majesty.

~On Time:
  ~ The only aspect of time that is eternal is now.
  ~ The one wholly true thought one can hold about the past is that it is not there.

~On Love:
  ~ Love waits on welcome, not on time.
  ~ ***What is not love is always fear, and nothing else.***
  ~ Exempt no one from your love or you will be hiding a dark place in your mind where the Holy Spirit is not welcome. And thus you will exempt yourself from His healing power, for by not offering total Love, you will not be healed completely.

~On Peace:
  ~ Illness is some form of inner searching. Health is inner peace.
  ~ No one who truly seeks the peace of God can fail to find it.
  ~ Peace of mind is clearly an internal matter. It must begin with your thoughts and then extend outward. It is from your peace of mind that a peaceful perception of the world arises.

~On Acceptance:
  ~ God's will for you is complete peace and joy; unless you experience only this you must be refusing to acknowledge His Will.
  ~ Heaven is here. There is nowhere else. Heaven is now. There is no other time.

Here is a great exercise to change the negative spiral in a relationship to an upward spiral and joyful connection. The essence of the exercise is the following:

Sit down with a person with whom you need to connect. Allow them to begin speaking first.

1) Truly listen to the other person without interruption until they have finished saying their concerns. It is important to connect on a heart level with the other person to truly understand what they really want to share.

2) You may wish to begin and end your dialogue by inwardly feeling, "I'd rather be joyful than right."
   Let go of any need to be righteous, confronting, defensive, fearful, resistant or arrogant. You may wish to say <u>what you stand for</u> (not what you stand against), please stand for peace and love too.

3) If at all possible state each feeling as arising from a fear. Let this person know what you are afraid of. Fears are sometimes easier to state and let go of than feelings. You may be surprised at what you both are truly afraid of.

4) Close your eyes sit quietly and connect with your heart and theirs and remembering your debt of gratitude to one another. Hold a space of love. Acknowledge memories of several compassionate or thoughtful things that this person did.

5) Think on what you would like to contribute to your relationship. Open your eyes and share your offerings. Focus on being present, connected and speaking from your heart. Focus on ways of creating the best relationship... possibly as a more heart-felt friendship, more truthful, intimate or whatever value you choose.

6) Accept this moment and your contribution to this process. Choose to have peace and trust with this process. "Be at peace with this child of God".....remember to *choose to be joyful rather than right.*

Consider the following~

~Many things that we have worried about have never happened.

~We alone create our thoughts, attitudes, feelings and experiences.

~We can decide to live with faith and trust in the process of life. We can trust that the Universe has a plan for each of us. (We don't have to play God.) We can allow life to happen. We can joyfully be with others accepting them and allowing them the freedom to be who they choose to be.

~If I want to make a difference, I can make it here in this very moment. I can unconditionally accept myself and others just as we are.

~We can be joyful with ourselves as we are in this moment.

~Peace of mind and serenity is reflected from the deepest parts of our being. It is a reflection of our deep connection to ourselves and our spiritual life.

~If we love and accept ourselves and others unconditionally, we celebrate our very existence. From this joyful place of being, we experience celebration, energy and vast resources to be whatever we choose. Our creative opportunities are limitless.

Consider releasing~

~Others know what is best for me.

~Blame, helplessness, guilt, powerlessness...

~Frustration, anger, resentment..... because you are choosing to be a victim....

Are you your own best expert?

~Are you free of negativity and fear?

~Are you beginning to celebrate all the change that is possible for you?

~Do you believe that life would be dull and boring if you weren't fearful?

~Who is in charge of your life?

Going Deeper:

~Questioning my belief systems helps me to release negative spirals and let go of beliefs that aren't beneficial. I may find some beliefs that are healthy for me. In this process I can begin to manifest what I really want.

~I can live free from "good" or "bad" and "right" or "wrong" beliefs.

~As challenging experiences arise, I practice unconditional acceptance as a first step and place to be. Then I create from my heart, my intentions, feelings, responses and solutions.

~I am aware when I am choosing guilt that I can let it go, love myself and understand that I am now and always doing my best.

~I am aware of any anger or reactions to others. I can decide consciously whether or not I want to continue to choose these ways of being. There may be some times when anger is appropriate. I can release it when I am ready.

~I continue to let go of past beliefs, reactions and ways of being. I consciously choose new ways of affirming and supporting myself, my health and my life. I continue to be present and just Be. ~I enjoy just Being.

I quiet the judging and fearful mind.
I quiet the stuffing … the numbing.
I quiet the endless, mindless chatter.
…. I let them all go, I breathe and become free.
I let them all go and become me.

I accept and feel my rage.
I accept and feel my grief.
I accept and feel my pain.
I accept and feel my fear.
…… Then I let them be transformed into love
…….and I just am…

I know what I feel.
I know what I want.
I know want I need.
I know who I am.
I recognize myself, my knowing and my Authenticity.
I recognize that I am an extraordinary "Child of the Universe."

I let love heal me.
I let love teach me.
I let love awaken me.
I let love fill my heart.
I let love empower and surround me.
….. I act with love, radiate love, I am love….
I love myself, honor myself and all life everywhere.
By Becky Mulkern ND

11

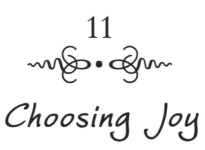

Choosing Joy

Joy is a net of love by which you catch souls.
~Mother Teresa

I originally named this chapter "Happiness is a Choice," but I no longer feel that it is an appropriate name. I have come to realize that happiness is part of the old continuum of operating from the mind. We are now moving beyond happiness into the evolutionary spirit of "joy." Happiness can be contrived just as being in a positive mood can be something that you are trying to do and the mind thinks you should be. Happiness feels superficial and more of a momentary pleasure. Usually people are happy because of something in their life. Joy is an expansive, passionate and an energetic way of being. *Joyful is what we are and what we hold in our heart.* When we enjoy, we are filled with joy.

Stop and think about it for a minute. Close your eyes and feel what happiness feels like….then let go of that and feel the essence of joy, feel how it live in your heart. Do you notice the difference? I notice a very big difference. Certainly most of us may not have contemplated this, but the difference is really "huge." Which state of mind would you prefer to live with, happiness or joy?

Think about embracing joy this coming week! Think about it often.

I began to question, "What is the opposite of joy?" Most people would say sadness or sorrow. I don't think that is necessarily true. Many possibilities come to mind from depression and despair to apathy, emptiness, complacency and loneliness. Others might say disbelief, guilt or even fear. Joy is a very spiritual word. Think of the word "rejoice." When I asked one friend she said, "joy comes from spirit and is deeper."

What percentage of the time do you choose to be serene and joyful? ...apathetic or depressed? In which states do you hold and feel more love? Are you aware of feelings of discomfort when you are not joyful? What prevents you from always choosing to be joyful? How loving do you feel toward yourself when you are joyfilled?

> We could never learn to be brave or patient
> if there were only joy in the world.
> ~Helen Keller

Based on what we believe, we consciously and unconsciously choose both joy and fear. When we choose fear, unhappiness and depression, we live without reverence for ourselves and we move away from what we want in a constrictive and fearful, "don't become too involved in life" way. When we choose joy, we are living in a place of love and wholeness. We move toward everything that we want in a creative, radiant and passionate way.

Let me offer a question: "Does our fear, apathy or despair about life really help to change them? It is very important to understand that choosing unhappiness is not bad or wrong, but is just a choice... whether conscious or unconscious it is a choice we make. We have many possible choices. We can spend more time being joyful and creative if we decide to stop living without joy. We can prioritize joy in our life. We actually don't have to have anything to be joyful about. We can just choose joy!

> Let your heart sing with Joy.
> ~Becky Mulkern ND

When I speak about being joyful...I consider it a state of love, unconditional acceptance and peace of mind. It is a state of being and an inner experience....some may say a connection to the spiritual or Divine. Bliss is an aspect of joy. When we totally allow a state of infinite joy that is when we reach a state of bliss. Bliss could be described as a state of being wholly present in supreme joy, peace and serenity, play and total momentary pleasure. There is an effortless, expansive and light-hearted place that lives within us that holds our infinite potential....a place of abundant life, health and connection. Feel the expansive quality when you speak of these feelings.

Just as optimal health is a far different state (joy, energy, vibrancy, healthy immune system, freedom from colds & flus, daily exercise, healthy posture, loving, compassionate, etc.) than disease and not merely the absence of disease. ***Real joy is far more than the absence of unhappiness or depression!*** It feels so much more energetic than happiness does. It feels more "rock solid' to me. What do you think?

Our joy comes from who we are. The more we judge ourselves the more dissatisfied and unhappy we may become. We may want others to change in order for us to choose joy. But though we are guaranteed that things will change (change is the only thing that we are truly guaranteed), they may not always move in the direction that we wish, so placing our joy on hold and waiting for someone else to change does not make any sense at all. No sense at all.

Most individuals become happy when they are getting something that they want or have reached a specific goal (conditional). They place their happiness as dependent on reaching certain goals. It is a conditional state of being. But in actuality, they are never happy because they always set more goals that would determine their happiness. Happiness is usually a state of mind that individuals create, which is determined by their reaching continuous goals.... one after the other.

> Things won are done, joy's soul lies in doing.
> ~William Shakespeare

Can you be enjoying your life without always having goals or reaching them? Can you just be joyful? *Joy is a state of being that is free from a focus on achieving.* Can you just enjoy the process? Would that be amazing, or would that be your normal state of being for you?

For many, unhappiness, depression, negativity and discomfort allow people some kind of reward, or attention, relief, etc. When we are anxious, in pain, distressed, or sad, often people help us, support us or give us attention. This may become a form of manipulation for some individuals.

As long as we place the key to our lives and emotional health in others hands or with other circumstances, then we are allowing ourselves to be affected or controlled by something outside ourselves. We are then a victim to external situations. Some individuals may even try to control others in order to create their own happiness. *But no one can make us joyful or non-joyful.* We alone hold the power to create what we want and how we feel.

> When one door of happiness closes, another opens,
> but often we look so long at the closed door
> that we do not see the one
> which has been opened for us.
> ~Helen Keller

Expectations are a major contributor to unhappiness, stress, and dis-ease. Expectations are based in fear. They can be unreasonable and based in low self-esteem, misperceptions and poor understanding. We can expect or want certain things from others to insure our happiness, but can we just accept others as they are and let go of all judgments, expectations and conditions in our relationships? If we didn't ever judge others, ourselves, and situations and wish that our life was different, would we ever be unhappy? Can we just totally love and unconditionally accept our life in the moment? Our joy, creativity and love comes from our feelings about who we are, our connection to others and all life. Truly loving ourselves is very necessary for a healthy and joyful life. This is not being self-centered, but being reverent and deeply thankful for all we truly have.

> There are those who give joy, and that joy is their reward.
> ~Khalil Gibran

Many individuals believe that if we lived with love and acceptance, we would become a passive individual. To the contrary, these states of being, lead us to more passionate, effective, energized, creative, clear, powerful, focused and conscious living. When we are at peace and living in the present moment, we are far more grounded, centered and able to effect change for ourselves more easily. We can clearly see what our present moment holds. When we are joyful as opposed to non-joyful, we are far more able to create what we want. We lose the "anesthetic of familiarity" and gain the "magic of reality" as Richard Dawkins, the famous evolutionary biologist might say.

We don't have to be angry and unhappy to be motivated to create change in the world. We don't have to be unhappy just because others are or to prove that we care about others. When we feel unhappy and depressed, we inadvertently share that energy with others and we promote more of the same. Our love, happiness and unconditional acceptance create far more lasting change than our unhappiness ever could.

> We are shaped by our thoughts;
> we become what we think.
> When the mind is pure, joy follows
> like a shadow that never leaves.
> ~Buddha

When we experience joy, we are living from our heart and choosing love and inner peace. Through our awareness we can feel joy more of the time. We can consume ourselves with living and choosing to see each moment of life as miraculous.

When I asked participants in my classes, "How can you bring yourself into a space of joy and peace?" They responded with these short answers: Breathe, walking, posture, prioritize more, change the environment, attitude, affirm, think positive, be alive and nature.

When we judge things as "bad or wrong" for us, we may actually choose to make ourselves non-joyful. Unhappiness is not in this moment if we can just stay in this moment. *Unhappiness itself is not bad or wrong, it is just a choice. What we may judge as bad or unfortunate is just an experience. This experience doesn't create our joy or unhappiness. An experience just "is"...how we judge it, feel it and live it determines what comes next...how we act.*

Within each moment in the fabric of life there is meaning and opportunity. We can choose to allow ourselves to feel joy or peace and to unlock the opportunities in the web of life that are there for us each and every moment of every day.

Love to faults is always blind, always is to joy inclined.
Lawless, winged and unconfined, and
breaks all chains from every mind.
~William Shakespeare

Take time to~

1) Think of times you chose to be negative, lonely and fearful. Why and how did this occur?
2) Think of times that you chose to be joyful, passionate and living in the moment. Why did this happen?

If you could go back in time now, would you change any of those experiences when you chose to be unhappy or fearful and instead choose to be in the moment and be joyful? Think of at least one experience that you could change your experience. See yourself doing it.

What choices supported fear or despair?......judgments, expectations, needing to be right. See yourself at times when you are fearful and negative deciding instead to choose to be filled with joy or peace instead. Would that be easy?

When are joyful, our open heart touches our true nature. Then we feel the miracle in the moment.

Joy comes from our feelings about who we are. It is present when we love ourselves and all life. If we didn't judge ourselves and our experiences, would we ever be without joy? Would we ever be without joy if we stopped judging that things should be different?

Our decision to be joyful is connected to our decision to release, let go of and transform what is not joy. Based on what we believe and the beliefs that we live by we are continually choosing our states of mind. *We can focus on heart-felt love and joy and what we want to create in our life.* We can release our choice of unhappiness, non-joyful states of being, and moving away from life and all that we really want. We can choose joy.

If negative states of mind are present, it is OK just feel them, experience them, be with them as long as you need to and then let them go and choose what you really want. *Feeling it is healing it.*

To get up each morning with resolve to be Happy
is to set our own conditions to the events of each day.
To do this is to condition circumstances
instead of being conditioned by them.
~Ralph Waldo Emerson
(Please change the word Happy to Joyful)

Creating Joy

1) Center your attention and intention in your heart and say to yourself: "I <u>am</u> joyful." (Release pursuing things and happiness. ...... "I will be happy when...." "That made me unhappy." "The new ....will make me happy.")

For some people happiness is a state of mind, that we offer ourselves when we have what we want. We could instead be joyful and peaceful <u>now</u> and indefinitely. We can choose to:

1) We can choose joy, value it and hold it now. We can choose….. JOY.
2) Feel your heart and the essence of JOY now… You are worth it. Connect with the Self that wants joy … feel it and live it.

Many individuals don't believe that they can be joyful on a sustained basis. What do you think?

A negative state of mind can truly come from our feelings about ourselves. If we didn't continually judge ourselves and our experiences or feel that our life was in some way lacking, would we ever be anything but joyful? If we stop wishing and thinking that our life should be different, and we are at peace with where our life is this moment, could we then be filled with joy? ….could we then move on to all of our true potential?

Beliefs that block Joy

~Something is wrong with me.
~I cause others to be………….
~I am not lovable.
~My sadness and anger means I care.
~I am a failure.
~Life is good and bad.
~I don't have enough……..
~I can't be happy.

Going Deeper~

~Have you become more aware of your fearful thinking? (Anything that is not love, joy and unconditional acceptance is based in fear.) Can you release and transform your fear?

~Are you taking time daily to be quiet and still and just to be?

~Can you just be joyful? Decide to be joyful for 1 week. Make it a priority. See what you find.

~Choose to be peaceful and joyful at times when you might not normally choose to. Choose to be accepting and peaceful rather than right.

~You become what you think about all day long. What do you spend your time thinking about?

~We always do our best in every circumstance according to the experience and wisdom that we have at that time.

~Everything that we learn and experience in life helps to enrich our lives and create our future.

~What grade are you in, in the school of life?

~Repeat often…."I am truly my own best expert. Only I know what is best for me".

~We often have many of the best answers to all our questions.

~When I choose to be conscious, accepting and peaceful, I am choosing to move toward everything that I want to create in my life.

~Living without joy is just a choice, it is OK. Negatively judging my feelings continues them. In moving toward negativity, despair etc., I then move away from what I truly want.

~If others criticize me, that is their choice. It has nothing to do with me unless I choose to let it be so.

~Can I just be true to myself?

~Are my needs met when I am not joyful?

~Who is responsible for my joy?

~If I live in my heart instead of my mind, I can enjoy joy.

~I am free to make choices that I are out of the box and out of the "norm."

~Joy is our destiny~

I can choose my beliefs~

~We are born with joy.

~I can encourage children to make their own best choices. This supports them to: learn autonomy, gain wisdom, be self-accepting and love themselves.

~In loving, I unconditionally accept others as they are. I easily respect others right to make their own choices.

~I love being unconditionally accepting. I am present with what is going on in my life so that I can choose what is next for me. Being present brings me peace of mind.

~I create my own joy or non-joy.

~Others' choices are a statement about them not me.

~Each moment presents opportunities to create life anew. In choosing to release fear, negativity and apathy, I open to my truly joyful and loving nature and creating everything that I can imagine.

~Beliefs create self-fulfilling prophecies. I wisely create my beliefs.

~I always do my best, according to what I have learned and experienced up until this time. This is true for others as well.

~Everything that I do contributes to my joy. Joy nourishes my heart and soul.

~I can choose to dance through life!

I believe in the sun—
Even when it does not shine;
I believe in Love—
Even when it is not shown;
I believe in God—
Even when he does not speak.
(written on a wall in a concentration camp)

12

Unconditional Love and its Miraculous Healing Power

One of the most loving individuals I ever met, was the minister in my church when I was growing up. His name was Reverend Muster. Unconditional love was written all over his face. He radiated love. It oozed out of every pore in his skin. You could behold it in his face and his eyes. He was the spiritual personification of love. I was blessed to have his example of love in my childhood, though that realization of that gift came in later years.

> Perhaps you think that different kinds of love are possible.
> Perhaps you think there is a kind of love for
> this, a kind of love for that; a way of loving
> one, another way of loving still another.
> Love is one.
> It has no separate parts and no degrees; no kinds
> nor levels, no divergencies and no distinctions.
> It is like itself, unchanged throughout.
> It never alters with a person or a circumstance.
> It is the Heart of God.
> ~*Course in Miracles*

What if you were awakened and empowered by the heart-centered truth of your real potential. Would you find that you could create and manifest everything that you desired? It is time to find out. By living from your heart and staying focused in love you will see that you are capable of all manner of abundance in your life. Indigenous cultures knew this was true.

Love is the capacity of the heart, the divine spark that animates each and every human soul. This spark is talked of by some cultures as the intelligence of the being and an access point to the spirit. We cannot think to glorify others and at the same time treat ourselves unjustly. We can't respect others and not ourselves. We have to truly love ourselves before we can be anything to anyone. How often do you think or say..."I love myself... I love me!" If we give ourselves love, then we will refrain from looking outside of ourselves for love. We refrain from ever looking again. If we are love, we live with love and we feel full of love. Without self-love and compassion, we have less love to give others. It is said that our heart is the "temple of God," so if that is true, think how differently we would all feel if we honored that every day. How different the world would be if everyone deeply loved themselves. Just imagine.... Even Darwin stated that sympathy was the "strongest instinct in human nature." Certainly sympathy is a great place to begin, if we are sharing empathy, joy, feelings and compassion.

> No one is born hating another person because of the
> color of his skin, or his background, or his religion.
> People must learn to hate, and if they can learn to
> hate, they can be taught to love, for love comes more
> naturally to the human heart than its opposite.
> ~Nelson Mandela, ~*Long Walk to Freedom*

Some generations have believed that self-love is selfish, vane, wasteful and narcissistic. Caring for oneself has previously been seen as negative and egotistical. Individuals who believe this may be left feeling powerless, empty, and lacking integrity. If we don't lovingly care for ourselves then who would do it? No one knows better than we what we need to be healthy and feel blessed.

We are living at a time when we are moving beyond the old paradigm of love. Maybe at times in the past, we carried love and felt love. Now there is an impulse toward each of us originating, being, and sharing unconditional heart based love. Unconditional love can heal our past and bring us all to a future filled with peace, respect, equality and joy.

An unreserved, positive self-adoration remains the essence
of health, the most important asset a patient must gain
to become exceptional. Self-esteem and self-love are
not sinful. They make living a joy instead of a chore.
~Bernie Siegel M.D.

As you think about your life in this moment, how does it feel? Are
you aware of any needs at this point, any feelings of incompleteness,
loneliness or emptiness? Do you look to others to provide for you,
what you cannot provide for yourself or to complete your "perfect
picture?" Do you look for things to complete your picture as well?
Is there a part of you that needs others approval for what you do
and who you are?

As we grow, evolve and become more loving beings, there
will be a natural love and support for ourselves that will exist at
all times. It will even be reflected in others connections to us. In
loving ourselves we will value who we are and not what we do.
We shall love ourselves unconditionally at all times, no matter
what. As we believe in ourselves and love ourselves, we shall have
an abundance of love to give and share with others. *We cannot
have healthy relationships with others until we have a healthy
relationship with ourselves.* Our loving presence will beneficially
affect those surrounding us. As we open to receiving love from
ourselves and the Universe, our Authentic Self is aroused and steps
forward into the light. We will feel the love through our whole
being.

If you want to love, take time to listen to your heart.
In most ancient and wise cultures, it is a regular practice
for people to talk to their heart..... rituals, stories and
meditative skills in every spiritual tradition..... awaken the
voice of the heart. To live wisely this practice is essential,
because our heart is our source of connection to
and intimacy with all life.
~Jack Kornfield, ~*The Wellspring of the Heart,
Body, Mind & Spirit Magazine*

Many individuals grow up believing the story that others are a necessary part of their feeling whole and complete. We certainly have learned to rely on the false notion that everyone has to find another person to complete them. For many, their sense of self has more to do with what they do and not who they are. We have learned to judge and measure ourselves in relationship to what we achieve and not according to what makes us ...us!

But our true sense of Self, has to do with our loving connection to our Infinite Self, "Oneness" and our connection to all that is.

> Oneness is the energy of LOVE that lies
> within and connects all of life, enabling us
> to recognize ourselves in everything.
> ~*Humanity's Team.org*

Our life does not gain meaning by what we do, but by what fills our heart and soul. The more we stay busy, the less connected we will be with ourselves, our feelings, our passion and our evolution. As we begin to suspend busyness and doing, and begin to connect with our Being and just "being," the more our evolutionary conscious will carry us forward. As we feel what is within us, and listen to what arises in our hearts, we grow in our awareness by deeply feeling (without judgment) what we feel and allowing healing in the present moment. ***By feeling it, we are healing it, not just the present moment but the past as well.***

As we stop believing our mind and our unhealthy ego when it tells us that we will be complete when, "we have the perfect job, relationship, etc." and we look to ourselves, God, and the universe for our emotional support, we begin to see that we have the opportunity to enter each experience with "worthiness for love" and support for ourselves. We can leave behind fear, pain, and feelings of inadequacy. Our choices and passion can shape our present moment and our tomorrows.

Fear can whisper in our ear continuously, that it wants to make us safe, but with love, we realize that we are already safe. Fear wants us to rely on "things" to feel good about ourselves, but the truth of love is that we need only to be here in this moment. Fear may cause us to conform, limit or compromise who we are, but when we settle into love, we are at home. With fear, we need guarantees and need to know what might happen, but no guarantees are ever good enough. If we live unconditionally with love in our heart and soul, guarantees are unnecessary.

Every moment of your life
you are offered the opportunity
to choose—Love or fear,
to tread the earth or to soar the heavens.
~*Emmanuel's Book 2*

I want to soar the heavens! Come and join me. Let us all fly!

Our relationship with others is like our relationship with ourselves. What we see in others, we may see in ourselves, whether we choose to or not. As we learn to look at ourselves with unconditional love and acceptance, without numbing or masking what is there, we begin to release the "old stuff" that we have accumulated. Healing begins as we evolve and base our relationships on unconditional acceptance, integrity and love. As feelings arise that are uncomfortable, we can be present, reprogram our vision and open our heart to true healing. In truly supporting and loving ourselves in healing, we may feel vulnerable before others, but no longer naked, fearful, guilty or embarrassed. Our total love, support and intimate connection with ourselves, creates an environment where there is only ease, safety and peace of mind. It is a place where we feel that what is happening is OK and perfect for our growth. We can enjoy celebrating ourselves as we move through these challenges. We are pretty amazing!

Our Evolution from our Mind to our Heart

All you need is love
All you need is love
All you need is love, love
love is all you need.
~Beatles

How wonderful that we are evolving back into a heart centered era. Long ago, many indigenous peoples lived exclusively with heart centered orientation and focus on "being" and knowing. As evolution shifted to mind orientation and focus on logic, science and "thinking," we lost touch with our hearts. This present evolutionary shift, from the mind to the heart, thankfully leaves behind seriousness, logic, polarity, fear, the "I," and ego centric living. We are being transformed as we shift away from the brain and the "I" that operates out of separation, as the most important aspect of life. While the mind speaks in words, the heart is present in living, feeling, and being. The heart is a sacred wellspring within our soul, a place of creation and connection with all life. It connects us to Oneness, the Universal life, and understands that equality in life means that all life is equally important. The heart energy connects us to our potential to create and have passion in our purpose. We feel the child-like awe in each moment as we see, live and experience life from our heart center.

And life is love. This mysterious quality of love
is all around us, as real as gravity.
~Jack Kornfield, ~*The Wellspring of the Heart,*
Body, Mind & Spirit Magazine

Just as we found a difference between the feelings of happiness and joy, let's see what difference you feel between orientation to the mind or to the heart.

Sit quietly for a moment and breathe deeply and relax. Slow the breathing down…long, slow and deep breaths. When you are ready, feel the quality and essence of your mind. What do you feel? How big does it feel and how far does its energy reach from your body? Is there a quality to it? What do you notice?

Then end this connection, breathe and be still. When you are ready feel the essence of your heart. What do you feel? How big does it feel and how far does this energy reach? Is there a quality to it? If you feel the energy is there any movement to it? What are the differences that you feel between the mind and the heart? Just be still with your heart for a while.

> Faith is an oasis in the heart
> which will never be reached
> by a caravan of thinking.
> ~Kahlil Gibran

When I was in Naturopathic School, we did a really interesting exercise (I hope you will think about doing this for yourself). We had to think about and present to the class how we wanted to be remembered after we died. I knew that I wanted to be remembered as a "loving" being. That was most important to me. I was very grateful that I grew up with an unconditionally loving Mother. Although she didn't often express love to me in words, I knew deeply in my heart that she was nonjudgmental and that she unconditionally loved and accepted me as I was. I was very fortunate. Because her love was not verbally expressed, I had to learn to do that on my own.

I can remember when my first born son was an infant I began telling my mother that I loved her. I would look in her eyes and say, "I love you." At first it felt really uncomfortable and a little strange, but through practice I became more comfortable with it and ultimately enjoyed expressing my love to her. At the same time, my mother became more comfortable with sharing her love too. It was amazing to have that opportunity to share our love with each other before she died five years later. I was very grateful.

My mother went through many challenges the last 10 years of her life. Over a period of time, she was in and out of the hospital. When I visited her there, I remember just being with her and experiencing total peace in my being. It didn't make a difference what she was doing. I was totally comfortable being there, whether she was asleep, we were talking or she was using the portable potty. I was never wishing that our lives were different. I was present with her and the circumstances. This was her challenge and I was comfortable with all of it. I was loved her and accepted her in each moment. That was quite a gift.

During the 5 years before my mother died, she was hardly ever without pain. She experienced a car accident as well as cancer, and previous to these she had a blot clot on her brain and nearly died. She was saved from dying from the blood clot when my family paid to move her by ambulance to another hospital. When I next saw her in ICU, I was nauseous and thought I was going to throw up. She looked 'one step removed' from death because she had nearly died. She was possibly only hours away from it, if she hadn't been moved. When the anesthesiologist saw her the following day, he thought that he was seeing a ghost. He thought that she had died.

During those years I cried often, because her health never seemed to improve and death seemed closer all the time. I had cried so much that when she died I never cried. I had already grieved her death for years. I think her death was a relief for both of us. I even knew the moment when she died. If I was in her presence, I was going to sing a classic spiritual song. A night after I had been with her, I was standing at my kitchen sink, and I began to sing the song. Within minutes, I received a call that she had just died. The strangest thing happened though after she died. I felt extraordinary joy, peace and bliss. My mother had just died...how could I? I talked to a close friend who was a psychic and she said that my mother was channeling her heavenly energy to me. Wow... it was truly amazing.... I felt so joyful!

> When man truly and purely loves,
> he automatically and willingly follows
> the invisible tugging strings of Divine love
> toward God.
> ~Paramahansa Yogananda

In Stephen Levine's book *A Gradual Awakening*, Levine relates how dying people feel the discomfort of people, who are uncomfortable with death and dying. The infirm would be just as happy to have these fearful individuals not visit or be around them. Many of the visitors' emotional discomfort, around death and dying, was disturbing to them, even when nothing was said. The dying preferred the unconditionally accepting to be present with their love, faith and unconditional respect for the process of life.

When I was growing up, I used to visit my Aunt Marjorie and Aunt Helen in the countryside of Massachusetts. My mother would leave me there for the weekend when I was fairly young. This was one of my favorite experiences of my childhood. They would take me off into the woods and show me the flora and fauna and talk about fairies and elves. We would see pheasants and foxes, many wild birds and explore the woodlands. I developed a love for the forests and nature through these experiences.

Around 40 years ago, I visited my Great Aunt Marjorie who was in the last days of her life. She was very lucid and said to me, "Do you know what life is all about, Becky…. love that is what it is all about." What she said has always been with me. I have always known in my heart that it was true. I believe that our time on this amazingly beautiful planet is all about learning to love and be loved in return.

We are now evolving toward an unconditionally loving and accepting world. I believe that we are closer every day. Sometimes it takes it takes challenges, struggle and loss before we realize what is really most meaningful.

What was very interesting in relationship to my Aunt Marjorie is that her spirit continues to be with me. When my second son was born, during the first 2 years of his life, I would look at him and see my Aunt Marjorie's face. There she was her face on his body…. I never expected to see her and wasn't looking for her, but there she was again and again. (This is my loving son who would always be happy to share or give away his last piece of cake….) He has always been very demonstrative of his love to me.

This was one of the many experiences that I have enjoyed that led me to believe in reincarnation and the multiple lives. I believe that we live many lives in order to learn our lessons and evolve into more loving, peaceful, and compassionate beings.

Relationships

And now abide faith, hope, love,
these three;
but the greatest of these is love.
~1 Corinthians 13

Expectations in relationships are often unrealized and unreasonable. They are often based in fear, lack of understanding, insecurities and misperceptions. The thought is: "If you loved me you would...." (This particular belief is very common.) Please understand though if people don't do what you want, it doesn't mean that they don't love you...it just means they are doing what they are choosing to do. What they are choosing to do may be an unconscious or conscious choice...but it is still their choice. They probably aren't even thinking about you when they do what they do. Many times in relationships, individuals are oblivious to their effect on those around them. If you want a truly loving relationship it is important to respect, allow and nurture others freedom to be, by accepting and supporting them so that they will do that for you as well. Healthy unconditional communication is certainly important too.

In an unhealthy relationship, the emotional connection is out of balance. Women who are afraid of their power and losing the relationship, sacrifice their autonomy for the partnership. Women may become self-sacrificing, vulnerable, service oriented, and selfless to an unhealthy degree. They sacrifice the "I for we." Men, on the other hand, may be threatened by intimacy and may focus on the "I at the expense of the we." This may leave men using their power in unhealthy ways. They may become tough, indifferent, dominant, unemotional, manipulative, and they may show emotions without vulnerability.

I once had an experience with a boyfriend that left me feeling sad, frustrated, rejected and unloved. I had given so much loving energy to the relationship and then I wanted to run away from it. I couldn't stop thinking about it. I was quite challenged because he wasn't communicating with me. I just needed some kind of resolution or to make a decision of where to go next. The solution just wouldn't come to me. I couldn't move on, let it go or know what to do next. I sat on the hill in the backyard late one afternoon and prayed and meditated about it. What came left me very peaceful and feeling that I had an avenue to proceed forward. The answer was just to love him ...pretty simple, pretty easy too. No expectations, no conditions just be loving. It felt so soothing and was certainly the best possible answer. I was very thankful. Answers have often come to me when I slow down, quiet my mind, pray, ask and listen. It is wonderful when we can get out of our own way.... We may both have been healed in that moment.

> Every loving thought is true. Everything else is an appeal
> for healing and help, regardless of the form that it takes.
> ~*The Course in Miracles*

When uncomfortable and negative experiences happen in relationships, we must remember not to take them personally. We can easily misinterpret and waste energy thinking others are "doing something to us." When we believe this is true we are choosing to be a victim. If we feel powerless, we are choosing to be a victim as well. Sometimes what is going on with others is about them and not about us. If we are feeling some kind of discomfort then it is about our own issues, not theirs. The easiest response is always love..... unconditional love. When we love, we are not saying that someone is "right" and someone is "wrong." When we are in the blame space we may become a victim. When we love unconditionally, we are just in a space of being at peace in our heart.

Many times in my life, I have placed myself second to others and have held back my true nature and feelings. Through unconscious conditioning and beliefs that I developed when I was very young

I created varying patterns of interaction in my relationships. They haven't always been healthy patterns. I was very shy growing up which I understand can be "over focus on self." My insecurities really kept me focusing on myself for "security's sake' and from stepping into the power that I held but didn't always use. In turn, I transferred this way of being into my relationships and how I operated in the world. Because I wasn't feeling "OK" about who I was, I might "try" to make someone love me to feel better about myself. (We cannot make anyone do anything so we should all stop that right now.) We are not only OK the way we are, we are totally perfect in each moment. We still can change and grow to a higher level of evolution and being, but who we are now is just "perfect!"

Even when we become angry or resentful, we can still carry love in our hearts, but if we carry extreme negative feelings we have moved out of the realm of love. Then there is no room for love and it will be harder to return to that space of unconditional living.

We give our power away when we hold resentment, anger, grievances, lack of trust and insecurities around relationships. These are inner obstacles and blocks. They prevent our loving and being loved. When we hold these negative emotions, we cannot step into the place of power that is available to us. These old negative emotions and experiences hold us back in a place of being a victim. We are unconsciously affirming that something has been done to us and we have no power over it. The self-fulfilling prophecy becomes, "we were powerless."

We have to reclaim our power if we are going to have healthy and thriving love relationships. Our core beliefs around love determine whether we have thriving relationships or are playing unconscious games and feeling victimized. If we continue patterns of shame, blame, feeling wronged or unworthy, we must heal the past before we can enjoy, co-create, be available and responsible for a healthy future.

If you have continued to create the same patterns over and over again in love relationships, what is the pattern that you are perpetuating? Are you holding unhealthy boundaries and past hurts or guilt and unresolved issues? Do you sabotage relationships or lack trust? Do you often feel rejected, abandoned or not good enough? Can you tell the truth, share feelings and open your heart? Do you give your power away, place yourself as second in the relationship or play invisible? Do you feel that you are "unlucky in love" or alone much or the time even when you have people around you? Do you dislike commitment, getting too serious or feeling vulnerable? What are your deep feelings around love and being loved? Do you feel worthy and deserving of a loving relationship and dedicated partner?

> You will become free if you fall in
> love with yourself right now.
> You are worthy of your love.
> ~Becky Mulkern ND

If you want to attract an unconditionally loving and thriving relationship then your values, self-worth, confidence, and feelings of desirability are all important. What you feel consciously and unconsciously, creates self-fulfilling prophecies. You have to recreate and change the old mind tapes and transform your self-identity around love. Shift and transform the old stories. Connect to the truth of yourself which is that you deserve to love and be loved. Can you share your feelings, feel worthy of love, release the past, affirm that you can change, transform the old patterns and create new and healthy ones? Generate and create new images, pictures and feelings around a thriving relationship. What would fulfilled love look like? How would it feel? Create the magic, joy and possibility for yourself. Write a new essay and see a new vision about your perfect love. Set new intentions that are different from the past, step into a new future... Be ready to give and receive. Release the old patterns and obstacles. Trust that you can attract your perfect love. Believe in yourself and feel willing to be loved, adored, blessed, and respected. Feel totally worthy of what you want.

When egos are free of fear (lovingly grounded in healthy individuality), there may be a balance of vulnerability, passion, understanding, respect, humility, and feelings of safety and security for both individuals. Open dialogue can serve to create and nurture an intimate relationship if it is grounded in unconditional love and acceptance. All dialogue and all questions should be grounded in love. A healthy relationship is created and nurtured by two emotionally healthy individuals. It may not start that way, but at least if both individuals commit to speaking from a place of unconditional acceptance, the individuals can evolve together. There would be no "hurting" each other if judgments and expectations are released or refrained from, and the union is based and held in unconditional love.

PEACE
When the power of love overcomes the love of power
the world will know peace.
~Jimmy Hendrix

If we are love unconditionally, we are accepting of others as they are. Our ease of accepting comes from our feelings about who we are. We understand that we ourselves and others are always "doing their best" at all times based on our life experience.

Erich Fromm author of *The Art of Loving* really captures the understanding of the balance of "I and we:" He believes that mature love is union, under the condition of preserving one's integrity and one's individuality. It requires "a state of intensity, awakeness, enhanced vitality." From there we manifest "an active concern for life and the growth of that which we love."

Without balance of giving and receiving, nurturing and release of egos, identity and autonomy are threatened and we become dependent on others approvals as a basis for our feeling of identity. This creates union without integrity.

We are all born to love and be loved. There is no other more important way. We are all worthy of love. This is the truth of who we are. As we release the old painful patterns and step into our authentic unconditionally loving self we will know the truth and feel the power of who we are. If we "be love" we shall experience more love than we could ever imagine. Let's live our evolutionary spirit and begin standing in love.

Core qualities in a healthy relationship

~ Valuing one another's individuality.
~ Both individuals are nurtured by the relationship: they express joy, health, sensitivity, good listening skills and are their true self. They value the relationship because it supports growth, evolution and trust.
~ Both individuals maintain interests and healthy relationships outside their relationship.
~ The individuals unconditionally support each other's interests and growth.
~ The relationship is woven into the totality of their lives.
~ There is an intimate friendship between the two individuals.
~ Freedom from expectations, allows it to develop as it will on its own. Both accept and cherish what their partner is giving to the relationship.
~ There is mutual respect, honesty, humility, compassion, appreciation and sincerity.
~ A balance and enjoyment of giving and receiving.
~ Living in the present and letting go of the past and future.
~ Holding and supporting personal integrity.
~ Actions that are often guided by the voice within or a spiritual connection.
~ Quick shifts occur during challenges. Feelings are not suppressed, overlooked or put "under the rug."
~ Joy, humor and laughter!
~ Genuine love for one another and oneself.

The healthy, whole and holy relationship comes from individuals who feel complete, whole and fulfilled. They come together to share and enjoy their love and nurture and support one another.

Many times I have found individuals in my classes saying "It will be very hard for me to love myself." They just couldn't love themselves as they were. One example is a client who was an illegitimate child….the product of her mother sleeping with a man for just one night. As a child, she was never accepted into the family, was an outcast, always received second-best. She felt rejection and was shown neither love nor care. This may have been due as much to the culture at that time as anything. She accepted the beliefs and judgments of others and over time treated herself the same way that others treated her! As she grew older she saw how unfairly she was treated by others but she continued to treat herself with judgments and dislike. Others excluded her from their love and she continued to exclude herself from her own love. She felt she was too old to change.

It is never, too late to change. We can all do it. Everyone is capable of so much more than they realize. Begin now. There are so many rewards awaiting you.

> Awakening the sensitivity that allows you to access
> universal information requires a flip of thinking: it
> requires that you look from above rather than from below.
> It requires an accurate knowledge of self. Yet you cannot
> know yourself until your images of self are dissolved,
> and only love is capable of that dissolution. Feel love
> being offered to you from the life that rises in your veins,
> feel love being offered to you in the sunlight that shines
> upon your home, in the rains that fall upon the fields
> that provide your grains, in the eyes of a child, partner
> or friend. The love available to you each moment is more
> than enough to dissolve the subtle ties that bind you in
> illusion. You are worthy, you are deserving of that love.
> *~Starseed the Third Millenium*

You can't wait for others to love you in order to love yourself. Love yourself and allow others to love you too. Love that we give to ourselves will come back from others as a reflection…. maybe ten-fold. *The key to loving ourselves is unconditional acceptance of everything without exception.*

> Your brother is the mirror in which
> you see your self-image.
> ~Course in Miracles

When we are living in fear we are not in a place of love. *To the degree that we hold fear, we are less affective in all that we do.* To the degree that we hold fear, we hold less love. We cannot hold both. They are juxtaposed:

Fear hides	Love responds
Fear separates	Love connects
Fear deflates	Love uplifts
Fear destroys	Love creates
Fear contracts	Love expands

As we travel through the light and darkness of our healing process, we inspire and ignite healing in others as well. This is our opportunity to lovingly support others in their healing process. We can choose to give up ideas of how things "should" be or controlling others or imposing our will on them. If we try to control others, we may find others trying to do the same to us. However if we free others to their own process, we are reminded that we have the same opportunity as well. Mutual unconditional support works great!

I remember one time years ago when I was asking my heart what I needed most in a loving relationship. I came up with "respect." Evidently, I was needing to do that for myself, but also wanting it from others. Just coming to understanding our needs and acknowledging what is missing in our lives, may be enough to bring the energy of that feeling and emotion toward us. So, what are two things that you need most in a relationship?

As we honor and respect others, we can release our obsessions and desires to manipulate, force, be aggressive or angry, hold up barriers, be defensive or to want things to be other than they are. We can hold love without seeking control. *Everything that is directed at us from others is either love or an appeal for healing, help, love and/ or acceptance, no matter what form it takes.* Many individuals have grown up without parents and/or role models showing them unconditional love. Whatever attention they received, be it positive or negative, they may have confused it with and think it was love. If they have not received unconditional love. they will probably live in judgment and fear and have an inability to be unconditional. That means that they will hold conditional feelings toward themselves as well as others. They will love you if...... They will love you if you conform to their wants and needs...... They will love you if you do what you "should" do. They will love you if you change. It is conditional, with fearful individuals who have not yet learned to be unconditional. Unconditional means, letting go of all expectations, judgments and conditions in a relationship. *We are offered the choice, again and again ... love or fear.... The choice is always ours.* What is your choice?

Intimacy

Enlightenment is the intimacy of all things.
~Diane Hamilton ~*Big Mind, Big Heart*

The true essence and quality of unconditionally loving relationships is that individuals respect, nurture, allow, and accept the right of each to be their authentic selves. We can be the initiators. If we see things in ourselves that we don't like, we can be more loving toward ourselves. The key to self-evolution is unconditionally loving and accepting ourselves and who we are right now! We are certainly more loving when we are free of judgment of ourselves and others. Love is a much higher frequency of energy than negativity and fear. In order to live with love, we have to transform and release self-defeating patterns and personal fears, while moving into the light and that higher level of energy.

I love this quote from *Emmanuel II*:

If you are living in the past, you are not present.
If you are living in the future, you are not present.
If you are not present, who is?
Without you, there is no intimacy.

Real intimacy reveals radical trust, vulnerability, effortless closeness, and operating as an Authentic Self. From this space, we can speak our truth and open to possibilities of true union. In being authentic, there is no personal drama to share and spread to others. There is no separation from reality, but deep presence in it. The shift is from personal identification and separation to unity and being an Integrated Being. With personal identification, the self doesn't always know how to be loving or a friend without operating from attachments, defenses, and old programs. When the shift occurs toward real connection, there is space for individuals to become more than they had once been…. to be spiritually unified.

Intimacy isn't created from our focus on it, but our focus on unconditionally loving. Intimacy comes from being comfortable with our desires and ourselves as we are. It comes from autonomy, feeling safe, healthy self-esteem, and knowing oneself. True intimacy involves a being that doesn't live at the expense of the relationship and a relationship that doesn't function at the expense of the being. There is no depth in intimacy without knowing yourself and having a clear sense of your healthy "I." Being a spiritually healthy individual supports a spiritually healthy intimate union.

The Runes talk about true partnership being achieved by "separate and whole beings who retain their uniqueness even as they unite"…. and who "let the winds of heaven dance between them."

Nothing is really more fundamental than love and being loving. When we compromise love or truth, we may be living in fear or feeling that something else is more important. Certainly we are disconnected from the flow, operating from our ego and not feeling love or loved. We may not be connected with our true essence, which is to love. As we release our "needs" and let them go, we reconnect with the spiritual and in feeling one with all life. We then will act with love and find that we do have everything that we need. Love can bring us back to our senses.

The need for intimacy springs from that portion
of you that has been cast from the Oneness.
It remembers what Oneness feels like
and is trying to find its way home.
~Emmanuel Book II

Children

Kahlil Gibran's book "The Prophet" speaks of children as coming through you but not belonging to you and how parents may give them their love, but not their thoughts, because "they have their own thoughts." But more significantly he speaks of parents as housing the children's "bodies but not their souls." How many parents would be capable of gladly and unconditionally doing this ….allowing their children to become what they are meant to become with the support and love of those parents. These are fortunate and rare children that have this opportunity.

What we should/could learn from children is the power of the moment. We don't have to be children to know the importance of play, laughter and momentary pleasure. Children live and play without goals, living joyfully with curiosity, and freely moving to their next adventure. Being in each moment and living spontaneously is the way of the child. What if we break free from the old beliefs, agendas, and habits, create new brain patterns, and transform our ability to play, create and recreate? We may find new freedom to play, laugh and just to be in each spectacular moment. We could spend our afternoons just being fresh and free like a child.

My boys were all very independent. They were very self-aware from the time they were young. I remember my youngest son saying to me when he was about 6 years old, "I know what is best for me Mom." I did learn to listen to him because he did!

Because of the freedoms that they were allowed they have not lived the ordinary life in an ordinary way. How wonderful! I allowed my sons the freedom to think and be and supported them to "think outside and beyond the box." Recently my oldest son started a new business and even hired the youngest son to help him. The youngest is very bright and has many wonderfully creative ideas. The newest business is a highly engaging social evolutionary web site that employs engaging ways for individuals to get to know themselves better. It uses peer reflection for raising self-awareness and supporting users to discover their strengths, recognize opportunities for growth and creatively change their lives. It will be released around May 2014.

Why are you here?

You may ask yourself: Why are you here. What is your purpose? What do you most want to be remembered for? or Who are you? These are all important questions to address as part of your growth and evolution. If you have read this book then I hope that you have become passionately inspired to see unlimited possibilities and infinite potential for yourself. It is time to leave the old outworn ways of being behind you and to explore how it feels just to be and to dream of what might be possible. Then *you will begin to see that you are what you are looking for.*

So what is your destiny at this time? What intentions and desires do you hold? Being quiet, meditating and allowing yourself to get in touch with your soul's journey will help it to unfold more easily. Open yourself to know the unlimited abundance and vast opportunities that are your birthright.

We cannot grow spiritually unless we deeply love and hold reverence for ourselves. As we open to profound loving of ourselves and all life, mountains move and environments change, and there is ease where there was difficulty. One of the biggest changes we can make is to just truly love ourselves.

Dostoyevsky

One of my favorite quotes on love is the following by Dostoyevsky. I have it in a place where I can read it every day:

Love all God's creatures, the world,
and every grain of sand in it.
Love every leaf, every ray of God's light.
Love the plants, love everything.
If you love everything you will perceive
the Divine mystery in things. Once you perceive it
you will begin to comprehend it better every day.
And you will come at last to love
the whole world with an all-embracing love.
~ Dostoyevsky, ~*The Brothers Karamazov*

Going Deeper~

~ When choosing to be unconditionally loving and accepting, know....you may never feel hurt.

~ Eliminate all "shoulds" in your loving relationships and in your life.

~Love people as they are, don't expect them to change (so that you can love them).

~Release "If he/she loved me, he/she would...."?

~*Expectations are a major contributor to unhealthy relationships.*

~Can you be joyful when those close to you make choices that are best for their life? *Do you understand that when someone loves you, their decisions may say nothing about their love for you.* When people make choices for themselves that doesn't mean that they don't love you.

~The more love and compassion I hold for myself, the more love I have for everyone.

~We always do our very best to love based on our life experience. We have unlimited potential to grow and evolve far beyond this present moment.

Loving , Honoring and Respecting Yourself~

~How often do you bless and praise yourself?

~Have you ever enjoyed looking in the mirror and expressing real love to yourself? Please try it…. Take some time to do it. Tell yourself, "I love you."

~Love yourself unconditionally, always. How does that feel?

~If situations come up where you are feeling that you have to be "right and in control" and you want to use some sort of force, instead let go and "melt" into unconditional love and see if you can still get what you feel you want or need.

~During the next week practice surrounding any uncomfortable situations with "light and love" or whatever feels right for you.

~Is there anything that holds you back from loving yourself to the greatest possible degree. (Painful incidents, judgments or unhealed hurts?)

> But we must start with ourselves:
> The moment you have in your heart
> this extraordinary thing
> called love and feel the depth, the delight,
> the ecstasy of it, you will discover
> that for you the world is transformed.
> ~I. Krishnamurti

13

Living with Gratitude and Reverence

> With sacred eyes we can see the beauty, the divinity
> and the meaning and purpose in this collective
> journey, as well as our own reason for being.
> With sacred eyes we can see the larger context
> without overlooking the details of the moment.
> With sacred eyes we can see the reasons
> for tough optimism and pragmatic hope
> within the chaos of our times.
> ~L. Robert Keck, Ph.D., ~*Sacred Eyes*

In some countries when individuals offer gifts, they give something that they have and deeply treasure, saying. "Take this please, it is the best I have." In our country sometimes people will say: "Take this, I don't need it anymore," or "I don't use it anymore" or "Take this I don't want it anymore." Think about how that sounds. What if we did offer our best and felt the joy in that! I did that recently, and I loved and enjoyed how I felt. I had a beautiful and very expensive shirt that I was no longer wearing, but I still couldn't let go of it. It was the most expensive shirt I had ever bought for myself, I really loved it and I had purchased it on a memorable trip to Colorado. I couldn't seem to part with it even though I wasn't wearing it. On my birthday when a friend was taking me out for lunch, I brought it in the car and was thinking about gifting it to her. I still valued it so much, that I was not sure I could give it away. I finally decided that I would feel much better giving it to my dear friend than keeping it in my closet. When I gave it to her, she immediately said she wanted to try it on and she wore it to lunch. She looked so stunning in it. It felt extraordinary to finally let it go and I felt such joy with giving that gift! It was a shirt I dearly loved and I gave it to a friend that I dearly loved. Win-win!

I was very blessed to gain gratitude during one of my biggest challenges. One spring, I spent 3 months lying flat on my back with a herniated disc and severe pain. It was actually one of the best vacations that I ever had. I couldn't and didn't do anything, not even read or watch TV. I just lay there and rested. I was at peace with "not doing." During that time, I experienced a tremendous amount of pain, enough that I took Percoset often just to ease the pain. On a scale of one to ten, it was a 12+.

A traumatic event had occurred previously had left me feeling harsh anger toward myself. It was soon after that when my back gave out. (I believe that it occurred because I wasn't supporting and loving myself.) The day that I felt the first pain, I was playing tennis ¼ mile away from my house and I couldn't even drive home. My friend had to drive while I lay back on the seat. That was it. I lay flat on a bed for almost 3 months.

I had never felt deep gratitude before this time. Through the intensity of this experience and connecting profoundly to my feelings, I became very appreciative and grateful during my healing process. Many blessings that occurred brought me to this place.... just to have someone bring me ice for the pain... I was so grateful. My son, Jesse, actually biked over mornings before school (he was in 4th grade) and made me breakfast. Wow...what an amazing gift. I was so grateful. Some friends planted my garden. Awesome! I remember when someone asked me if they could do something and I said, "Oh, if you could please sweep the kitchen floor that would be so nice." (I could feel the dirt on my bare feet.) I became so grateful for everything....so grateful.... so thankful.

I didn't feel as if I was born with gratitude (though I was taught to write "thank-you" letters growing up). Maybe we have to experience something deeply moving to bring us to this place. After healing my back, I could feel gratitude in every cell of my being, and felt so thankful and blessed in gaining it too. Being grateful is now an important aspect of everyday life for me.

> The principal that provides us
> the greatest abundance is appreciation.
>
> True spirituality ...is generosity, consideration,
> compassion and many other profound virtues.
>
> Our real nature is to express all of them.
> Life is a gift. Treasure it.
> ~Pa'Ris'Ha, ~*Hawk on the Wings*~

Most people in the United States are unaware of how very fortunate they are. They are very wealthy compared to the rest of the world. Let me share with you some statistics that may have you thinking about how grateful you are for what you do have:

~If the Earth were a community of 100 people...
  1 person would own 50% of the world's wealth...
  50 people would share only 1% of the world's wealth...
  15 are hungry and seriously malnourished...
  16 have no drinking water...
  39 have no basic sanitation...
  15 are unable to read...

<u>If you have food in your refrigerator, clothes in your closet, a bed to sleep in, and a roof over your head you are better off than 83 % of the people on this planet.</u>

WOW!! How does that make you feel? Are you grateful?

In years past, I watched a documentary about teenagers from the slums of New York City who visited the slums of India. The New York teens thought they were disadvantaged and lived in poverty and until they saw what real poverty was. They had no idea that there were teens their age that lived in makeshift cardboard buildings and tent like structures with few belongings, no drinking water, and no refrigerators. They broke down and cried when they saw real poverty.

When I was vacationing in Mexico, I visited a hammock-makers house outside the city where I was staying. He was a joyful, smiley faced man who wove beautiful hammocks and traveled daily by bus to the city to sell his hammocks. His house had very little furniture, no refrigerator, a few chickens running around and very little food in sight. A couple of soda bottles were on the counter. Yet he appeared totally happy and the children looked healthy....

> Studies have shown that having gratitude
> can make you 25% happier
> and can cause you to be
> immune to anger, disappointment
> and frustration.

When we acknowledge the amazing fullness and the richness of our lives, we are filled with peace, joy, gratitude and unconditional love. We are less apt to see a loss in many circumstances. We accept where we are and see only what we have gained. In living free of regrets, we are thankful for all that life has given us and continues to bring us. We can experience each moment as full, creative, dynamic, enriched, and an opportunity for unlimited potential to express itself. We truly understand that we need nothing more than this present moment. As we receive and accept everything as a gift, we more easily support ourselves and hold gratitude for life and all that we have. This state of being further opens the door to abundance, unlimited opportunities, and the whole universe.

As we grow, learn and evolve spiritually, we leave behind misery, lack, old limiting belief systems and impossibility. It is time! We then begin to feel a very deep and encompassing sense of gratitude. As it increases, our joy and peace of mind do as well. As our peace of mind and joy increases, we begin to feel more gratitude and appreciation than we ever thought possible. As we consciously evolve, we realize and feel our inner power for creating, as well as the universal and Universe-given power to fulfill all our dreams.

We are co-creators. As we trust the power of love and creativity, we work synergistically with the universe in creating all that is possible for ourselves, humankind and life on earth.

As we realize our fulfilled hopes and dreams, our gratitude knows no bounds. We feel the wellspring of love, creativity and gratitude filling every cell of our being. We are finally truly aware of all that we have!

As individuals grow, learn, and evolve spiritually, they often display a very deep sense of gratitude for what life has brought them. As they travel on their individual journeys, their sense of peace becomes deeper, their gratitude more encompassing, and their joy and serenity are beyond what they could have thought possible. As we evolve, we understand our inherent power for creating, as well as the universal power available to help us fulfill our dreams. As we work synergistically with the universe and the Divine, we trust this creative process. As we truly realize that all our dreams can be fulfilled, our gratitude feels amazing.

As we realize who we are, our gratitude grows. As we experience more gratitude, our sense of peace and joy increases. Our inner peace grows, as we feel connected with our gratitude and Authentic Self. Every cell of our being feels alive. Yet even when we experience overwhelming events, we know we can choose to focus on all that we are grateful for and all that we have. We feel a bottomless well of gratitude that we can invoke at any time.

Reverence

When I experience the miraculous beauty of the natural world, it affects me deeply. How can anyone remain unchanged, when they watch a glorious sunset with colors ranging from bright turquoise blue to brilliant orange, yellow and deep reds and pinks? As I stand there and experience this beauty, something in me at that moment seems to unite with that glory that is all around me. Experiencing that moment to the exclusion of all else is life changing. I have felt the deepest gratitude for being blessed to have such an experience in really seeing the "Glory of God."

Because of the love we feel for all people and for Mother
Earth, in difficult times when so much destruction is
happening we can also see a world full of opportunities.
Our hearts seek to awaken an expansive spiritual power
—the sacred inner power that will enable us to cooperate
with others and change what seems impossible to change.
~Arkan Lushwala, ~The Time of the Black Jaguar

Native and indigenous peoples have always demonstrated
deep reverence and gratitude for the "sacred" world in which
they live. In their ceremonies they show their appreciation for the
"Great Spirit," the Universe and the world around them, that has
provided so much abundance. In reflecting on this, I believe it is
because they experience a world far different than most people
in my culture. In industrialized nations many are living in such a
superficial, materialistic, self-focused way. They see little outside
of themselves and their needs. Native peoples though see and feel
life very differently. They acknowledge the life in all of nature....in
rocks, trees, rivers, mountains, etc. It is a dominant aspect of their
everyday life, not something they do once a week or once a year. It
is not a discipline, but a way of being that permeates every aspect
of their being and living. They live a deeply reverent way of life.

Imagine a culture that is holds gratitude for everything that
comes their way. Everything. It is time for all of us to demonstrate
gratitude for our blessings…..
For one day be thankful for everything that you receive. See if
your life feels different after that day. Be thankful for the gas for
your car, the food you eat, the friends that call you, the work that
comes your way, the air you breathe, your heart that continues to
beat, etc. There is a lot to be thankful for! Does your life change at
all just by being thankful?

Purpose

If we are truly aligned with who we are, being passionate, living from our heart and following our dreams, then we are living our true purpose and destiny. Even if you have not found your ultimate passion, if you are aligned with these aspects, you are on the road to your highest potentials and possibilities.

If you have not yet connected with your true purpose, try seeing with a new and different perspective. Think about how you want to feel in the future and feel it now. Get in touch with the essence of who you are and what you love from a different point of view. How would you feel if you loved what you are doing in life. How would you feel if you were at peace. How would you feel if you had a loving family and loving friends? How would you feel if you were serving and bringing value to society, your community at large and the planet? (profit could be secondary) Ask your own questions. This may help you to form your own picture of your purpose. Your trusting connection to the Infinite Intelligence will help your evolution to occur.

We are moving from the Dualistic World Grid to connecting with our heart and the "Consciousness Grid," where we will be deeply connected with all life on earth... Oneness. In this place we shall have a deeper realization of our connection to the Universe and the meaning of life. We will live with a sense of knowing that is beyond words.

> Religion can never reform mankind
> because religion is slavery.
> ~Robert G. Ingersoll (1833-1899)

If we are truly living our purpose, there is no faltering, doubt, wasted energy or impossibility. All of our energy is directed at and utilized with being our purpose and living from our heart. We all crave this more than most anything else... to serve, contribute and be all that we can be. If our heart is full and we are living with true joy and spiritual connection, our spiritual energy will radiate out to the whole universe. Some individuals experience very "large" lives and some contribute to the whole, just by being in a space of love, compassion and unconditional acceptance. One is no better than another. We are all equal in the eyes of the universe.

Kevin Cashman said that purpose is the "spirit seeking expression." That is why we are here on earth. *We each have a very unique contribution to make that no one else can make.* Let's do it! Our spirits are longing to express our joy. We are here to love all that we do. No one else can do what you are here to do. Enjoy it! Express yourself and your uniqueness! We will all be enriched by your contribution.

Abundance

This new evolutionary era is calling for us to rewrite our abundance matrix program. Just as you can reprogram your computer, it is time to reprogram many of your ideas and beliefs about what an abundant life means. We can no longer live with the idea that separation and competition are paramount. Winning, thinking mechanistically, personal profit, an economy that works for the 1%, believing in scarcity and materialism are ways of the past. We have learned a great deal by thinking that they held value, but we can see now that we are better off to bless these limiting beliefs, let them go and move forward. We have been told that they were important and/or necessary, but that is not true.

The world is a very abundant place, but with blinders on we may only see what we are programmed to see and believe. If we experience wanting, control or uncertainty and we believe in limitation, lack and struggle, then we may experience that around us. *If "want" is our motivating factor then we are interpreting life as incomplete and lacking.* Living in survival mode, feeling separate and disconnected may not prove fruitful either. If we believe that we are already whole and that we live in an abundant universe where there is plenty for everyone, then we will experience that in our life. The mind is not the Self. Our programing is not who we are. If we stay connected with the source of our abundance, live it and hold it in our heart as our basic nature, then we will feel the difference. It is not something that we have to figure out (mind), get or pursue. If we release "lack" and "unworthiness" mentality, we can hold heart-felt compassion, trust in the unknown, and feel our abundant nature. In keeping our thoughts, feelings, beliefs, energy, and actions aligned with our heart and the abundant life that we have, we will always see an abundant world. There are infinite resources. We are energetic beings with no limitations and boundaries. Both energy and life are meant to flow through us. We have to allow it, promote it, feel worthy of it and celebrate.

Some people say that *having rests on giving.* Certainly we will be more aware of the fullness of life if we share what we have, rather than hoarding it or worrying about losing it. If we share and give what we feel is lacking in our lives...we shall have more of it come to us. It is in sharing that we feel the fullness of life and will want to share more. *There has to be a balance between giving and receiving, breathing in and breathing out......*even both talking and listening. Many individuals are typically givers and have a challenge with receiving, while others are typically takers or receivers and may not enjoy giving. We can learn to feel comfortable with and enjoy both receiving and giving. This is important to keep the flow going in our life. If we do one aspect more than the other, our life will be out of balance. If our life is out of balance it may lead to dis-ease.

When we are given a gift, we have the opportunity to return our heartfelt gratitude. To me this is one of the best gifts that I can give. If I am really present in the now, I enjoy saying how grateful I am for gifts from others. That is a true gift!

Native Americans believe that having "giveaway" ceremonies benefit the earth, the universe, life and all beings. This keeps life energy circulating and supporting an abundant and flourishing life on earth. During their ceremonies, they give what is of special value to themselves, rather than something they no longer need or want. They do this fairly often to produce an abundant life for all and prevent stagnation and lack. They believe that this benefits even their crops, food, water and everything that comes to them. When I have parties, I sometimes have individuals bring something to share with others. We place the gifts on the table and let others gather what they would like. It is a fun experience and a way of gifting things that we would like to share. We have had such fun with this.

Our views of success and failure affect the prosperity in our lives. If we don't feel successful or that we could ever be successful, we won't attract (the energy of) financial success. Successful people often think in the "I can" mode and their energy vibration may be much higher than those individuals who focus on lack or "I can't." Disconnect from what isn't working and doesn't serve you. Free of ***doubt or reservation, focus on what you want to create.*** This allows you to more easily create all that you could ever want.

Money is energy and representational of what we believe about ourselves and life. Money demonstrates our beliefs related to worthiness and manifestation. It speaks of our wants, beliefs, fears and needing. It can be useful, but it certainly can't buy our peace of mind. Our financial prosperity may show how limited we feel, the impossibilities that we may believe in or how full our life is and how optimistic we feel about our future. If we believe that life provides for our needs, then that will affect what we receive. I certainly don't mean that you sit in a corner and just affirm, but you are free of doubt, actively creating and holding gratitude for all that you have and for all that is coming.

One thing I love about this evolutionary time is "community helping and supporting community." Why not share resources and encourage mutual support? If we work together with connection and cooperation, we all benefit. We all have expertise in different areas. Why not work for the whole and the individual? I have found that having support with different aspects of publishing this book has been heart-warming and awesome. I just haven't had the time or expertise to do it all. Sons and friends have helped with tech work, editing, photos and getting the word out to others. I have used *Indiegogo*, the largest crowd funding organization to help me raise money for editing, publishing and marketing this book. By doing this...I am saying, "I can" and I am creating a community to help me with my goal. At the same time, I am getting the word out about what I am doing. Through this process, I have already started advertising my new book before it is even published. It feels like a "win-win" situation. I am so thankful for the support of friends and family in this project.

We can create a shift through reshaping our intentions and feeling grateful. If we utilize our higher mind and higher power, we can feel the essence of what we want to create in our lives. If we create a new and dominant thought in our beings, we can create a magnetizing force that attracts energy from the "field of all possibilities." As we release old paradigms and struggle, we can change the field of energy around us to what we want manifested now. Abundance, joy and miracles are here now.... The Divine/Universe and I are the co-creators and source of my abounding and infinite abundance. Seeing yourself sharing your gifts and blessings is part of the whole package. Sharing, receiving, feeling blessed, holding grace and compassion, loving service to others...this brings it full circle. Miracles arrive from higher thinking and connection to the quantum field where possibilities manifest. Think in unlimited ways to allow prosperity to come from unexpected places. Have faith and embody abundance.

> Follow your bliss and the Universe
> will open doors for you
> where there were only walls.
> ~Joseph Campbell

Abundance is what we hold in our heart and soul. It is about how we experience life as our true self. When we are guided by our heart, abundance (that doesn't mean just money) flows easily. When we are a powerful creator and centered in our heart, we understand that there is an inexhaustible amount of love and creative energy coming from the Universe. In feeling worthy, we know that abundance comes from within us, and creates the impulse for our life to be full of many possibilities. When we experience our life as full and feel the love energy that is present, we can really think about what we would love to be experiencing (Now)! Feel the expansive energy of love and abundance.

When we work with interconnected and collaborative minds and hearts, we all benefit. We can then celebrate what we all create individually and collectively. Abundance is really an energetic quality full of worthiness, gratitude and celebration! Abundance is our birthright. We are radiant and worthy beings. Have courage and dream big!

Affirmations~

~I am ready to heal NOW.

~Everything that happens is for my highest good.

~I always have everything that I need and more.

~I experience all my challenges peacefully, harmoniously and lovingly in Divine perfect time.

~I am thankful for all that I learn.

~I allow and support myself to be all that I can be.

~Whatever I release and let go of is transformed and replaced with love.

~My life is filled with infinite possibilities and opportunities.

Going Deeper~

~Do you often spend more time thinking about what is lacking in your life than what you have? (You can easily change that.)

~Can you count on yourself unconditionally, through all experiences?

~How do you respond to big challenges? (a downward spiral?...or an upward spiral?)

~How do you respond to life's every day challenges? (a downward spiral or an upward spiral?)

~Review your beliefs about prosperity—are they limited or limitless? Can you do an upgrade?

14

The Creative Power of Prayer

It is in proportion to our trust in the Divine
that the Divine Grace can act for us.
(*unknown*)

Over the years, many studies have been performed on the effects of prayer. It was found to positively affect healing rates of wounds, heart attacks, blood pressure, headaches, growth of white blood cells, and anxiety. Prayer affected various life forms including fungi, bacteria, water, yeast, red blood cells, seeds, plants, algae, mice, and chicks. Interestingly enough it didn't matter if the prayer was done in the presence of the life form or at a distance. Studies have even proved that prayer can transcend distance and time. Nothing was capable of stopping the effects of it, not even a lead-lined room.

Larry Dossey MD, who wrote many books on prayer, feels that many doctors are "spiritually malnourished." He suggests that doctors pray for their patients, which he feels might even help speed their recovery.

Genes are not the absolute controllers
they are represented to be.
Biology, in other words, is not destiny.
~Larry Dossey

Studies found that even ordinary people had the ability to bring about physiological changes in other living organisms through prayer. Dossey believes that this suggests that everyone possesses innate healing abilities, at least to some degree. In referring to prayer, Dossey said that, "There is great mystery here....in the strongest possible sense ... something unknowable ... something essentially beyond human understanding."

Prayer is something that we can always do when we feel powerless. It is especially appropriate when everything seems beyond our control (which might be OK). It is a more beneficial activity than focusing on our fears and what we don't want to happen. Prayer gives us something we can do in times of challenge. Some people say, "Turn it over to the Universe, your Higher Power or the Divine Will. However it works for you, don't hesitate to use it. *The ego's illusion of power is released when we turn to prayer.* Through prayer we are admitting that there is something beyond ourselves that is more powerful than we are. We can still be responsible and creative in many ways, but the Divine can help and guide us in the process if we will only but ask. *~Ask, and it shall be given you......Mathew 7:7.*

> In Quietness all things are answered and
> is every problem quietly resolved.
> ~*Course in Miracles*

Although in the "Course in Miracles" prayers are spoken of as always being answered, we may not always realize, visibly see the result, or always understand the answer that comes, because of our desire to have a specific outcome. We may be receiving help without realizing that we are. Things are sometimes more mysterious than we might believe. Be very specific about what you really want or need for the best outcomes.

Although not everyone believes in God or the Divine, I find it very interesting that some scientists come full circle through their work. Through their study and understanding of science and physics, many have come to believe that there is something beyond ourselves that is in charge of the universe. I love the following quote by the brilliant scientist Max Planck:

> Gentlemen! As a physicist, who has his lifelong served
> a sober and objective science....out of my researches
> into the atom, I will say the following: There is no

such thing as matter on its own. All matter comes and
persists only through a force, which brings the particles
into vibration...in the tiny sun-system of the atom...
so we must assume that behind this force there is a
conscious, intelligent Spirit. This Spirit is the basis of all
matter.......But as Spirit cannot exist for itself alone, and
to every Spirit there belongs a Being, so we are forced
to assume Spirit-Being. But as Spirit-Being also cannot
exist out of itself alone, and must have been created,
so I am not shy in naming this mysterious creator, as
have all peoples of all the ancient cultures,—God!
*(some words of the physicist Max Planck (1858-
1947) delivered to a scientific audience and
translated from the journal, Lebendige Erde,
No 3/84 page 133.)* ~Max Planck

In reading this again, (I do love this quote) it led me to reflect on
the mystery of crop circles and now there are "snow circles" out in
the world too. How wonderful! Though some people have taken
credit for making them, some are definitely not man-made. They
are awe-inspiring and lead you to realize that there are many things
that are beyond our understanding or any logical explanation. I love
the mystery of it all.

When praying, you may want to think of prayer as connecting to
the Unified Field, God, Infinite Intelligence, Source or communion
with the Sacred Universal Spirit within all life. Anyone can use
prayer as a way of being and connection with the Divine. It is a
spiritual path to a reality where many have released and dissolved
challenges in their lives. You have heard the saying, "Let go and let
God." Well, that means that you may really have to let go of control
in order for prayers to be answered. We can't always know how
things are supposed to be resolved with prayer or how our prayers
should be answered. We have to release fear of the unknown,
control, and limiting perspectives. They may limit the Universal
Intelligence's ability to respond to our prayers. Let go, breathe and

let your prayers be answered.... We are always connected to the Divine. Our nature is the love that is available to us from the Divine. Don't question that you can pray and be heard. Just let go of any beliefs that may block your union with the Universe.

> There is never a time
> when love, power and guidance
> is unavailable to you,
> only times when you are closed to it.
> *~New Teachings for an Awakened Humanity*

You may wish to pray for love, healing, renewal or for other people. The real truth is that we are already whole and perfect, so you may wish to pray for recognition of your wholeness and perfection. Always embrace and acknowledge the wholeness of yourself and the loving being and perfection that you are.

We can certainly pray for many things...healing for others or ourselves, but sometimes it may be better if we just ask for peace of mind that allows us to unconditionally accept what is happening in our lives. The more deeply peaceful we are, the more love we can hold and share. We could ask for freedom from doubt or to have faith and trust in the process that is occurring in our lives. We could ask to be able to transcend and transform the process that surrounds us. By connecting to the love and well-being that is present in the Universe, we trust ourselves and all that may unfold in this moment. We could even ask for limitless mental strength to transform our challenge. Prayers do create miracles and change outcomes, so exercise your rights.

> Prayer from the heart can achieve
> what nothing else in the world can.
> ~Gandhi

Prayer isn't something that should be done once a week at church, I believe it is best on a daily basis. Through prayer, we can touch and embrace others with our love and healing light. Through our unconditional acceptance of their challenges we may help them to transcend them as well. In the process of prayer, we can even offer our love to the Infinite Intelligence. What a wonderful idea… creating a circle of love…the giving and receiving…

When our prayers are answered, certainly we can offer our love and gratitude for the outcomes both before and after. We are always given so much every day….half of our prayer time could be spent in gratitude for all we have.

I love affirmations and visualization as ways to transform any doubt or negative ideas. Continually affirm what you want or want to believe in…..for example: "I am always supported by the Universe," "Blessings are bestowed on me every moment," "I am blessed by all that I have and will have," "I am always connected to love and the Field of Infinite Possibilities."

Please allow yourself to incorporate prayer and gratitude into your daily life and see how everything changes for you.

> To keep quiet and concentrate, leaving the Force
> from above to do its work is the surest way to be
> cured of anything and everything. There is no illness
> that can resist that if it is done properly, in time and
> long enough, with a steady faith and a calm will.
> (*unknown*)

Prayer has always been an important aspect of my life. I have had different prayers that I have loved and used. I have created ones that served my needs at particular times as well. One that I have loved and shared is the following by Isabelle Hickey:

> I clothe myself in the robe of Light,
> composed of the Love, Power and Wisdom of God,
> not only for my own protection, but that so all
> who see it or come in contact with it
> will be drawn to God and healed.
> ~Isabelle Hickey

There are many ways to pray or utilize prayer. Certainly emotional or psychic protection are important for our health and wellness. We can ask for protection from negative energy, people or experiences. I often call in the Arch Angels (Michael, Ariel, Raphael and Gabriel) to support, protect and/or heal me or to take away negative feelings that I might have. I have often asked them to surround and protect my house and me.

One time I experienced extreme fear that I knew was not mine. It felt as if I was possessed by an entity. I tried a number of things to eliminate this energy but nothing worked. It wasn't until I called in the Arch Angels that the healing occurred. When I did call to them to eradicate this energy, heal and protect me, I experienced them pulling this fearful, dark entity out of my body and away to the light to be transformed. Two of the angels pulled him out of my body and away from me. I felt very different afterwards. They fear was gone. I saw it leaving. I thanked them for the healing and blessed them with my gratitude. It really worked!

Some affirmations can be similar to prayer. For example: Onc might wish to say:

> Divine Love now dissolves and dissipates every wrong
> condition in my mind, body and affairs. Divine
> Love is the most powerful chemical in the universe,
> and dissolves everything which is not of itself.
> Florence Shinn, ~*The Game of Life* (written 1925)

Going Deeper~

~Do you fear not having enough in your life? Do you feel lack?

~Do you feel you need more money? Will you be unhappy without it?

~Does money buy happiness or joy?

~Are you envious of individuals that have more money than you?

~Have you a balance of giving and receiving in your life?

~Do you feel worthy of financial success and prosperity?

~Are you noticing that beliefs and assumptions that you have held for years no longer serve you?

Release and Let Go of~

Everyone else comes before me.
I don't deserve...
I am not worthy...
I have to struggle and work really hard...
Money is the root of all evil.
I am always in debt.
I never have enough.....
I enjoy giving, but I am challenged with receiving.

Iroquois Thanksgiving Prayer

We return thanks to the rivers and
streams, which supply us water;
We return thanks to the sun, which has
looked upon earth with a beneficent eye.
We return thanks to the moon and stars, which
have given us light when the sun was gone.
We return thanks to our Mother, the
Earth, which sustains us.
We return thanks to the Great Spirit, in
Whom is embodied all goodness,
and Who directs all things for the good of His children.

15

The Approaching Age
of Agelessness

People don't grow old, when they stop growing
they become old.
(*unknown*)

Some generations have been deeply programmed to live under the laws of collective conditioning and to believe in aging. We are the only form of life that is consciously aware of thinking about aging and mortality. We are now stuck in an unhealthy "aging" belief system.

We are constantly speeding up and slowing down the process of aging, healing and disease. Our deepest beliefs and conditioning are constantly triggering physical health changes. Stress alone creates nutrient depletion and many unhealthy changes in the body. Unless we have a focused desire to create wellness and change our response to stress, we may move into the future with deteriorating health. On the other hand, we may reach a point at which we desire to create shifts in our thinking and choose other responses to stressful experiences. We can raise our energy and direct our lives toward optimal health and healing, and in turn, longevity. One third of our life is directed by genetics and two thirds is affected by choice. If that is true then we do have tremendous power over our future wellness. I have heard that even genetics can be beneficially affected by our choices. So, please understand that your health is not predetermined.

> We are not victims of aging, sickness and death.
> These are part of the scenery, not the seer,
> who is immune to any form of change.
> ~Deepak Chopra M.D. ~*Ageless Body, Timeless Mind*

What our mind thinks and feels certainly influences every cell in our body in speeding up and slowing down the aging process. We can change our biology by what we focus on. Whatever thoughts that we think, create biochemical changes.....distressed mental thoughts get converted into biochemicals that create dis-ease and certainly the opposite is true.

Beliefs about life and death are constantly being reinforced in our cultures and affect our thinking and beliefs. When individuals over 60 go to the doctor and they tell the doctor of their symptoms... the doctor will often say, "Well you are getting older..." In my practice as a Naturopathic Doctor, I do not accept age as a reason for symptoms or disease. I will accept that you haven't taken care of your body, that you haven't eaten a healthy diet, and that you have had a lot of stress, but you shouldn't get sicker as you grow older. It is not predetermined.

One day I was listening to an audio tape by Deepak Chopra and I heard him say, ***Research has proven that the body actually shouldn't age.*** He went on to say that it is how we treat it, what it is exposed to and all the stresses that contribute to the aging process and disease. Stressors (Physical, chemical and emotional) are a huge factor in this process, as they shut down circulation, change physiology, poison our bodies and affect all systems in many detrimental ways. One of the most important factors I believe that would change everything else is living in a state of unconditional love. If you are in an unconditionally loving state, how could you feel stressed? The world would be a very different place if everyone lived with an unconditionally loving heart.

Agelessness comes from releasing fears as they arises, and living in a state of unconditional love. Look at the age lines on some individuals faces do you think they are caused by love or fear, compassion or anxiety?

And still there is the human heart that seeks to know love.
That is the voice of transformation.
That is the voice of truth.
Fear is the frightened child.
Love is the flame of holy remembering.
~Emmanuel Book II

Eating an optimally healthy organic diet made from local and fresh foods and a generally healthy lifestyle are ultra-important for maintaining and achieving an ageless quality. When we take time to thoughtfully feed and care for ourselves it is a win-win result. We can feel really excited that we are taking time for our sacred self and in turn reap the rewards of health.

Last summer I enjoyed a four day hike with a friend over the White Mountains and Presidential Range in New Hampshire. These mountains are in my backyard, so to speak. Some of my favorite hikes are there. We hiked over 9 peaks in 4 days and 7 peaks in 2 days. We stayed overnight at the mountain huts. I hadn't done any multiday hikes with a backpack since my broken leg 9 years previous, so I told my friend that a moderate pace or less was what I was interested in. I was thrilled that I felt great during the whole hike. I was never tired or in pain. There were no leg cramps or muscle spasms. I woke up each day ready for the day's hike. We swam in mountain lakes and rivers and enjoyed every moment. It was an amazing four days. I was especially excited about how awesome I felt because I am presently in my 60's. I have such gratitude for still feeling so healthy. I believe that we don't have to deteriorate with age, but that we can live vibrantly until we decide to leave this planet.

I truly enjoy taking care of the amazing physical body that I have been given. I feel very blessed with the health and strength that I have. I certainly have been rewarded for all my efforts.

The more fully alive we want to be, the more fully aware we have to be. Life is awareness and consciousness. Living fully comes from total presence. Imagine being really present and enjoying each moment totally. Aging comes from a place of limited awareness and fear. In being human, we learn about boundaries, limitation and beginnings and endings. Life is full and ever changing. We have the opportunity to live a spiritual life in a human body. That is the nature of being human.

> We who bore the mark, felt no anxiety about
> the shape the future was to take. All of the faiths and
> teachings seemed to us already dead and useless. The
> only duty and destiny we acknowledged was that
> each one of us should become so completely himself,
> so utterly faithful to the active seed which Nature
> planted within him, that in living out its growth he
> could be surprised by nothing unknown to come.

Although we might not have been able to express it, we all felt that a new birth amid the collapse of this present world was imminent, already discernible. Demian often said to me: What will come is beyond imagining.....

Then our day will come, then we will be needed. Not as leaders and lawgivers—we won't be there to see the new laws—but rather as those who are willing, as men who go forth and stand prepared wherever fate may need them.

....But no one is ready when a new ideal, a new and perhaps dangerous and ominous impulse makes itself felt. The few who will be ready and who will go forth—will be us.
~Herman Hesse, ~*Demian* (1919)

Are you ready?

16

Putting it All Together

The following is a quote that I love, because it is simple and gets right to simplicity of truth:

> And so to the future, and so to tomorrow.
> What shall it be my friend, what shall it be?
> The entire universe is at your disposal, quite literally.
> Oh yes, of course it is available to everyone,
> but so few know that.
> You have found it out through your recent struggle,
> so what shall it be?
> Settle for nothing less than what you truly desire,
> and do not be afraid to ask for what you feel
> will bring you joy and fulfillment.
> ~Wingate Paine, ~*The Book of Surrender*

Thoughts for leading a Conscious & Celebratory Life

1) Bless the world of duality for all it has taught you and leave it behind. Joyfully release it all: good, bad, right, wrong, success, failure, and all the rest.
2) Intend and choose how you want to feel: loving, joyful, awake and conscious, full of potential and ready for limitless possibilities.
3) Be authentic, be your true self, be honest and unconditional with yourself and others.
4) Live free of limiting beliefs that you haven't consciously chosen. Consciously choose the beliefs that determine your life.

5) Look at your experiences consciously. They may be in your best interests whether you realize it or not. Change your perspective, perception and intentions when you need to.

6) Create loving relationships free of expectations, conditions and judgments.

7) Be present each moment of the day. Enjoy awareness of your breath, body and heart. Quiet your thinking mind and enjoy quiet time daily. Breathe slowly and deeply. Be here now.

8) Listen to your mind's internal dialogue. Consciously choose your thoughts and be aware of what you want to say. Rephrase what isn't creative and say what you really mean.

9) Enjoy knowing and loving yourself. Live with unconditional acceptance, love and personal integrity.

10) Accept what comes to you. Take time to thoughtfully choose what you will do next. Accept and feel each step. Everything is always OK. You are safe. Each moment provides another opportunity! Don't plow through life...flow with it. Accept life's natural order and cycles. Let Divine order come with effortless ease.

11) Understand that you can have what you want by focusing solely on what you want to create. As you let go of fears, bless them for teaching you so much. Listen to your heart and follow your dreams.

12) Choose joy. Slow down...... each moment is precious. Hold gratitude for all experiences and opportunities.

13) Allow yourself to joyfully give the universe or Infinite Intelligence some issue, fear or consideration that has been on your mind and in your life. Totally and unconditionally give it up!! Thank the Universe for graciously accepting and transforming it.

14) Hold gratitude and celebration in your heart for all that you have and for all that life brings to you.

15) Intend your life to be full of unlimited opportunities, peace, love, gratitude, respect and JOY.

16) Be creative. It is all up to you. You have unlimited potential and infinite opportunities!

17) Lighten up...enjoy laughter, humor and joy in your daily life.
18) Life is an Opportunity...live and enjoy it! It is a sacred experience.

Our deepest fear is not that we are inadequate.
Our deepest fear is that we are powerful beyond measure.
It is our light, not our darkness that most frightens us.
We ask ourselves, Who am I to be brilliant,
gorgeous, talented, fabulous?
Actually, who are you *not* to be? You are a child of God.
Your playing small does not serve the world.
There is nothing enlightened about
shrinking so that other people
won't feel insecure around you. We are
all meant to shine, as children do.
We were born to make manifest the
glory of God that is within us.
It's not just in some of us; it's in everyone.
And as we let our own light shine, we unconsciously give
other people permission to do the same. As
we are liberated from our own fear,
our presence automatically liberates others.
~Marianne Williamson, ~*A Return To Love: Reflections
on the Principles of A Course in Miracles~ Harper
Collins, 1992. From Chapter 7, Section 3 (Pg. 190-191).*

17

Living from Our Heart and Celebrating Life

We have the potential to embody our magnificence.
~Ernesto Ortiz, ~*Akashic Records*

It is time for us to celebrate our magnificence. Though we are spiritual beings having a human experience, we are first and foremost spiritual beings. The physical is just a manifestation of our thoughts, words and desires. As we recognize our true brilliance and light, we will move on to the next dimension, our next level of evolution, our next journey. It is already happening and is unstoppable. We can all begin to celebrate our graduation, the return of love to the earth and the return to "Oneness." The more we reverently celebrate our birthright the sooner we may all move on to this next dimension.

As we begin to identify our truly unrealized potential, we understand that we are in the beginning stages of seeing the grandeur of ourselves. Walter Russell was one of those rare individuals who tapped into the Universe and his "magnificence." He was able to do in one lifetime what would normally take 5 or more lifetimes to accomplish.

Deepok Chopra also talks about the "Field of all Possibilities" a place where we can step beyond the strictly physical world and tap into a place of all possibilities.

Walter Russell understood how the character of true genius manifested:

Can you give me the secret of life? I asked. (Glenn Clark)

He hesitated, then replied. "Yes, I believe sincerely that
every man has consummate genius within him. Some
appear to have it more than others only because they
are aware of it more than others are, and the awareness
or unawareness of it is what makes each one of them
into masters or holds them down to mediocrity. I
believe that mediocrity is self-inflicted and that genius
is self-bestowed. Every successful man I have ever
known and I have known a great many, carries with
him the key which unlocks that awareness and lets in
the universal power that has made him into a master.
(Walter Russell)

What is that key? I asked.

That key is *desire* when it is *released* into the great eternal
Energy of the universe.

I have read Glenn Clark's book about Walter Russell "The Man
Who Tapped the Secrets of the Universe" many times. It is one of
my favorite books. Walter Russell is a man who believed that he
could do anything that he set his mind to and even when friends and
individuals told him that what he was proposing to do was totally
impossible. He never veered off course. Again and again he seemed
to do the impossible in both art and sculpture. He was an unusual
and divinely gifted man.

We are moving toward a time when we will recognize
and acknowledge the Divine Universe, our Oneness and the
unconditionally loving self in one another. In doing so, we can
honor each other by greeting one another with the respect and
reverence of the following Nepalese Greeting (whether we say it out
loud or in our minds). Many people use it these days as a greeting
or farewell (even on emails):

Namaste = I honor the place in you
in which the entire universe dwells.
I honor the place in you which is of love,
of truth, of light, and of peace.
When you are in that place in you,
and I am in that place in me,
We are One.

If we can wisely live from our heart while trusting in our spiritual connection then we can interact with life optimally, creatively and productively with each experience that we encounter, without exception.

We are truly far more than we had ever imagined.
~Becky Mulkern ND

We are presently in a moment of monumental shift, evolutionary transition and a tremendous leap forward for humankind. This is an extraordinary moment in the history of the earth and the universe, though it is merely a moment in eternal time. While the human body is presently offering resistance, matter is changing rapidly to prepare itself for a new manifestation of being.

What if this last issue isn't our current rate of progress;
what if, as we shall soon see, it's really our
linear brain's inability to comprehend our
current rate of exponential progress?
~Peter Diamandis & Steven Kotler,
~Abundance - The future is better than you think

The impulse of evolution is awakening us and pushing us to transcend the present model of life. ***Everything is breaking down, transforming, and is ready to be reborn.*** It is time to regenerate, rejuvenate and recreate society to a sustainable, just and evolved place, with social, scientific and technological aspects moving to a new level of efficiency and creativity.

The focus of this period is living from a loving heart and being in union with the Divine Forces that are at work now. Your transition will be easy if you live each moment in a state of Being, receptivity, trust and inner peace.

> So what is about to unfold in the future will come
> very soon, probably, and according to the Mayansand
> all the rest of the tribes, this will happen between
> now and the late 2015, and nobody knows when.
> Only Mother Earth knows the truth of that
> situation. But we have made it into the new Unity
> Consciousness Grid. Life will soon be very different.
> ~Drunvalo Melchizedek, ~*The Mayan Ouroborous*

Our conscious evolution and greatest growth occurs as we choose to totally let go of fear, judgment, limitation, and negativity. We can instead, joyfully choose acceptance, integrity, unconditional love and dynamic Presence. We have been given the sacred gift of life for which we are responsible. Let us hold gratitude and celebration for this gift. As we take a stand for this new era, we awaken and move from the "I" to the "We," from the individual to the collective. We can then hold the Unity of Oneness in our collective heart.

We are shifting from limitation and an ego-based consciousness to an unconditionally loving Sacred Self that operates from its higher self and divine love. There is no other course. You can choose to respond any way you like to your life experience. Why not choose love? The choice is yours. You can be an instrument of Divine Love and feel the "aliveness" coursing through your being. If you unconditionally love yourself, others and all life, how could you ever doubt or see anything as wrong? God/Goddess/Source does not judge you. Why have you judged yourself? Let it all go. Be grateful that you can transform your life and move on. If you begin to feel doubt or fear, feel it and experience and acknowledge it as something you are finally releasing and leaving behind. Love that part of yourself and the inner child that has experienced so much pain. Acknowledge the pain as a teacher and communication from your inner self. Love and honor that self and breathe out the old pain and negativity, release it. Be transformed and born anew.

Recently, I baptized myself, in the cold late September waters of the Swift River. I consciously released the old feelings and experiences and asked for what I wanted to replace them....joy, love, awareness, prosperity, and renewal. You can do these types of rituals yourself as an intention of what you want to create for yourself. Rituals solidify our intentions, by making it conscious and three dimensional. By living it, speaking it and doing it, we bring it to us.

Remember that the universe always responds with a "Yes" to whatever you say and affirm, whether it is creative or destructive, whether you want it or don't want it. Continue to do your best and as you rise to higher aspirations. Visualize what you want for yourself and the collective world. Trust in yourself and the process of life, as you spiral upward toward unlimited possibilities and opportunities. Celebrate your unlimited power to create.

One of my favorite writings that I have on one of my doors for all to see is the following:

Warning Signs of Good Health

1) Persistent Sense of Humor
2) Chronic Positive Expectations; tendency to frame events in a constructive light
3) Episodic outbreaks of joyful, happy experiences
4) Sense of spiritual involvement
5) Tendency to adapt well to changing conditions
6) Rapid response to and recovery from stress and repeated challenges
7) Increased appetite for physical activity
8) Tendency to identify and communicate feelings
9) Repeated episodes of gratitude and generosity

10) Continuing presence of support network
~James Greenblatt MD, Newton, Massachusetts

In the past, when we chose to live with conditional feelings, we came to realize that what the ego had told us about life was not true. It was all based in fearful illusion. With the ego's effort to gain power, security, importance and control through its uncontrollable chatter, we realized, that the ego told us only what we "should fear" and "should do." When we finally understood that the only thing that we want to control is the ego itself, we let go of running after how life "should be," and we delighted in living each moment as it is, choosing to be fully present and alive, and thankful for the gift of each day.

Recently I was walking in the woods of New Hampshire, marveling at the beautiful fall foliage. The yellows of the leaves were brilliant with the sunlight shining through them. It was a spectacle to behold. I began to think about how lit up and alive the woods seemed and then the word "delight" came to mind. It was delightful to make this connection. So whenever I think of the word delight from now on I will think of that fall day in the woods when the leaves were alive with color and spiritual light and I felt "delighted."

> Follow your bliss and the Universe will open doors
> where there were only walls.
> ~Joseph Campbell

As we transform the subconscious mind's memory bank of life's fearful experiences and negative voices, we discover an inner identity and gentle voice that is spiritually uplifting. As we let go of limiting beliefs, the voice supports and guides us toward living with unconditional love and acceptance. If we choose daily meditation, prayer, serenity, conscious choice, introspection and being we can feel calm in the middle of chaos. This is a place where we aren't trying to be or affirm anything. We experience our true essence of simply being authentic and living it. We feel whole to the core of our being.

I was thinking lately about the word 'chaos' and its significance at this evolutionary time. There are many individuals who are very challenged by the changes that are occurring. They are fairly disturbed and believe that the present environmental shifts and climate change will bring terrible outcomes. (It can be helpful to really get in touch with and feel the sadness, fear and anger around these issues.) It led me to wonder. Can we see this time as an evolutionary shift into a beneficial and greatly needed change as well as the end of an outdated era? Can we shift our perception and see the creative energy movement, and not just the destructive energy downfall? We often see what we expect to see. Can we look closer and see that the chaos is really not chaos at all? It is the crumbling of limiting and destructive energies and outworn paradigms that no longer serve us. New structures and frameworks are being created that will be blessings to serve us sustainably. Can we see that Grace is involved in the process of change? Can we hold our focus on what we want to create? I believe that we can and must do this. Many others believe this as well. Join us and let's create what is possible for our collective future.

Now is a time for your faith, trust, and heart to become truly active and unshaken by the changing circumstances. As we grow stronger in our trusting the future, we become aware of the gentle voice that is guiding us on our spiritual journey. Our inner self has power, purpose and energy to connect us with Source and the Universe. We are evolving and spiraling upward toward enlightenment and a more expansive outlook. We are moving beyond the ego and limited identity. We are evolving toward the highest expression of who we are and a global and universal love that will heal our planet and all life.

When man truly and purely loves,
he automatically and willingly follows
the invisible tugging strings of Divine Love
toward God.
~Paramashansa Yogananda

As we question the truthfulness of all that we were taught, we release alignment to the "crowd" and we realize that we have a larger identity and a deeper connection to all life than we had formerly realized or experienced. We joyfully leave behind our limited and fearful views and we become truth seekers, "fringe dwellers" (Stuart Wilde) and/or "Wayseers." (Watch *The Wayseer Manifesto* on You Tube.) As such we no longer fit into society as it has been or make motions to try to. If you recognize in this process, that you are feeling disquieting and uncomfortable feelings that aren't yours, you may want to consciously separate yourself from the "mass consciousness." We only identify with the "mass consciousness," when we lose our integrity and fall asleep. Lift your awareness up, go within and consciously choose love, integrity, and being.

Our minds and hearts desire to live and thrive in dimensions of consciousness, where we have the deepest love and respect for ourselves and all life.

We now have the opportunity to evolve from beliefs in the "norm" and collective limiting identities, to an inner self that displays increased compassion, greater reverence and a peaceful consciousness. As the collective consciousness shifts we easily let go of the old masks, phony facades, and the need to be anything other than who we are. We can value honesty, integrity and equality as important aspects of our new and thriving world.

Many times we will be tested to see if we have really moved on, or whether we are still connected to old beliefs, habits and fears adopted in the past. The ego will raise its little head again and again to see if we really have let go of our need to live in fear and impossibility. It may be relentless too, if we still choose to hold onto fear as a motivator. We will be challenged again and again to release and let go of old aspects of our being that do not serve us. Issues that we don't deal with directly, may return to haunt us, until we resolve them, make changes, let them go and move on. As we move toward living from our heart, we may feel very different, and at times we may feel a "void" or emptiness in ourselves, as the old is gone and the new is not yet in place. Be patient with yourselves during this time and allow for the transition and rebirth into your new extraordinary life. This process may feel as if it is taking too long, you may become impatient but welcome the change with an open heart and celebration as you await your divine destiny.

Heaven is here. There is nowhere else.
Heaven is now. There is no other time.
~The Course in Miracles

In reading this book, you may now have gathered new tools and ideas about how to shift into your new life. Accept and support yourself totally, as you grow and evolve. Be clear and unconditionally loving with yourself and others. Through your loving attitude, the power of the universe will be introduced into all your actions and thoughts. As you operate lovingly from your heart center, you will feel a far greater connection to your inner knowing. In linking to life through love, you will find your sense of knowing to be deep and true. Utilize reason and intellect if you like along with your intuition, to support it, but not to lead it or determine your actions. The intellect is meant to implement actions of the heart, not to determine them. As you trust your intuition, you will find yourself connected to the dynamic and living powers of the universe. The universe is supporting your greatest self and unlimited potential to transform your dreams into reality.

I am always doing things I can't do.
That is how I get to do them.
~Pablo Picasso

Life doesn't occur from struggling or holding on, so relax your mind, your heart and your body. Choose to release struggle and to flow with whatever comes to you in your life. Understand that this doesn't mean that you are passive or that you are closing your eyes to life or you think only good thoughts. It means that you look at whatever comes to you and whatever you see in the world, whether its hunger, violence or war and you choose your action or non-action, motivated by love (not tension, anger, hate, resentment, etc.).

Thoughts that are empowered by love, bring empowering solutions and responses of love, gratitude, reverence and the understanding, that do make a difference. *To the degree that fear and anxiety affects your motivation, to that degree, you are less effective in all that you do. For when you actions are motivated by fear, love is denied from all that you do.* When we are connected to fear, we are no longer fully present. If at any time in self-reflection, you doubt your power and think less of yourself, then you are living in the past or the future—and you are not fully present. You are isolating yourself in fear.

Release your fears, release your worries and settle into love. Embrace and hold it in your heart, radiate it and never let it go. Be love....

And always remember these things, my dear:
Remember you have free will.
Remember you have light and so you shall remain.
Remember there is no right or wrong,
Only Divine truth;
Remember that if you ask, you shall receive.
Remember!
~Flo Calhoun, ~*I Remember Union*

One prayer/invocation that I have been drawn to say at times on a daily basis is the following. Even though it was written many years ago, I believe that it is more appropriate now than ever, to support us in focusing on the profound shift that is occurring:

From the point of Light within the mind of God Prayer

From the point of Light within the mind of God
Let light stream forth into the minds of men.
Let light descend on Earth.

From the point of Love within the heart of God
Let Love stream forth into the hearts of men.
May Christ return to Earth.

From the center where the Will of God is known
Let the purpose guide the little wills of men—
The purpose that the Masters know and serve.

From the center which we call the race of men
Let the plan of Love and Light work out
Any may it seal the door where evil dwells.
Let Light and Love and Power restore the plan on Earth.

We are beginning the process of birthing a fully worthy, unconditionally loving, and conscious humanity. They know and understand that fear is an illusion that we no longer need to embrace. With the seeds of potentiality within them, they will joyfully give birth and co-create the new paradigm for the individual and the collective evolution as a whole.

We can look at what Gandhi said about this new social order for a truly free post-colonial India. Gandhi had a trinity of insightful ideas.

The first was *sarvodaya, "the Upliftment of All."* Sarvodaya includes the care of the Earth, of animals, forests, rivers and land as well as people. For Gandhi, life was sacred. He advocated reverence for all life, for humans as well as other-than-humans.

The second aspect was *swaraj* or "Self-government." It brings about social transformation through small-scale, participatory structures of government as well as focusing on self-discipline, and self-transformation. He believed that a moral, ethical, ecological and spiritual foundation were necessary to build good governance.

The third part of the trinity was called *swadeshi,* or "Local Economy." He opposed mass-production but supported local production by the people. He believed that every member of society should be engaged in work in small manufacturing organizations that fed the body as well as the soul. He understood that excessive economic growth would destroy the fabric of life and the integrity of the natural world. This last aspect of social order has me thinking about all the new small organic farms that are popping up all over my community. This promise of a sustainable future warms my heart and soul. We are fortunate where I live to have so many young and passionate individuals who want to contribute to a sustainable world. It is awesome. I truly celebrate them.

> Many assume that the coming millennium is to be a
> period of low technological emphasis; they are right
> in so far as the vast abuses of the industrial era are
> concerned. But they are wrong in that science and
> technology throughout the millennium will come to
> better serve the human race as they have ever done at
> their best in the past. They will serve the purposes
> of the creative intelligence in ways yet undreamed
> of. When debilitating assumptions of history are
> pulled out from beneath human genius, it will be
> like a ship lifting anchor or a bird taking to the air.
> ~Ken Carey, ~*Starseed - Living in a Posthistoric World*

There is a global unity forming. It transcends all groups, whether they are faith-based, functional or cultural. Individuals are waking up to being aware of the creative renewal arising and beginning to understand their role in this process. If you are attracted to being a part of this new evolutionary unity and evolution, understand that Spirit, social, scientific, technological and the mystical are all vital to this process. You may be attracted and drawn in to this evolutionary journey and unification through magnetism. It is time for us to visualize and dream a new world that is sustainable, socially just, unconditionally loving and compassionate. We can create a world that healthily sustains us and all life. Let us all trust and believe that we can all do this......

> *Although the world is entering a time*
> *of great change and crisis,*
> *the future of humanity is not dark*
> *and will never be hopeless.*
> *Every person must make the long journey*

through the darkness and confusion of the present
seeking the glowing light
that has guided the masters among us
since the beginning of time.
It is the flame of true healing, hope, wisdom,
joy, peace, cooperation, enlightenment and love.
It represents the new day that is dawning
upon the earth.
All those people who point the way
to the whereabouts of this
Sacred, special light
will always be remembered and respected
by all those who have ever walked the earth
and sought the higher values and potentials
of our universe.
You will know when you have seen this light or have felt
the truth of one of its emanations
in something that you have learned.
Draw that spirit of that light into your heart
that it may radiate from within you
awakening your higher self,
guiding your path, reaching out to all who
are within the sphere of its glow.
It is through working in harmony
with this silent energy
that you will find the deepest peace and security,
in all places and through all times,
that can be known on earth.
You have chosen to be a leader,
and countless people,
most yet unknown in your life,
are already turning their eyes and hearts to you
for guidance, love, protection, knowledge,
healing and strength.
The future of mankind is truly in the hands
of enlightened new leaders

> *throughout the world.*
> *It is in* <u>*your*</u> *hands.~*
> *~Khangsar TserongM'ing,*
> *(Healing Preist and Martiall Arts Master*
> *Litang, Kham, Tibet, 1826-1924)*

Are you one of these leaders? If so, you are deeply valued at this time. Join the movement toward creating our amazing collective future.

We can change our beliefs and perception, but can we understand what is true and what is not? Here is one for you to think about. We talk about the sun as if it is rising and setting every day, but that is not at all true. We know that the sun actually is not moving, it is we, on the earth, who are spinning through space. It appears that the sun moves because of the way the earth is spinning in space and the sun appears to set at the end of the day. Yet it is easy to forget that the sun doesn't rise and set every day. How many other things do we perceive or believe that are not really true? Are you aware of the illusionary aspects of your life?

The following quote is about *Crow Medicine (referring to the bird)* from *Medicine Cards*, by Jamie and David Carson:

> Human law is not the same as Sacred Law.
> More so than any other medicine, Crow sees that
> the physical world and even the spiritual world, as
> humanity interprets them, are an illusion.
> There are billions of worlds. There
> are infinitude of creatures.
> Great Spirit is within all.

We are presently in a time of fundamental change and dynamic evolution. We are shifting to higher levels of creation and expression. Indigenous cultures all over the world have prophesized this time for hundreds and thousands of years. We all have unique and valuable gifts to offer, commit to and contribute to this monumental time.

The collective heart of humankind is "sick and tired" of living in fear, competition and powerlessness and is asserting its desire to evolve, live from the heart and love unconditionally. As we open our minds and hearts and shift our focus and motivation from fear to love, we can actually feel the love that is available to us and through us. We become overcome with joy, when we realize our spiritual connection and inheritance. We then know that that nothing can ever harm us. We are immortal, radiant and one with all life. We are caretakers of the earth, powerful and compassionate. We are responsible for bringing love, peace, acceptance and understanding into each and every moment of our collective lives. *We are truly far more than we had ever imagined.*

As a Naturopathic Doctor, I see a correlation between an individual's health and the wellness of our planet. As we leave behind our numbness, unconsciousness and lack of feeling and we show greater respect and reverence for the community of life, we will all experience improved health and wellness in body, mind and spirit.

The present dynamic change is like moving from an "old and worn out" robot to a new and life sustaining garden and paradigm. It is the difference between *The Mechanic and the Gardener* as Lawrence LeShan said in his book of that name. The mechanistic way of living is an outlived model that has been with us for over 1500 years. The model is based in science and logical left brain thinking. It rejects the spiritual life, subtle energies, nature and all life as worthy of respect and reverence. It loves pragmatism, science and evidence based information, even when the science isn't "good science."

The gardener is the lover of life and the natural world. Gardeners support a flourishing Earth and Universe that holds the land and all life as sacred. They live from their heart and treat life with care, respect and love. They love laughter, celebration, connection and being. Gardeners understand that all life is "One," we are all connected, and "what I do to you, I do to me." They know that we are all interconnected in the web of life.

How can we be healthy if we don't live as gardeners and treat ourselves, other individuals, animals and all life with reverence and respect? We have important choices to make. If we are truly awake and conscious, the choice is easy. As gardeners, let us plant seeds now for a future filled with joy, opportunities, love and unlimited potential for us all.

We have reached the end of a 13,000 year "yang" age cycle and are moving into a "yin" based age. Yin and Yang are aspects of Chinese science and philosophy that involve the interconnection and interdependence of the many aspects of life and the natural world. They are opposites that complement and transform each other. You cannot have one without the other. Neither is better than the other. We learn from all aspects of both of them. There is a vital balance that exists between the two that perpetually strives for harmony. When one reaches fullness it is transformed into the other....day transforms into night, a seed into a plant, life into death, etc. endless cycles of transformation, movement and change. (Change is the only thing that we are guaranteed in life.) The ending yang age has reached its fullness and widest expansion. It was symbolized by focus on the physical body, the external, moving fast, doing, expansion, focus, aggression and male qualities. With its ending, it has already begun transformation into the yin qualities of the feminine, mothering, creating, slowing, yielding, softness, internal and contracting movement, passivity, the earth and being. With this movement toward the feminine aspect, we see women stepping up and taking a larger part in the transformative process. Women are stepping into their power and finding their voice. They are speaking up for change and embodying what they want to see in the world.

The fear based worlds are falling apart and causing some individuals to experience growing pains. Those who remain resistant to the present and future changes, and aggressively fight "against" the shift and evolutionary change, will be challenged. If they do everything in their power to keep the status quo, the transition will not be easy for them. They need to let go, accept, allow, and align with their Divine Nature. The status quo cannot and will not remain. The old constructs are falling away and everything is presently in flux, change and transformation. The problems dissolve as we evolve... Some individuals have already become the essence of the new yin age and are feeling a little impatient that change isn't occurring fast enough. Many light-workers are thirsting and hungry for the new and healthier world. Those in the forefront can help birth this new age and support the fearful and resistant to welcome it with grace and celebration. We all have unlimited potential to create a future "extraordinaire." Let's do it!

> Cosmic forces, Mother Earth and thousands of
> awakened human hearts want to change everything
> and bring it back to its healthy state.
> This is a wave that will continue growing
> until it breaks in the shore of time.
> Nothing can stop it.
> It is life seeking to continue living.
> It is us seeking to continue living.
> ~Arkan Lushwala, ~The Time of the Black Jaguar

One of my favorite examples of this new era is the website "Playing for Change." If you want to be uplifted with joy and music, tune into this site. Mark Johnson started it in 2002 when he saw street musician Roger Ridley playing "Stand by Me," on a street corner in Santa Monica, California. Roger said to him, "I'm in the Joy Business, I come out to be with people." Presently, the site has videos of very talented musicians from around the world playing music together. The videos also include worldwide children's choirs singing together. Playing for Change has created schools and scholarship programs for 700 children, who have weekly music and dance lessons. Videos of musicians playing together from around the world are seen in Rwanda, Nepal, Mali, Africa, Brazil and throughout Europe. Their PFC band even played on the "Tonight Show." Look for Grandpa Elliot if you want a real treat!

> Never doubt that a small group of thoughtful,
> committed citizens can change the world.
> Indeed, it is the only thing that ever has.
> ~Margaret Mead

The year of 2012 was a profound turning point in our history. It marked the beginning of a new era of peace, love and truth for humankind and planet Earth. It began a time of monumental uplifting and evolution in human consciousness and the direction of our collective future. So much is happening that I am in awe of the speed of this change and shift.

There has been a rise in women's power as signified by organizations such as *One Billion Rising*. Women are feeling empowered to make a difference all over the world. *Microcredit* has revolutionized the ability of women to be entrepreneurs, start businesses and provide for their families. Wow... this is a huge opportunity for many women.

Certainly the broader acceptance of gay rights and gay marriage is slowly spreading worldwide. We can finally embrace both the masculine and feminine energies in a balanced and healthy way, while accepting everyone for their unique differences.

There are many new startup companies. Crowd source funding has changed the economic dynamics for many individuals and businesses. CouchSurfing, a peer to peer hospitality exchange with over 7 million members in 207 countries, has certainly allowed individuals from all over the world to connect and share homes, ideas, and thoughts, and in turn meet individuals they wouldn't normally meet. As we get to know people from all walks of life, we realize how similar, different and connected we all are.

Healing of indigenous peoples' cultures is occurring as individuals realize the many wounds previously inflicted on these peoples. In the US there has been more attention on and recognition of racial prejudice and the profiling of many young men and women.

Movies on African Americans have come to the forefront to relate the prejudices of the past. Many prejudices are still present though as we see in immigration reform issues. President Obama has recently been speaking on social and economic inequality, which he has not addressed previously. An increase in the minimum wage seems imminent nationwide.

Wind mills, solar power and organic farms are springing up all over. We are finally consuming less gas and oil than in previous years as energy efficient cars are beginning to make a difference. Recycling is recognized as important, necessary, and cost effective. More people are doing it all the time. The alternative has been very expensive and has cost us dearly, but change is happening rapidly.

Our heart-felt connection to the Earth, both the microcosm and the macrocosm and our respectful choices effect social and economic justice, peace and sustainability. How we treat ourselves and others affects the whole world. As we treat ourselves with love and compassion, our personal wellness becomes part of a global model for health, wellness and sustainability.

Let go of the old model of thinking, that says we are broken, wrong or need to be fixed. The Kingdom of Heaven is within us… we just need to wake up, love and honor life while letting go of the old and untrue illusions. Open your arms, welcome your birthright, and embrace yourself as a whole and Divine being. Align yourself to the truth and with joyful enthusiasm express who you are. … There is nothing more to attain…

One of the most important things that we can do at this time is to just "Be." By this I mean, to connect with your spiritual nature, Infinite Intelligence, the Universe, God, Great Spirit, the Divine or whatever brings you to a deep state of peace, inner knowing and fulfillment. In this place we can "be" without judgment, expectation or negativity and connect to our Authentic Nature. It is a meaningful time to be spiritually self-assured. That means that whatever is going on, you are as solid as a rock. Even if chaos, upheaval, and monumental shift and change occur, you can proceed forward, without doubt or fear, while being spiritually self-confident about our individual or collective future. There is no room for doubt and fear. Let's raise our creative energy at this time. Let's all passionately visualize the future that we want to see, a future filled with love, joy and health for all. This is our birthright. Each moment counts in this period of shift, change and evolution. We are all creative factors in the evolution of the planet and the universe. We all have unique gifts to offer that are a valuable asset to the world. "Step up" and share these your profound gifts. Life will continue to be creative no matter what happens... but now is the time to choose to be a dynamic and powerful participant. Be a reservoir of joy and a creative impulse for change. We are radiant stars, pure spiritual light and worthy of the love that is available and waiting for us.

> Your time is limited so don't waste it living someone
> else's life. Don't be trapped by dogma, which is living
> with the results of other people's thinking. Don't let the
> noise of other's opinions drown out your own inner voice,
> have the courage to follow your heart and intuition.
> ~Steve Jobs, *June 2005*
> *Stanford University Graduation Speech*

We are evolving from doing and thinking to knowing and being...how wonderful!

What if in 20 years or more your grandchildren or the younger generations of your family ask you what you did to help promote this amazing shift and change that occurred when the old world was dying and falling apart and the new world was still in transition. What would you say for yourself? What would you like to say for yourself? There is time to get on board if you haven't already. If you were in your all your glory, what would you be doing now to contribute to this time? How would you thrive?" Open your heart, connect with pure Source energy and freely allow for infinite possibilities and the unknown to support your answer. We all need your contribution and participation. You are a unique and valuable part of the whole. Join us.....

The year of 2014 is a profound time of personal and global awakening as new universal vibrations awaken our earth consciousness. Our planet needs all of us to serve and open our hearts and minds to allow for our true destinies. This time will be remembered for years to come as an evolutionary turning point on this planet. We are creating and participating in a new and sacred world paradigm that is based in our heart. Heaven is truly here on earth.

We are presently creating our own future ... a better future for us all. In this very exciting time of changing consciousness and spiritual enlightenment, individuals and groups are speaking out and "stepping up." We are now no longer saying what we are "against" but what we are "for." As we embrace ourselves and the "Sacred" in all things our heart sings and feels the Oneness of all life. Old institutions and conventions are falling away as we create a whole new and amazing paradigm that will work for us all (the 100% of us!). A new world is being born in which the whole web of life matters! The effects of all this change are slowly and increasingly becoming visible as they manifest themselves.

In the morning before the sun appears on the horizon, we gradually see nature and the world around us as the darkness fades. Soon the mountains are alive with pink alpenglow and areas in the distance are glowing with the sun's early morning light. Soon the sun appears over the horizon the world is saturated with its golden light. The light that has always been there, has suddenly erased the darkness and becomes visible to us all. We are presently leaving the darkness behind and returning to ourselves and a world of light.

The present unstoppable momentum of social, economic, environmental, and spiritual evolution and change is only now beginning to appear at the surface of our knowing. Very soon a global tidal wave toward a new and amazing paradigm will be visible for us all to see and celebrate. Now is time to prepare for the party..... You are invited!

18

Acknowledgement of Participation in Life is an Opportunity

As a believer in choosing to consciously and joyfully evolve you have embraced~

~ *Letting go of old belief systems, judgments, fear and expectations.*

~ *Understanding that you have unlimited choices and infinite possibilities.*

~ *Supporting and unconditionally accepting yourself and others at all times.*

~ *Loving yourself totally and unconditionally.*

~ *Creating and celebrating your life and this time in our evolution.*

~ *Empowering yourself and others at all times.*

~ *Opening your heart to life and all opportunities and possibilities.*

~ *Thoroughly enjoying your process of growth and conscious evolution.*

~ *Creating a new paradigm of sustainability, justice, peace, power, wisdom, reverence, and love for all life.*

~ *Living with Joy as your destiny.*

~ *Choosing to live life as a sacred opportunity.*

Congratulations, Blessings, Love and Joy!!!

You have it all……….. I wish you well and send you forward with unconditional love and light.

May unconditional love and joy fill your heart and soul and may you be blessed in all of your life. May you bless the world and all life with your presence.

I love you all……

> ~You may say I am a dreamer.
> But I am not the only one.
> I hope that someday you will join us
> And the world will live as ONE~
> ~John Lennon, ~*Imagine*~

Epilogue

As I was finishing my book the Universe threw me another unexpected lesson. As I began the fund raising project for the editing, publishing and marketing of my book, my clients seemed to dry up...no one was calling and I was having cancellations as well. Though that income diminished, the bills were certainly there. I became fearful and challenged to live what I have asked others to believe in: "The Universe takes care of us. Have faith and trust that everything is just as it should be. Everything is perfect and in Divine right order. Don't struggle, resist or push against what is occurring...flow with life." Wow! It became a great challenge for me.

I have always been taken care of and provided for by the Universe, even when finances were challenging, my life has been rich and abundant in so many ways. I have always had money to pay my bills even if it was later than sooner. Practicing unconditional acceptance has been a wonderful and enlightening gift for me to learn.

As everything proceeded with the challenge of what appeared "no income," I kept focusing on being in the moment and holding gratitude and love in my heart for all that I had. I kept working many hours daily on the book and letting go of everything else. While focusing on giving, I would place my heart into healing for our planet and solar system. This would keep cycles of giving and receiving in a "flow." I did some outdoor early morning healing meditations that were sincerely heart-felt. The first profound one that I did left me feeling that the Universe was out there supporting and loving me. After the first meditation in my back yard, I walked down the hill to the beach. As I was walking along the beach, a bald eagle flew close in front of me. It flew across the river and landed in a tree. It stayed there for a while and then flew up the river in the same direction that I was headed. Within a few minutes as I walked along the shore I saw the eagle again across the river high in a tree. I was watching the eagle when another very large bird flew off from 20 feet below it. I believe it was a juvenile eagle! Two eagles! Wow!

Another day after a heart-felt meditation for Mother Earth, a bald eagle flew down the river in front of me as I approached the beach. Seeing these mature eagles were signs to me, of acknowledgement from the Universe. In Native American medicine, the eagle symbolizes the power of the Great Spirit. It symbolizes living in the physical earth realm, while staying deeply connected and balanced with the spiritual realm. Eagles represent conquering your fears and a "state of grace achieved through hard work, understanding and a completion of tests of initiation which result in the taking of one's personal power…. a trial of trusting one's connection to the Great Spirit… to take heart and gather courage to soar above the mundane levels of your life…. and to follow the joy your heart desires." (from the *Medicine Cards* book by Sams and Carson)

What is interesting is that I have had time to focus on the final editing stages of my book. This has made quite a difference in the final outcome. The extra hours that I have placed in the final editing has contributed to many changes, additions and subtractions that may not have been possible. The final editing which I have done myself was quite a project, but allowed me to add information and meaning that would not have been possible if I had paid the publisher to do it. It really worked out in my favor. I am so pleased with the book as it stands now. This is my contribution to our evolutionary process. I hope that you enjoy it as well.

My intuition and my angels have been telling me that this is an important book for our evolution because it will guide and support individuals and young people, to flow easily through this time, and on to the next era. It is a hopeful and instructional guide for the time we live in. I feel blessed that it might be. I do know that what I have taught individuals has made a difference in their lives because there is great truth in my words....

In the meantime, I feel very grateful, blessed and supported because financial and emotional support has arrived from many unexpected directions. I see the universe working in so many miraculous ways. Have faith that you are always being taken care of by an abundant universe, and celebrate the gift horse that is always there to take care of you.

I have a few more books in mind already, so that is where my heart and soul are headed. I have always loved teaching and supporting others...this is my opportunity!

I hope that you are blessed with a life full of infinite possibilities, endless opportunities, and abundant joy. Thanks for participating in our collective evolution! You are unique and wonderful Child of God. You are dearly loved.

Soon we shall see how the future unfolds for us all.... I can feel the growing joy already!!

Printed in the United States
By Bookmasters